St. Louis Community College

Forest Park
Florissant Valley
Meramec

Instructional Resources
St. Louis, Missouri

Disfigured
Images

Recent Titles in
Contributions in Afro-American and African Studies

Anne, the White Woman in Contemporary African-American Fiction: Archetypes, Stereotypes, and Characterizations
Anna Maria Chupa

American Policy and African Famine: The Nigeria-Biafra War, 1966–1970
Joseph E. Thompson

Wines in the Wilderness: Plays by African American Women from the Harlem Renaissance to the Present
Elizabeth Brown-Guillory, editor and compiler

Education of the African American Adult: An Historical Overview
Harvey G. Neufeldt and Leo McGee, editors

The Wealth of Races: The Present Value of Benefits from Past Injustices
Richard F. America, editor

Black Music in the Harlem Renaissance: A Collection of Essays
Samuel A. Floyd, Jr., editor

Telling Tales: The Pedagogy and Promise of African American Literature for Youth
Dianne Johnson

Ethiopia: Failure of Land Reform and Agricultural Crisis
Kidane Mengisteab

Anancy in the Great House: Ways of Reading West Indian Fiction
Joyce Jonas

The Poet's Africa: Africanness in the Poetry of Nicolás Guillén and Aimé Césaire
Josephat B. Kubayanda

Tradition and Modernity in the African Short Story: An Introduction to a Literature in Search of Critics
F. Odun Balogun

Politics in the African-American Novel: James Weldon Johnson, W. E. B. Du Bois, Richard Wright, and Ralph Ellison
Richard Kostelanetz

Disfigured Images

*THE HISTORICAL
ASSAULT
ON AFRO-AMERICAN
WOMEN*

Patricia Morton

Contributions in Afro-American and
African Studies,
Number 144

GREENWOOD PRESS
New York • Westport, Connecticut • London

Library of Congress Cataloging-in-Publication Data

Morton, Patricia.
    Disfigured images : the historical assault on Afro-American women
  / Patricia Morton.
      p.   cm.—(Contributions in Afro-American and African
studies, ISSN 0069-9624 ; no. 144)
    Includes bibliographical references and index.
    ISBN 0-313-27296-4 (alk. paper)
    1. Afro-American women—Historiography. I. Title. II. Series.
E185.86.M64   1991
305.4'08996073—dc20   90-20701

British Library Cataloguing in Publication Data is available.

A paperback edition of *Disfigured Images: The Historical Assault on
Afro-American Women* is available from Praeger Publishers, an imprint of
Greenwood Publishing Group, Inc. (ISBN: 0-275-93885-9).

Library of Congress Catalog Card Number: 90-20701
ISBN: 0-313-27296-4
ISSN: 0069-9624

First published in 1991

Greenwood Press, 88 Post Road West, Westport, CT 06881
An imprint of Greenwood Publishing Group, Inc.

Printed in the United States of America

The paper used in this book complies with the
Permanent Paper Standard issued by the National
Information Standards Organization (Z39.48-1984).

10 9 8 7 6 5 4 3 2 1

To David, Denise, and Neil

Contents

Preface

What readers will find in this book is not a history of Afro-American women, but rather an exploration of how their historical story has been told—and frequently mistold—from the late nineteenth century to the late twentieth century. Thus, this is an exploration of how black women's history has figured in a century of American historiography.

My study acknowledges that fictional and popular media have played a major role in shaping the culture's image of black women's history. However, the primary focus of this book is on the literature of fact that, in America, has been titled as scholarly and thus identified with the discovery and communication of truth. My findings suggest that from the late nineteenth century and well into contemporary times, this literature has said much about black women's history, and yet has presented little fact and much fiction.

A great deal that was said was comprised of caricatures—of little substance but of substantial import. Indeed, what was said over time in a vast body of historical and social-science literature has shaped, updated, and endorsed a distinctive and profoundly disempowering, composite image of black womanhood. This image is best described as mythical in the sense that it was constituted of images that became deeply interwoven into the shape of a story. And this constituted a story of damaged and damaging womanhood that began with slavery and seemed to have no end. Through images the black American woman has emerged in this historiography as a natural and permanent slave woman.

This study hopes to illuminate the role of American scholarship in the shaping and making of this story out of racial and sexual mythology. My findings argue that this body of literature is a telling mirror of the deep and persistent divisions and injustice in American society.

The historical and social-science sources that are of interest to this study, presenting Afro-American women in an historical vein, are treated herein not as secondary sources but as primary sources. These include not only the sources of yesterdays, but also today's reconstructions of black women's slavery history. It is by viewing this literature as a whole, that historiography becomes a rich window looking into continuity and change in American culture's perceptions of gender and race, as signified and epitomized by its image of black womanhood. Thus, my exploration concludes by examining why and how during the closing decades of the twentieth century, American scholarship has turned finally to slay the old myths by writing black women's history as it should be written.

This book cannot include the wealth of studies that are at last bringing the realities and diversity of black women's history to life, but it does hope to forward recognition of this new field of American scholarship. And while this book hopes to deconstruct and demystify the myths long underpinning the black woman's image, the author fully acknowledges that the realm of myth is by definition profoundly illogical and subjective. Therefore, readers are encouraged to regard this as only one possible interpretation, and in turn to develop their own.

Finally, readers should be warned that much of the material unearthed by this book is ugly. Indeed, to discover such profoundly dehumanizing constructions of reality embedded in American scholarship is painful. Yet this too is part of history. And it seems best to confront such material directly rather than to ignore and deny its existence.

Most of the sources examined herein still sit on the shelves of our libraries, quite ready to convey the most grotesque impressions to future generations. Thus, it is important to acknowledge openly the role of the literature of fact in the shaping and endorsement of racism-sexism. Thus we may also emphasize the responsibility of the scholarship of today to contribute to a future in which both reality and discourse contradict the grotesque shapes of the past.

Introduction

It should be emphasized that this book is not a history of Afro-American women. It is not the black woman's story. Rather, it constitutes an exploration of how her history has been constructed by the stories told in a century of American scholarship. My findings argue that in imagery, Afro-American women have figured to a surprising extent in American historiography—surprising in the sense that it is frequently assumed that women have been largely invisible in the traditional discourse of history. Yet in its images, the black woman's history has both figured and been profoundly disfigured.

As William Van Deburg has shown, long after the slavery era Afro-American people remained identified in the American popular mind by the equation of "blacks with slaves and slaves with blacks." He has noted that these images have been "forwarded by writers of fiction, history, and drama," while today the popular media continues to "endorse traditional stereotypes" of "Uncle Tom and his kin."[1] However, American racial stereotypes have been fully inclusive of black women, and Van Deburg might well equally have pointed to "Mammy and her kin."

Certainly the old slave Mammy lives on as a most popular historical image of black womanhood. Providing a steady diet of mammies, the pancake-box Aunt Jemima represents the modernization and yet continuity of this old-time figure. Once very dark, obese, and grinning, today she still presides on the product label, increasingly lighter and brighter, but still in a bandanna and grinning. Mammy remains a valuable emblem from a marketing perspective because of her image in the American popular mind. Simultaneously perceived as both a real, historical person and a legend—as the most devoted and beloved of servants—her presence on the label assures that the product must be both good and all-American because she is steeped in American history.

But while a most beloved image, the Mammy is by no means alone as a symbol of contemporary black womanhood. As Mary Helen Washington has pointed out, "stereotypes about black women abound like weeds in this society." And as Alice Walker has noted, Mammy is accompanied by a plethora of images including " 'Matriarchs', 'Superwomen', and 'Mean and Evil Bitches'. Not to mention 'Castrators' and 'Sapphire's Mamma'."[2]

During the last two decades a host of studies have unearthed such derogatory images and demonstrated their falsity. And the struggle of Afro-American women to name and define their own identity has been manifest in the growth of black women's studies and in a wealth of literature, both scholarly and creative. Yet as Mary Helen Washington has observed of the stereotyping, "the habit still persists."[3] Afro-American women seem to be particularly and persistently typed, as Barbara Smith and Gloria Hull have noted, by the image of mindlessness. Belonging to the two groups historically labeled as intellectually inferior, as women and black, they continue to find their intellectual capabilities doubly discredited.[4]

Indeed, the author was told of a recent social event at an academic institution during which it was offered as a humorous student observation that "black women writers" was a contradiction in terms. Faculty present apparently could not, or at least did not, challenge this student "joke," arguing that it was, after all, only a joke.

Along similar lines, I have been advised by well-meaning colleagues that to challenge such stereotypes black women must begin to write their own history, as if these colleagues were unaware that the new field of black women's studies, fully inclusive of history, comprises an exploding scholarly field. That such misconceptions persist confirms what Smith and Hull have aptly described as the oppressive "cultural-political value system in which Afro-American women have been forced to operate." And these perceptions remain all too evident today.[5]

In America black men have been equally subject to stereotyping, and both sexes have been typecast by racist mythology. Moreover, as Kate Millett has pointed out, blacks as a "race" have frequently been labeled by the same set of traits ascribed to the other historically marginalized group—women. Both blacks and women have been associated, for example, with "inferior intelligence, an instinctual or sensual gratification, an emotional nature both primitive and childlike," and with "a contentment with their own lot which is . . . a proof of its appropriateness."[6] Yet my findings argue that Afro-American women have also figured in imagery in significant ways as distinctively different from either black men or white women.

My findings suggest that the persistence and peculiar shape of the images today identified as "myths" of black womanhood can only be fully understood as the legacy of both racism and sexism working together over a long period of time. These have grown from the Afro-American woman's unique position, in Deborah White's words, "at the crossroads of two of the most well-developed ideologies in America, that regarding women and that regarding the Negro." As White has pointed out, it was during the era of slavery that these ideas "were molded into a peculiarly American mythology."[7] Thus, like Van Deburg, this historian has pointed to slave-rooted images as foundations for the myths of today. Yet it seems time not only to bring specific attention to the slave-rooted symbolizations of Afro-American *women*, but also to ask how Mammy and her kin have been perpetuated into contemporary times. To answer this question there is good reason to devote new attention to the role of the media of "fact" as a vehicle of their transmission; that is, to American scholarship.

As numerous studies have shown, scholarly discourse has by no means been free of racial mythology. William Van Deburg has demonstrated that American historians have, until recently, largely continued to reiterate time-honored stereotypes of slavery and race. However, such stereotypes are often treated as if gender neutral, while woman's image in American historiography has rarely been examined as yet. It is generally presupposed that women have been left invisible in this traditionally male-dominated discourse, in what is often identified as "His-story." But such assumptions have not been verified by research. And there are especially good reasons to investigate how Afro-American women may have figured in the story of American history, in light of recent recognition that they have been assigned a prefabricated history. The question is where it has come from.[8]

This book commenced when its author encountered Michele Wallace's observation in her 1979 book, *Black Macho and the Myth of the Superwoman*, that Afro-American woman had been assigned "a hell of a history to live down."[9] Because Wallace's portrayal of that history seemed both persuasive and shocking, it pointed to a further question: What role might historians themselves have played in the shaping of that hellish historical story? After all, historiography is not just past history. As William Van Deburg has demonstrated of the historiography of race and slavery, this provides a window onto American culture which not only illuminates the society's racial values over time, but also "to some variable degree creates, shapes, confirms, and strengthens them."[10]

Frances Fitzgerald has also pointed to the interaction between historians and American popular culture. As she has indicated, in the nineteenth century historians openly transmitted values and moral lessons together with "facts." During the turn-of-the-century decades, however, in concert with the professionalization of scholarship, historians came to see and present themselves as the "scientists" of the past. Their role was to discover the facts and to transmit them as objectively as possible. But as Fitzgerald has found, their subjectivity and moralism thereby, in effect, went underground. Still "themselves a part of history, in that they reflect the concerns, the conventional wisdom and even the fads of the age that produced them," historians continued more subtly than before to transmit and endorse the values and assumptions of their culture. Moreover, because history has traditionally played such a prominent role in education, generations of American children have grown up perceiving history books as having, in Fitzgerald's words, "much more than other books had the demeanor and trappings of authority."[11]

Therefore, this study began as an investigation of how Afro-American women may have figured in the past in American history books. However, it soon led into a wider body of scholarly literature as it became apparent that a distinctive, slave-woman portraiture pervaded more than the history texts. It became clear that the equation of black women's history with a prefabricated slave womanhood has played a major role in American research on race, commencing with sociological analysis of what became known in the early twentieth century as the "Negro Problem." Thence, not only historical explorations of slavery, but also social-science interpretations of race came to present virtually a uniform, preencoded story of the black woman's past, complete with a set of slave-women stock characters who merged into caricatures of black women after slavery.

My findings suggest that well into contemporary times this fundamentally backward-looking story has underpinned the literature of slavery and race, in effect continuing to endorse racist-sexist mythology by presenting the old images as fact. But liberal thought has long emphasized that it is through learning the facts that we are freed from false beliefs and myths, while scholarship presents itself and is generally accepted to be the medium of fact. Thus, if the literature of fact has transmitted a set of prefabricated, slave-rooted images of Afro-American women, it has thereby brought particularly powerful trappings of authority to these images that may entrap even the most liberal elements of American culture.

Certainly, as Michel Foucault has played a leading role in illuminating, scholarly discourse may constitute a compelling face of power.[12] Reasoning that women's continuing marginalization has been perpetuated by our omission as full human beings from the recounted story of the past, feminist historians have been inspired by perceptions that, in order to make claim to an equal place in the present, women must also establish a claim to the past. But it has less often been recognized that black women have not simply been excluded from American historical discourse; instead, they have often been included as images, but rarely in substance.

My findings argue that Michele Wallace is correct—Afro-American women have been assigned a "hell of a history to live down." As Deborah White has pointed out, history "is supposed to give people a sense of identity. . . . It should act as a springboard for the future." Those who share in her hope that it will finally achieve this for "black women who have been given more myth than history" may best forward that aspiration by recognizing the particular challenges and peculiar pitfalls which confront this endeavor.[13]

This recognition may also be advanced by acknowledgment that even the most antiracist scholarship has not been free from these mythical perceptions. In this sense, this book will not entirely support the views expressed by some studies that black-authored scholarship has long been much more progressive than has white-authored scholarship.

It is agreed that as William Van Deburg and John David Smith have shown, early black historians were pioneers in combating the proslavery historiography that, in effect, endorsed white supremacy. Nineteenth-century Afro-American historians rejected the portrait of slavery as a benevolent, paternalistic institution by emphasizing its fundamental cruelty and damage. Yet this antiracist historiography also frequently portrayed profoundly degraded, dehumanized images of slave women. However, this book hopes to explain why such images lived on in black- as well as white-authored scholarship, by pointing to perceptions of gender which crossed the color line.[14]

Much of the literature examined in this book is male-authored. This is because in the past American scholarship has largely reflected the traditional male control of public discourse. However, this book is not intended as an attack on "His-story." Instead, its findings argue that even the modern women's movement has by no means been immune to the spell of slave-rooted myths of black womanhood. It recognizes that the struggle to slay the old myths has become today an endeavor that links male- and female-authored scholarship.

It should also be clarified that the attention paid to myth by this book does not presuppose that all myths are necessarily completely false. Myth is itself an ambivalent concept, simultaneously defined as "without foundation in fact, imaginary, fictitious," and also "as a story or belief that attempts to express or explain a basic truth."[15] Generally when I speak of the myths of race and the myths of black womanhood, I am referring to myth in the first sense. However, in another sense myths do signify subjective, perceptual reality, constituting metaphorical representations of how the world is perceived that are based upon both experience and emotion. They may, in the words of Northrop Frye, provide "justifications of our desires, and at the same time hold up before us images of cosmic forces that preclude the possibility of any perfect gratification of them."[16]

Myths may also serve to justify our fears or to alleviate anxieties by projecting what is feared onto others. Racist mythology has functioned in this sense, to rationalize racial oppression and justify scapegoating. And racist mythology has long been pervaded by the images known as stereotypes.

Both stereotypes and myths are fundamentally pictures in the mind created out of imagination, although while the myth tends to mystify reality, the stereotype tends to simplify reality. However, both have pervaded the story of black women's history in a way that leads today's scholars to use these terms interchangeably. This book largely follows that practice. But its findings also point to the conclusion that over time, a distinctive set of slave-rooted stereotypes have, in the literature of fact, become integrally woven together into a composite image that is appropriately described as mythic. This composite image has emerged as more than the sum of its parts by taking on the shape of a story of damaged and damaging womanhood. And this story reveals much about society's linking in myth of both gender and race.

Finally, it should be noted that the realm of myth is not readily challenged by reason precisely because it does symbolize subjective and psychic reality. Thus, as Elizabeth Janeway has found, the old images of man's world and woman's place remain strikingly impervious to logic because underpinned by images of gender as natural and permanent. As Nina Auerbach has discovered, "the myth of womanhood flourishes . . . in the vibrant half-life of popular literature and art." In Auerbach's view, these myths live on largely because they "live below the formulated surface" of their age rather than crystallizing "into explicit gospel or precept which the conscious mind can analyze and reject."[17]

However, Auerbach may set up a mistaken dichotomy between fiction and the literature of fact. While scholarship does constitute an era's officially "formulated surface," it does not follow that myths do not also reside beneath its surface and shape. Certainly there is little reason to believe scholarship is immune from the human propensity to create myth. As Barry Barnes has pointed out, the human mode of perception is to read the world "as an assemblage of symbols." For the raw materials used in their construction of knowledge, scholars turn to "existing knowledge and existing cultural resources," which include both contemporary symbols and "old knowledge."[18]

Moreover, historians are particularly reliant upon old knowledge. As well, they familiarize the past to the present by developing it in terms of the cultural symbols known to their contemporaries. The historian also frequently makes the past intelligible by presenting it in the form of a story, which involves the exercise of imagination. Hence, as Hayden White has observed, historical writing actually has much in common with fictional literature in presenting "verbal fictions." And in deciding which out of all possible "facts" to include in his or her story, the historian is influenced by the values of contemporaries regarding what is significant. Thus, in sum, the writing of history draws heavily upon "the myth, fable, and folklore . . . and literary art of the historian's own culture." As Claude Lévi-Strauss has advised, "a clairvoyant history should admit that it never completely escapes from the nature of myth."[19]

Myth has been central both to the shaping of American history and to its recording. Alfred Stern has observed that "myths have been used for centuries in writing history as well as making it."[20] However, if we are unable to liberate ourselves from this historical habit, perhaps we may at least recognize and exercise it with an ever more acute sense of responsibility when we acknowledge the role of American historiography in shaping the "hell of a history" which has been assigned to black American women. By exploring the discourse of yesterday's literature of fact we may also forward our understanding of the discourse of today, by recognizing the subtexts pervading the dialogue—or struggle—between present and past, which continues to shape the reconstruction of history. Doubtless, in confronting the legacies of racism and sexism together, those who struggle finally today to place black women rightly in history face a difficult challenge.

NOTES

1. William L. Van Deburg, *Slavery and Race in American Popular Culture* (Madison: The University of Wisconsin Press, 1984), xi, 158.

2. Mary Helen Washington, ed., *Black-Eyed Susans: Classic Stories by and about Black Women* (New York: Anchor Press, 1975), ix; Alice Walker, *In Search of Our Mothers' Gardens* (New York: Harcourt Brace Jovanovich, 1983), 237.

3. Washington, *Black-Eyed Susans*, ix.

4. Gloria T. Hull and Barbara Smith, "The Politics of Black Women's Studies," in Gloria T. Hull, Patricia Bell Scott, and Barbara Smith, eds., *All the Women Are White, All the Blacks Are Men, But Some of Us Are Brave: Black Women's Studies* (Old Westbury, N.Y.: The Feminist Press, 1982), xviii.

5. Ibid.

6. Kate Millett, *Sexual Politics* (New York: Avon Books, 1971), 86.

7. Deborah White, *Ar'n't I a Woman?: Female Slaves in the Ante-Bellum South* (New York: Norton, 1985), 27.

8. Van Deburg, *Slavery and Race*. On scholarship and race see, for example, Stanford M. Lyman, *The Black American in Sociological Thought* (New York: Putnam, 1972); George W. Stocking, Jr., *Race, Culture and Evolution* (New York: Free Press, 1968); Alexander Thomas and Samuel Sillen, *Racism and Psychiatry* (New York: Brunner/Mazel Publishers, 1972); Eleanor Engram, *Science, Myth, Reality: The Black Family in One-Half Century of Research* (Westport, Conn.: Greenwood Press, 1982); and John H. Stanfield, *Philanthropy and Jim Crow in American Social Science* (Westport, Conn.: Greenwood Press, 1985).

9. Michele Wallace, *Black Macho and the Myth of the Superwoman* (New York: Warner Books, 1980), 133.

10. Van Deburg, *Slavery and Race*, xii.

11. Frances Fitzgerald, *America Revised: History Textbooks in the Twentieth Century* (Boston: Little, Brown & Company, 1979), 20, 7.

12. See, for example, Michel Foucault, *The History of Sexuality*, trans. R. Hurley (New York: Pantheon Books, 1978); and Hayden White, *Tropics of Discourse: Essays in Cultural Criticism* (Baltimore: The Johns Hopkins University Press, 1978).

13. White, *Ar'n't I a Woman*, 167.

14. Van Deburg, *Slavery and Race*; John David Smith, *An Old Creed for the New South: Proslavery Ideology and Historiography, 1865–1918* (Westport, Conn.: Greenwood Press, 1985).

15. *The Random House College Dictionary*, revised edition (New York: Random House, 1977), 882.

16. Quoted in White, "Forms of Wildness," *Tropics of Discourse*, 1975.

17. Elizabeth Janeway, *Man's World, Woman's Place* (New York: William Morrow and Company, 1971), esp. 29–36; Nina Auerbach, *Woman and the Demon: The Life of a Victorian Myth* (Cambridge, Mass.: Harvard University Press, 1982), 10.

18. Barry Barnes, *Interests and the Growth of Knowledge* (London: Routledge and Kegan Paul, 1977), 12, 18.

19. Hayden White, "The Historical Text as Literary Artifact," in Robert Canary and Henry Kozicki, *The Writing of History: Literary Form and Understanding* (Madison: University of Wisconsin Press, 1978), 42, 55, 45.

20. Alfred Stern, "Fiction and Myth in History," *Diogenes* 42 (1963): 98. See also, for example, Patrick Gerster and Nicholas Cords, eds., *Myth and Southern History* (Chicago: Rand McNally College Publishing Co., 1974).

1

The Myths of Black Womanhood

It is only recently that attention has been paid to the black woman's image in the American popular mind. During the civil rights era a new anger was brought to the myths underlying American racism, and historians turned with a new zeal to delete racial stereotypes from American history. However, the anger and protest focused largely on the derogatory labeling of the black man.

John Blassingame, for example, called for the writing of a black-authored story of the past because the white-authored version was replete with "myths which have distorted the image of the black man." He charged that black Americans had, in images, long been "lynched and castrated" by white historians.[1] If Blassingame's androcentric perspective appeared in his choice of language, it was also revealed in his own historical work. In particular, and most effectively, he challenged the old stereotype of the slave as a "Sambo": "indolent, faithful, humorous, loyal, dishonest, superstitious, improvident, and musical . . . a clown and congenitally docile." This historian argued that in reality Sambo was essentially an invention of the antebellum Southern white imagination to alleviate fears of black rebellion and provide relief from "the anxiety of thinking about slaves as men."[2] Yet Blassingame's perceptive analysis of this and other images of slave men did not show how relief was obtained from the anxiety of thinking about slaves as women.

Generally in such studies the existence or significance of distinctive symbolizations of black women was denied by omission rather than by commission. However a 1976 book, *Sexual Racism*, moved toward explicit denial. Its author, sociologist Charles Stember, argued that sex was central to American racism. According to this analysis, the white man's sexual jealousy of black men was the basis for his racial hostility, while his jealousy was reflected in and inflamed by the myths of black male hypersexuality. In Stember's view, it has "clearly" been upon the black male, and not the black female, that the mythology of black sexuality has "largely focused."[3]

Stember argued that as early as the colonial era of the American past, white perceptions of black men as, in effect, superstuds, were "concretized in myth into specific anatomical and physiological details—his penis was larger, his sexual capacity greater, his desire harder to satisfy." In Stember's view, the notion that black women were similarly hypersexed was not "threatening in a male-dominated society," and hence "the notion of black sexuality has centered on the black male."[4]

According to Stember's book, for these reasons racist insistence upon the protection of white racial "purity" has historically focused upon the black male. It was he who seemed to pose the threat of racial "mongrelization." Hence, the image of the rapacious "black brute"—the violator of white female purity who could be controlled only by lynching—in effect midwifed the birth of racial segregation, in Stember's view.

As Stember and others have noted, the stereotype of the black male rapist has long survived the dismantling of segregation. But not all would agree with him that "though parallel myths developed around the black woman, they are neither as widespread nor as specific."[5] Instead, as Angela Davis has pointed out, the male rapist image has long been complemented by "its inseparable companion: the image of the Black woman as chronically promiscuous."[6]

As attention is brought to the society's linked symbolizations of black manhood and womanhood, the distinctiveness of the black woman's image in the American mind also emerges. Deborah White has observed: "If she is rescued from the myth of the Negro, the myth of woman traps her. If she escapes the myth of woman, the myth of the Negro still ensnares her."[7] What must be emphasized, however, is that from this dual set of myths the black woman has emerged as significantly different in her image from either black men or white women in America.

The "ultrafeminine" image of white womanhood can perhaps best be captured in the American South, where this and other American value systems have long been written in capital letters. The patriarchal prescriptions for womanhood may be best conveyed in brief by Rosemary Daniell's portrayal of the Southern white woman as the "manipulative magnolia," describing

all the women whose roots I shared—as netted in one mutual silken bondage. Together, we were trapped in a morass of Spanish moss, Bible Belt Guilt, and the pressures of a patriarchy stronger than in any other part of the country. . . . Like most southern women, I had grown up feeling that only relationships with men were worth serious pursuit.[8]

In contrast, patriarchy and the gentle workings of feminine wiles are not central to the black woman's image, but matriarchy and domination of men are. Far from pursuing relationships with males, her masculinized traits and aggressive behavior drive them away from her—if they survive her emasculation of them. Neither a magnolialike figure nor a shrinking violet, in her image she resembles more closely the Venus's-flytrap that entraps and devours its hapless victims.

At least, so Afro-American women were told—or interpreted what America was told—by a major publication of 1965 known as the "Moynihan Report." Because this was a major formulation of what has since been widely identified as "the Myth of the Black Matriarchy," the Moynihan Report and its reception deserve our attention.

As Assistant Secretary of Labor and Director of the Office of Policy Planning and Research in the Johnson Administration, Daniel Patrick Moynihan presented reform of the Afro-American family as crucial to the "war on poverty." In an earlier book coauthored with Nathan Glazer, *Beyond the Melting Pot* (1963), he had already outlined the thesis of black familial decrepitude that would be fleshed out in his 1965 *The Negro Family: The Case for National Action*, which became known as the Moynihan Report. Although Moynihan may well have intended that his generalizations apply only to impoverished blacks, *Beyond the Melting Pot* already suggested their wider applicability, characterizing black parents, for example, as ignoring and resenting their children "as Negro parents . . . so often do."[9]

That study, which in 1964 won the *Saturday Review of Literature* award as a major contribution to improving race relations, also emphasized and related high rates of black motherhood out of wedlock and of mother-led households to offspring poorly socialized in the values and norms underpinning American achievement and the work ethic. *The Negro Family* largely only expanded upon this picture, with particular emphasis upon what it called Negro "matriarchy." But in the context of rising black nationalism, and viewed as a policy-making document, it was the Moynihan Report that touched off a raging controversy.

Critics charged that the report wrongly and damagingly presented black Americans as the cause of their own problems. The report did present the "deterioration of the Negro family" as the heart of the "tangle of pathology" which perpetuated poverty and antisocial behavior. Familial "disorganization" was presented as the major source of weakness in the contemporary black community.[10]

By disorganization, Moynihan meant especially the rule of black mothers. In his 1965 report he clarified his view that it was the "black matriarchy" which was the core of the problem, imposing "a crushing burden on the Negro male."[11] In *Beyond the Melting Pot* he had already explained this supposed fact of contemporary life by pointing to the past. Slavery, by denying the legality of slave marriages and separating spouses, was said to have created the "fatherless matrifocal pattern" which continued after emancipation when black women found it easier than their men to find jobs and secure "favors" from whites. Moreover, the former were said to have been less damaged by racism because as women they were used to being underprivileged. Hence, "the problem of the Negro in America is the problem of the Negro man more than the Negro woman."[12]

Expanding upon such notions in his 1965 report, Moynihan argued that, unable to fulfill the masculine role of provider, demoralized black fathers deserted their families. As a result, he claimed, matrifocality increased, together with sexual promiscuity and illegitimate births. In his view the slave-rooted matriarchy had become a self-perpetuating institution. Contemporary black women were said still to be relatively advantaged, enjoying more familial power, educational and professional success, and greater psychic well-being than their men. According to Moynihan, the male children of mother-led homes were in particular jeopardy. Lacking male role models, they grew up sexually confused and demonstrated antisocial behavior including juvenile delinquency, crime, poor educational achievement, and welfare dependency.

Furthermore, the impact of poverty and powerlessness was said to be especially damaging to black masculinity because "submissiveness is surely more destructive to the male than the female personality." In support of this observation Moynihan noted that "the very essence of the male animal, from the bantam rooster to the four-star general, is to strut."[13]

Not surprisingly, the report advised black men to join the military to regain their manliness. The armed forces offered "an utterly masculine world . . . away from women." The forces offered work, and Moynihan was interested in promoting the employment of black men "even if this meant that some women's jobs had to be designed to enable men to fulfill them." Moynihan's message was clear: both inside and outside of the family, it was essential to establish the authority and "manliness" of black men so that Afro-American gender relations corresponded to the normal patriarchal relations of the American way. And what he wrote had an unmistakable air of authority and plausibility.[14]

Indeed, Moynihan presented his "black matriarchy" in a matter-of-fact, commonsense way. The appearance of this image in his report, essentially as a fact which could be taken for granted, stemmed in particular from its presentation as the natural outcome of history, and from his references to such eminent scholars as Stanley Elkins, Thomas Pettigrew, and E. Franklin Frazier. These sources appeared to substantiate as conventional academic wisdom Moynihan's account of the historical evolution and dynamics of his dominant black female/emasculated black man paradigm. Thus, his thesis seemed to be firmly based upon history and upon officially endorsed reality. It seemed, as observed by Lee Rainwater and William Yancey, editors of

The Moynihan Report and the Politics of Controversy, to say "nothing new." They were therefore surprised by the controversy which it inspired.[15]

At first sight, however, some seemed to find the report quite noncontroversial. For example, in her 1965 article in the *Negro History Bulletin*, Ann Allen Shockley accepted it as a taken-for-granted truth that under slavery the black woman had become the "family matriarch," and that "matriarchal patterns" remained "predominant today." But Shockley pointed optimistically to eventual fulfillment of the black woman's dreams in finding "her likeness and identification in that of other women."[16] According to an article in *Ebony*, the "immediate goal" of contemporary black women should be to establish "a strong family unit in which the father is the dominant person."[17]

However, some were quick to perceive the Moynihan thesis as perpetuating myths which were damaging to black Americans. The contributors to Toni Cade's 1970 anthology, *The Black Woman*, pointed out that it was "fallacious reasoning that in order for the Black man to be strong, the Black woman has to be weak." They charged that the erroneous female power/male weakness paradigm which cast black women as castrators and black men as emasculated was "popularized through the highly publicized and highly touted work . . . by Moynihan." His report was "dividing black men and women" in their struggle against racism: "Moynihan stopped that force and Black men began to look upon their women as a strange breed who were against them."[18]

Cade's book reflected the consciousness-raising effect of the Moynihan Report. As a publication in which black American women spoke out for themselves in support of each other, this anthology reflected their increasingly outraged recognition of how they figured in the American mind.

By the mid-1970s American social science had undertaken the revisionist family research which led to identification of the "Black Matriarchy" as a myth. As will be discussed later in this book, it was argued by these studies that most contemporary black families were not mother-led. It was pointed out that it was ludicrous to speak of matriarchal control if the husband and father was absent, because who, then, was being controlled?[19]

For black women themselves, the matriarchy image provoked a mounting sense of injustice and anger. It seemed to label them as to blame, in Joyce Ladner's words, "for all kinds of alleged social problems which . . . they did not create." In the view of this sociologist, that they were the hard-working backbone of the black family should be cause for celebration rather than blame.[20] As Frances Beale charged, it was worse than foolish to label black women in this way, since "a matriarchal system is one in which power rests firmly in the hands of women." In contrast, black women were doubly oppressed, "victimized on two counts: they are women and they are Black."[21]

Yet it became increasingly clear that the matriarchy mythology was but the tip of the iceberg, while as Robert Staples pointed out, "in no other area is there . . . so many stereotypes and myths, than that of Black female sexuality. . . . The image . . . is that she is the most sensual of all female creatures." Contributors to Cade's anthology pointed with particular outrage to this: "She has been . . . called 'loose', hot-blooded, 'wanton', 'sultry', and 'amoral' . . . [and] used as the white man's sexual outhouse."[22]

Moreover, as Joyce Ladner observed, the sexual image fed into the matriarchal one, resulting in a figure simultaneously labeled as an immoral procreator of bastards, a castrator of men, and as a woman of superhuman strength.[23] These images seemed oddly to shade into each other, creating a composite picture both irrational and yet with its own underlying coherence.

As Michele Wallace pointed out, the sex-object image and the stereotypical, loyal old Mammy were both symbols of black female collaboration with the enemy. As slave-rooted images of black women who "had never been able to close their legs to a white man nor deny our breasts to a white child," the images blended into those of the matriarch who "had not allowed the black man to be a man in his own house."[24]

In Wallace's view, the composite picture that emerged in total from the "hell of a history" thus assigned to black American women was Amazonic:

From the intricate web of mythology . . . a fundamental image emerges. It is of a woman of inordinate strength. . . . Less of a woman in that she is less "feminine" and helpless, she is really *more* of a woman in that she is the embodiment of Mother Earth, the quintessential mother with infinite sexual, life-giving, and nurturing reserves. In other words, she is a superwoman.[25]

According to Wallace, this mythology was the reason for the apathy of many black women to feminism. Their view of themselves as more oppressed by racism than by sexism was reinforced by the belief that they were already liberated Amazons, and that the black male's oppression was greater. Wallace claimed that feelings of guilt about their seeming excess of power over the black male were feeding their support of male domination.

As well, other studies emphasized the contemporary black woman's internalization of the society's damaging images of her. Together with chronic socioeconomic deprivation, the pervasiveness of derogatory images was said to erode her self-confidence, to promote her negative self-identity as a loser, and at best, to inspire anxiety and confusion over her own identity.[26] Accordingly, Joyce Ladner advised that a "frontal attack" must be made on the myths of black womanhood as much as against "hunger and . . . brutality. Ultimately, all of these injustices are interdependent."[27]

Others focused more on the social and political functions of these conceptualizations as pillars of racial inequality. In Mae King's view, the "politics of sexual stereotypes" revolved around four central figures: the sex object, the "tragic mulatto" who failed in her misguided attempt to pass as white, the inept and comical domestic servant, and the masculinized, domineering matriarch. Together these shaped the composite picture of a defeminized female failure. As well, according to King's analysis, this portraiture functioned to discourage the white male from marrying the black woman and having to share his status, property, and power with members of the subordinate caste. In this way, the devaluation of black womanhood reflected and perpetuated the "power distance" between whites and blacks.[28]

But however the cultural imagery was interpreted, its origin seemed to circle back to the past. As Barbara Christian observed, the "invidious" black matriarchy mythology appeared to be but "another variation of the image of the mammy." As was increasingly recognized, such "companion myths are not recent in their origins."[29]

Studies of the film industry have shown that, among the stereotypes of black Americans historically pervading American motion pictures, Mammy was very prominent. Played by Hatti McDaniel in the 1939 blockbuster, "Gone with the Wind," she was popular enough to win an Oscar, while as Edward Mapp has observed, "Hollywood, prone to replicate successes . . . wrapped a bandana around the head of each working black actress." The parade of screen mammies, cast as jolly and warm, also typed them as huge, tough, and masculinized enough to emphasize the ultrafemininity of the white female stars.[30]

Included among the visual media's cast was also the "exotic mulatto," usually played by a white woman. Like Mammy, this seductive figure flourished especially during the depression era at a time when the public sought escape from realities into fantasies either comical or sexually titillating. In post–World War II America, the exotic mulatto became on the screen a more tragic figure, modeled after "Pinky" of the 1949 movie of that title. Foiled in her attempt to pass into white society, exposed as a "Negro," she often met with a sad fate, or at least lost her white man.

As well, the postwar Mammy was updated into the shrewish "Sapphire" figure of the popular "Amos 'n' Andy" radio and television series. With "colored folks" this caricatured figure became a bossy "black bitch," although remaining a faithful servant to the white family. Thus, the Mammy became an explicitly matriarchal figure who "wore the pants" in her own home and made a fool of her man.

Indeed, as Edward Mapp noted in the early 1970s, on the screen, "the thin line between black mammy and black matriarch may be distinguished largely by whether the old girl is presiding over a white or black household." He noted too that by then the female mulatto had moved back toward her exotic sex-object image, used and abused by men in the new sexploitation films. In sum, Mapp pointed to "a tragic history of stereotyping and a steady procession of mammies, maids, miscegenists, matriarchs, madams and assorted 'make-it-for-money-types.' " But what he discovered as a "half-century of screen humiliation for the black woman" led others still further back in time, and into other media of transmission.[31]

According to Karen Sue Warren Jewell's findings, the screen Mammy had evolved from a stock character of late nineteenth-century fiction. But in the written media she had been a capable figure, performing a valuable role for white families. In contrast, in the visual media she became more depreciated—an inept and comical character capable only of the most simple, menial labor. In Jewell's view, as this Aunt Jemima figure became the most prevalent film image of Afro-American women, it became the popular culture's central symbol of black womanhood, typing black American women as tough and defeminized and born to perform menial service for whites.[32]

However, it has become increasingly apparent that however she has been updated, the Mammy's origins circle ultimately back to the Old South. As Barbara Christian has found, the Mammy constitutes "one of the most dominant images to emerge in southern life and literature."[33] As well, recent studies by Christian and others have cast new light not only upon Mammy but also upon her kin.

These studies have demonstrated that, in Catherine Clinton's words, "sex is as critical a factor for understanding social relations in the South as race," by discovering the webbing of images of black and white women which were a basis for Old South mythology. It is also increasingly clear that the one set of images cannot be fully understood without the other, just as the Mammy and the Lady were integrally related figures.[34]

As Clinton has shown, the Lady idealization of Southern white womanhood propped up both slavery and patriarchy. According to this symbolization, the plantation mistress was, from patriarchal perspectives, an ultrafeminine creature: delicate, sexually pure, and devoted above all to her family. Dependent and deferential to men, the Lady was, in her image, rewarded by being protected, worshiped, pedestaled, leisured, and advantaged.

Clinton argues that in reality the plantation mistress was a hard-working and capable woman, responsible for the management of slaves and assigned a host of onerous responsibilities. These included the production of the numerous offspring which were essential to the status and perpetuation of the patriarchy. The master's children also had to be, and be known to be, racially pure; that is, of all-white ancestry, in a society which based slavery upon black ancestry. Thus, that the plantation mistress conform to the Lady ideal was essential to white male supremacy and to the maintenance of slavery. In Clinton's words, "slavery exaggerated the pattern of subjugation that patriarchy had established."[35]

In Clinton's analysis the Lady has emerged as strikingly akin to her slave sister in her subordination by white male supremacy, but as blinded to reality by the patriarchy's use of "near-identical ideological warfare" against both women and slaves.[36] In the context of this warfare, the Old South's image of slave womanhood emerges as a powerful weapon of white male domination over both free and enslaved women.

For example, while white Southern culture was pervaded by a double standard which prescribed female purity and yet ignored the white man's sexual exploitation of black women, the plantation mistress blamed the slave woman, not the master, for miscegenation. But as Clinton has illuminated, the society's image of black womanhood preshaped this response by labeling slave women as unrestrained, lascivious creatures avidly seeking sex with their masters or anyone else. Clinton has pointed out the Mammy image as the basis for society's "constant harping" upon the theme of the white male being "suckled at black breasts." This assigned "black women to an animal-like state of exploitation: Mammies were to be milked, warm bodies to serve white needs—an image with its own sexual subtext."[37]

Thus, the master could rationalize his violation of black female sexual purity as no violation at all. The plantation mistress dared not challenge the sexual double standard. If she failed to act in accordance with the prescribed Lady role, she risked incurring the same stigmatization that was attached to black women in a culture that conceptually divided all women into "ladies, always white and chaste; and whores, comprising all black women (except for the saintly Mammy) and any white woman who defied the established social constraints on her sexual behavior." In short, Clinton's findings argue that the "racist sexual stereotype" of black womanhood propped up the white man's sexual control over all women.[38]

Similarly, and by exploring the Old South through its literature, Minrose Gwin has found that "as obverse images in the popular mind, the chaste belle and the lustful female slaves evolved into rigid stereotypes." As Gwin has argued, "the virgin/whore dichotomy which was imposed upon white and black southern women must have deeply affected their images of themselves and of each other." The women of each race were thereby rendered a "fractured self," denied a full and diverse identity by the culture of patriarchy, and encouraged always to reject their racially designated female other. Therefore, Gwin has pointed out, "just as black women were forced to be strong, white southern women often were compelled to appear weak."[39]

Barbara Christian has demonstrated that Mammy was essential to the Lady ideal. The plantation mistress did require the assistance of slave women in domestic work and the care of children. But as well, the Lady image was made credible by providing the Lady with an idealized servant companion who was assigned complementary moral qualities of religious piety and asexuality, and yet contrasting physical attributes. Christian has found that as a stock character of Old South literature, the slave Mammy was invariably cast as superreligious and loyal to "her" white family, and also as physically strong, tough, obese, and ugly. Her masculinization highlighted the Lady's ultrafemininity. In short, the Mammy and the Lady were two sides of the same coin. In Christian's words, "if one was to be, the other had to be."[40]

Deborah White has also pointed to the Mammy as complementing the cult of domesticity which relegated white women to home and family. As she has noted, Mammy's image was as the foremost Big House slave. A maternal figure, she loved the white children whom she nursed and raised, while she was also in charge of all domestic management, in effect as the "surrogate mistress and mother." In reality, White has argued, no one slave woman served all of these roles, and "the reality of Mammy and female household service does not square with the Mammy legend."[41] But in her image, Mammy simultaneously symbolized the ideal slave and the ideal woman.

Moreover, in White's view the Mammy's desexualized image was fundamental to the defense of slavery as an institution that promoted racial affection, but not, as Northern abolitionists charged, illicit sexual intimacy. This figure was all the more essential to the South's romanticization of slavery as an extended white-black family because of the female slave's Jezebel typing as a lascivious woman who invited the white man's sexual attention.

As White has pointed out, the Jezebel image evolved in part from the physical conditions of slavery, as the slave woman necessarily hitched up her skirts to work and was forced to disrobe for inspection at slave auctions, in a society which equated increasing layers of clothing with female respectability. Also, the master's interest in her ability to procreate new slaves rendered her sexuality and fecundity matters of public discussion.

But as well, by labeling the female slave as a Jezebel, the master's sexual abuse was justified by presenting her as a woman who deserved what she got. The white man could also deny the challenge posed to patriarchal mythology by this woman who could do "man's work" by labeling the slave woman as a sexual animal—not a real woman at all. However, the more she was treated and viewed as a Jezebel, the more essential Mammy became as the counterimage of slavery's racial intimacy. Thus, as White has illuminated, Mammy and Jezebel were also two sides of the same coin of Southern mythology.[42]

Moreover, as Catherine Clinton has pointed out, as a figure assigned masculine attributes and substantial authority, the Mammy was the other side of the same coin which typecast the slave man as Sambo. Because the only Old South image of black power was Mammy, who devoted her power to collaboration with whites, the Sambo figure was a major figure of the society's "emasculation of slavery."[43] In image, Mammy confirmed Sambo: the stereotypical, docile, demasculinized slave man. Thus, these linked representations rendering slave women as other than womanly and slave men as other than manly stripped the enslaved of a gender identity.

In short, it is now apparent that the oppression of slavery cannot be fully understood without complementing attention being paid to Uncle Tom and his kin by paying equal attention to Mammy and her kin. The Old South sought to alleviate its anxieties not only about seeing slave men as men, but also about seeing slave women as women. Moreover, because the sexual dynamics of slavery can no longer be ignored, it also becomes increasingly clear that, as Barbara Christian has pointed out, "the racism that black people have had to suffer is almost always presented in peculiarly sexist terms. That is, the wholeness of a person is basically threatened by an assault on the definition of herself or himself, as female or male."[44]

This constitutes a most dehumanizing assault. Elizabeth Fox-Genovese has emphasized that for human beings, gender defines "their innermost identities, their ideals for themselves, and their views of the world." Sexual identity lies "at the core of any individual's sense of self."[45] And attention to the historical continuity of this assault points to the modern myths of black womanhood as truly "nothing new."

Indeed, as Deborah White has observed of the modern woman's image as "a domineering black woman who consumes men," it circles back to the Jezebel slave-seductress figure, while "her assertive demeanor identifies her with Mammy."[46] And as Bell Hooks has noted, "Just as the nineteenth century white public had portrayed black women as embodying all negative traits that were usually attributed to the female sex as a whole while portraying white women as embodying all positive traits, the twentieth-century white public continued this practice."[47]

Recent studies have emphasized both the continuity and the damaging consequences of society's assault on black womanhood for relations between black men and women. In Bell Hooks's view, through the matriarchal mythology "white racist oppressors" have been able to forge bonds "of solidarity with black men based on mutual sexism," by scapegoating the black woman for the black man's inability to play the traditional masculine role in a racist society. Thus while "negative images of black women . . . affect all Americans," they also promote special "divisiveness between black men and black women."[48] Michele Wallace has argued that from the "hell of a history" assigned to Afro-American women have emerged the images of black female strength and black male weakness that created "the myth that they were weak because we were strong."[49]

In addition, recent feminist research has emphasized the divisive consequences of these images for all American women. They have functioned to perpetuate, in the words of Phyllis Marynick Palmer, an overriding "dualism of female identity." Her analysis begins with the paradox that the women's movement seems often simultaneously to use black women as symbols of female liberation and to criticize their failure to support the movement. As she has noted, the nineteenth-century black abolitionist and women's rights leader, Sojourner Truth, is a popular feminist emblem. Hence, Palmer has asked, why has the feminist movement embraced black women "as images of strength and pathos" while often ignoring their own views and needs?[50]

In answer, Palmer has turned to society's historically dichotomized conceptualization of black and white womanhood, which assigned to white women the idealized attributes of "true womanhood," and cast black women as fallen womanhood. Barbara Welter has pointed out that during the nineteenth century the Victorian cult of "true womanhood" prescribed not only female domesticity, but also chastity, piety, and dependency on and deference to men, together with other patriarchally prescribed "feminine virtues." Thus, Palmer has noted, the "good" woman was by definition "pure, clean, sexually repressed and physically fragile." In contrast, the "bad" woman was by definition the woman without male protectors, who provided for herself. The black woman was therefore de facto the bad, unwomanly woman, cast in Palmer's words as "dirty, licentious, physically strong, and knowledgeable about . . . evil."[51]

Palmer's analysis goes further to argue that in America the elevated status of white womanhood has been crucially reinforced by this racial representation of bad womanhood in a way that has provided important psychological incentives for conformity to "woman's place." In Palmer's view, American white women have historically accepted the constraints of that place because the black-white, bad-good categorization has so powerfully reinforced their elevated self-image.

In this context the simultaneous use of Sojourner Truth as a feminist symbol and the failure to incorporate black women into the feminist movement becomes more comprehensible, according to Palmer. Sojourner Truth continues to be perceived in accordance with this set of historical perceptions as a version of Mammy, a powerful figure who uses her power in service to and in nurturance of whites: "The image of white woman being cradled in a black woman's arms has . . . exerted a lasting appeal." But Mammy-cum-Sojourner is also a defeminized figure who reflects continuing assumptions that black women deserve their inequality because they are losers as women.[52]

In short, Palmer argues that the psychological rewards of the white woman's pedestaled image remain crucial today. Therefore, while black women may be embraced as symbols of female strength and pathos, they are still not embraced as equals. And until this still-immense perceptual barrier dividing "good" and "bad" women is transcended, American women will not be able to make common cause.

In sum, recent analyses have pointed to the power of racist-sexist mythology to divide women from women and to separate white Americans from black Americans, as well as to construct barriers separating black men and black women. However, to challenge fully these perceptual barriers dividing person from person, it is essential to recognize that they have been very deeply embedded into an edifice all the more durable because apparently built out of history and solid and reliable fact. What follows will argue that American scholarly discourse has played a major role in constructing as factual a story of black women's history that has endorsed the culture's most derogatory myths of Afro-American womanhood.

What follows is, therefore, a reconstruction of how Afro-American women have been cast in the stories of others; it is by no means the black woman's story. Therefore, it hopes not to deserve the same kind of criticism that Alice Walker has expressed of Michele Wallace's book for focusing on male-authored writings and considering "the male version of reality enough," and for attempting to apply stereotypes which "cannot possibly fit creative, moving, thoughtful, and evolving 'human beings.' "[53]

A substantial part of my investigation does focus upon the stories men have told about women. But as the historian, Winthrop Jordan, has pointed out, the expression of "sexually-oriented beliefs about the Negro in America" has been largely "male in genesis and tone."[54] In reality, to examine American scholarship is to examine what has been, until recently, largely a man's world.

Of course the ugly, grotesque images unearthed in this study do not fit real human beings. Yet even the most depowering myths of femininity may stem from aspects of womanhood perceived as threats to male-defined order.[55] Thus, Nina Auerbach has criticized the zeal of feminist scholarship for slaying these representations: "Gleefully . . . we identified pernicious 'myths' and 'images' of women" in order to bury them by a deluge of facts and statistics. Instead, Auerbach has suggested that by retrieving this "lost world of belief" we may discover "a less restricting facet of woman's history than the social sciences can encompass." Truly, this cultural historian has shown that the mythological Victorian woman is "too strong and interesting a creature for us to kill."[56]

It may be as well that the mythological black woman-cum-slave woman is both strong and profoundly revealing. Certainly she reveals much about the manipulation of black woman's history in American historiography.

NOTES

1. John Blassingame, ed., *New Perspectives on Black Studies* (Chicago: University of Illinois Press, 1971), xi, 208.

2. John Blassingame, *The Slave Community: Plantation Life in the Antebellum South*, revised edition (New York: Oxford University Press, 1979, orig. pub. 1972), 225, 230.

3. Charles Stember, *Sexual Racism: The Emotional Barrier to an Integrated Society* (New York: Harper and Row, 1978), 60.

4. Ibid., 57, 55.

5. Ibid., 57.

6. Angela Davis, *Women, Race and Class* (New York: Vintage Books/Random House, 1983), 182.

7. White, *Ar'n't I a Woman?*, 28.

8. Rosemary Daniell, *Fatal Flowers: On Sin, Sex, and Suicide in the Deep South* (New York: Avon Books, 1984), 17.

9. Nathan Glazer and Daniel Patrick Moynihan, *Beyond the Melting Pot: The Ne-*

groes, *Puerto Ricans, Jews, and Italians of New York City* (Cambridge, Mass.: Harvard University Press and MIT Press, 1963), 50; Daniel P. Moynihan, *The Negro Family: The Case for National Action* (Washington, D.C.: United States Department of Labor, Office of Policy Planning and Research, 1965).

10. The controversy over the report is introduced in Lee Rainwater and William Yancey, eds., *The Moynihan Report and the Politics of Controversy* (Cambridge, Mass.: MIT Press, 1967), 24. Moynihan's "The Negro Family: The Case for National Action" was reprinted in this book, pp. 47–94.

11. Moynihan, "The Negro Family," in Rainwater and Yancey, *Moynihan Report*, 75.

12. Moynihan and Glazer, *Melting Pot*, 38.

13. Rainwater and Yancey, *Moynihan Report*, 16.

14. Ibid., 88, 29.

15. Ibid., 19. Moynihan's references to these scholars in substantiation of his thesis may be found on pp. 62–65.

16. Ann Allen Shockley, "The Negro Woman in Retrospect: Blueprint for the Future," *Negro History Bulletin* 79 (1965): 55, 56, 62.

17. Quoted in Paula Giddings, *When and Where I Enter: The Impact of Black Women on Race and Sex in America* (New York: William Morrow & Company, Inc., 1984), 329.

18. Toni Cade, ed., *The Black Woman* (New York: Mentor/New American Library, 1970), 93, 114, 145.

19. See, for example, Robert Staples, "The Myth of the Black Matriarchy," *The Black Scholar* 1 (1970): 9–16; and Staples, *The Black Family* (Belmont, Calif.: Wadsworth, 1971).

20. Joyce Ladner, *Tomorrow's Tomorrow: The Black Woman* (New York: Doubleday, 1971), xx, 33.

21. Frances Beale, "Double Jeopardy," in Cade, *The Black Woman*, 117.

22. Robert Staples, *The Black Woman in America: Sex, Marriage and the Family* (Chicago: Nelson-Hall Publishers, 1973), 37; Toni Cade, *The Black Woman*, 81–82.

23. Ladner, *Tomorrow's Tomorrow*, 30; Ladner, Foreward to Staples, *The Black Woman*, ix–xiv.

24. Wallace, *Black Macho*, 134.

25. Ibid., 154.

26. See, for example, Christine Carrington, "Depression in Black Women," in La Frances Rodgers-Rose, ed., *The Black Woman* (Beverly Hills, Calif.: Sage Publications, 1980).

27. Ladner, Foreward to Staples, *The Black Woman*, xiii.

28. Mae King, "The Politics of Sexual Stereotypes," *The Black Scholar* 4 (1973): 12–23.

29. Barbara Christian, *Black Women Novelists: The Development of a Tradition, 1892–1976* (Westport, Conn.: Greenwood Press, 1980), 78; Jean Carey Bond and Patricia Peery, "Has the Black Male Been Castrated," in Cade, *Black Woman*, 114.

30. Edward Mapp, "Black Women in Films," *The Black Scholar* 4 (1973): 42. See also, for example, Donald Bogle, *Toms, Coons, Mulattoes, Mammies, and Bucks: An Interpretive History of Blacks in American Films* (New York: Viking, 1973); Thomas Cripps, *Slow Fade to Black: The Negro in American Film, 1900–1942* (New York: Oxford

University Press, 1977); and Gary Null, *Black Hollywood: The Negro in Motion Pictures* (Secaucus, N.J.: The Citadel Press, 1980).

31. Mapp, "Black Women in Films," 43, 42.

32. Karen Sue Warren Jewell, "An Analysis of the Visual Development of a Stereotype: The Media's Portrayal of Mammy and Aunt Jemima as Symbols of Black Womanhood" (Ph.D. dissertation, Ohio State University, 1976); see, for example, 93, 125.

33. Christian, *Black Women Novelists*, 8.

34. Catherine Clinton, *The Plantation Mistress: Woman's World in the Old South* (New York: Pantheon Books/Random House, 1982), xv, x.

35. Ibid., 6.

36. Ibid., 15.

37. Ibid., 202.

38. Ibid., 204.

39. Minrose C. Gwin, *Black and White Women of the Old South: The Peculiar Sisterhood in American Literature* (Knoxville: University of Tennessee Press, 1985), 46, 4, 11, 14.

40. Christian, *Black Women Novelists*, 12.

41. White, *Ar'n't I a Woman?*, 49, 56.

42. Ibid., esp. 27–61.

43. Clinton, *Plantation Mistress*, 202.

44. Christian, *Black Women Novelists*, 252.

45. Elizabeth Fox-Genovese, *Within the Plantation Household: Black and White Women of the Old South* (Chapel Hill: The University of North Carolina Press, 1988), 42.

46. White, *Ar'n't I a Woman?*, 166.

47. Bell Hooks, *Ain't I a Woman: Black Women and Feminism* (Boston, Mass.: South End Press), 180.

48. Ibid., 80, 66–67.

49. Wallace, *Black Macho*, 196, 173.

50. Phyllis Marynick Palmer, "White Women/Black Women: The Dualism of Female Identity and Experience in the United States," *Feminist Studies* 9 (1983): 153–55.

51. Palmer, "White Women/Black Women," 157; Barbara Welter, "The Cult of True Womanhood, 1820–60," *American Quarterly* 18 (1966): 151–74. For nineteenth-century definitions of femininity see also Carroll Smith-Rosenberg, *Disorderly Conduct: Visions of Gender in Victorian America* (New York and Oxford: Oxford University Press, 1985).

52. Palmer, "White Women/Black Women," 153.

53. Walker, *Our Mother's Gardens*, 323.

54. Winthrop Jordan, *White Over Black: American Attitudes Toward the Negro, 1550–1812* (New York: W. W. Norton & Co., 1977), 150.

55. See, for example, Mary Douglas, *Purity and Danger* (London: Routledge, 1966); and Sara Delamont and Lorna Duffin, *The Nineteenth-Century Woman: Her Cultural and Physical World* (London: Croom Helm, 1978).

56. Douglas, *Purity and Danger*; Nina Auerbach, *Woman and the Demon*, 2–3, 12.

2

A Century Ago: The Foundations of Sexism-Racism

A century ago the literature of fact became more inclusive of Afro-American women than we might expect. This chapter examines why and in what sense they were of interest to the white-authored account of history.

Certainly the presence of women in the American past has by no means been evident in a traditionally male-dominated historiography. Thus, today's women's historians charge that in "His-Story," women have been largely "invisible." And it has been assumed that black American women have been even more excluded than others. In Gerda Lerner's words, "belonging as they do to the two groups which have traditionally been treated as inferior by American society—Blacks and women—they have been doubly invisible."[1] Yet such presuppositions have not been substantiated by research. It also seems possible that precisely because of this dual membership, black women have been of more interest than we might assume.

It has often been recognized that black Americans have, in fact, not been invisible in American historiography, but rather, unfortunately visible as racist stereotypes. In the words of Herbert Aptheker, "a racist society breeds and needs a racist historiography." Aptheker has pointed especially to the historians of late nineteenth-century America as those who prepared the ground for popularization by fictional and film media of stereotypes of black inferiority. It is with that radical racist era that this book commences its investigation of black women in American historiography.[2]

This is not to suggest that racism suddenly entered historical discourse a century ago. Instead, as William Van Deburg has found, from the beginning of American history "the first American historians foreclosed historiographical and sociological possibilities with their 'unthinking decision' to equate blacks with slaves and slaves with blacks." But in turn-of-the-century America, historiography became more explicitly racist than ever before. It was during this era, which saw the institutionalization of what contemporaries and historians have known as "Jim Crow" segregation, that as I. A. Newby has pointed out, historical writing became a pillar of Jim Crow's defense.[3]

It was also during the turn-of-the-century decades that the writing of history, like other fields of American scholarship, became professionalized. Scholars were increasingly expected to be educated experts rather than gentlemen amateurs. As the intellectual elite entrusted with the production and communication of knowledge, they shared their ideas in teaching, in journals, and in learned associations, and gained their livelihood and reputations from the official and academic institutions to which they were attached.

Moreover, the writing of history was increasingly seen as a science, based upon the collection and strictly dispassionate interpretation of evidence. As the science of the past, the writing of history took on the authority of scientific objectivity, supposedly freed from subjective and value-laden perspectives to discover the facts. It is in this context that turn-of-the-century historiography comprises the starting point of our investigation of how black American women have figured in this discourse of "fact," in recognition that the new professionalism was encouraged in large part by the same forces which gave birth to Jim Crow racial segregation.[4]

By the late nineteenth century American racism had been codified and legitimized, especially in association with social Darwinism; that is, by the doctrine which applied Charles Darwin's thesis of the survival of the fittest in the struggle for survival to races as well as to species. This functioned to rationalize American expansionism and rule overseas, which were cast as the "white man's mission" to civilize the lower races. However, it also served to justify racial control at home in an America focused upon what today's historians have characterized as "the search for order."[5]

As R. H. Wiebe and others have shown, turn-of-the-century America's overriding sense of the advance of disorder and chaos stemmed from the pace and scope of the changes associated with the growth of industrial capitalism, the movement of people and power from countryside to city, and the growing centralization, bureaucratization, and secularization of life. At a time when life seemed increasingly out of the individual's control, these aspects of modernization seemed to cast old values and certainties into serious doubt.

In a society which seemed in danger of losing its coherence, causes of the problem of disorder were avidly sought, and scapegoats were readily found in the vulnerable groups most easily targeted as un-American. Thus, the influx of new, non-Northern European immigrants was met by a flood of nativism. Similarly the swelling migration of Southern blacks to the North fed perceptions that what had once been viewed as the South's problem had become, in the early twentieth century, the nation's "Negro Problem." And the professionalization of American life, from social welfare and law to scholarship, was fed by the same set of perceptions and forces. Designated as posing problems of social control, the new immigrants, the poor, and the Negro were to be examined and managed by the new, professional experts. In this context, the society's historians and social scientists became in effect the experts entrusted with discovering the past and present causes of, and solutions to, disorder.[6]

Moreover, in the late nineteenth-century South what Joel Williamson has characterized as a veritable "rage for order" made racial control a crucial security blanket. As white supremacy became institutionalized by racial segregation, the "uppity Negro" who failed to know "his place" was scapegoated as the great menace to order. In this context the image developed and flourished of the black man as a rapacious "black brute" who savagely despoiled "the flower of white womanhood." This symbolization of Negro menace served to justify, and also fueled the swelling of lynching—the mob terrorism which constituted the ultimate weapon of white rule.[7]

During this radical racist era, despite the historians' professed commitment to objectively discovering the past, as Newby has found, "anti-Negro ideas came to pervade the study of nineteenth-century American history."[8] The distinguished historian, James Ford Rhodes, for example, was lauded by his colleague W.E.H. Lecky for his desire "to do justice to all sides and to tell the exact truth." Rhodes's work was characterized by prodigious research; seen as a scientific historian par excellence, he became president of the American Historical Association in 1898. Published from 1892 to 1922 in nine volumes, Rhodes's *History of the United States* was acclaimed by scholars and public alike. It was also pervaded by his expressed conviction that Negroes constituted "one of the most inferior races of mankind."[9]

Certainly Northern as well as Southern late nineteenth-century white-authored history provided its stamp of official approval to the culture's symbolizations of black inferiority, endorsing, for example, the image of the Negro rapist, especially in its portrayal of the aftermath of slavery's abolition. Portraying the post–Civil War decade as "Black Reconstruction," historians delineated the supposed horrors of "Negro rule" during the brief post–Civil War period when, protected by the federal Army's occupation of the South, some blacks held political office.

Leading in the formulation of this portrait was the respected historian, William Archibald Dunning, and those who studied under him at Columbia University. According to Dunning, the freed blacks were not "on the same social, moral, and intellectual plane with the whites." Hence, their inflamed ambitions for equality led to "the hideous crime against white womanhood."[10]

This portraiture was fleshed out especially by Dunning's former student, the Southern historian, Walter L. Fleming. Fleming's picture of Old South slavery as a benevolent school teaching blacks how to be useful workers and providing them with moral training, was complemented by his story of the post abolition era as a tragic time when the ex-slaves ran amok, confirming that the Negro could not cope with freedom. Indeed, according to the Dunning school of historiography, the freedpersons were not only a menace to whites but also to themselves as they regressed to their African ancestors' savagery. Evidence of their deterioration without slavery's civilizing restraints was provided especially by their sexual depravity.[11]

This was the vision of Reconstruction portrayed in the popular novel *The Clansmen*, authored by the Southern radical racist, Thomas Dixon. Dixon's portrait became the basis of the 1915 epic film, "The Birth of a Nation," which as a national blockbuster success did much to nationalize the image of rapacious black male hypersexuality. During this radical racist era, generally seen by today's historians as stretching from the late 1880s to the 1920s, sexual racism crystallized more explicitly than ever before into American racial mythology. The historian Joel Williamson has referred to this period as the "crucible of race"—as the clearest genesis of the conceptualizations which long continued to underpin American race relations.[12]

During this era it was emphasized by racist writers that the Negro wanted civil equality because what he really wanted was sexual equality; that is, sex with white women. This conviction constituted, in Newby's words,

the fundamental fact of anti-Negro thought. No discussion, diatribe or treatise was complete without noticing it, and every idea, action, and policy was examined in light of it. . . . Anti-Negro writers, in short, were universally concerned with the sexual aspects of racial problems.[13]

Newby has rightly pointed out that for these perceptions "no glib explanation will suffice." But he and most other historians of the radical racist era have focused almost exclusively on black male symbolizations of sexual racism. Concentrating on these, Newby, for example, has assumed that the central object of Jim Crow segregation was "to protect pure and undefiled maidenhood . . . from the crimes of brutal black assaulters." According to Lawrence Friedman, racist writings emphasized the black male menace to white womanhood but "rarely mentioned sexual relations between white males and black females."[14] Yet in reality, white-black miscegenation usually involved the pairing of white man and black woman. And in light of the era's obsession with racial "purity," it seems unlikely that this pairing was ignored.

This was the time when what is known as the "one drop" doctrine flourished. To understand this bizarre set of notions, it should be remembered that while in America individuals have been designated as either white or black, the person known to be of mixed racial ancestry, no matter how white in appearance, has also historically been labeled as black. It has followed that the mixing of "black" and "white" blood has been conceptualized not as leading to the whitening of the black race, but to the blackening and "Negroization" of the white race. But during the late nineteenth century the supposed menace of "Negroization" was symbolized especially by the "one drop" rule which may best be captured in the popular novels of Thomas Dixon.

In Dixon's words, "a pint of ink can make black gallons of water" because "one drop of Negro blood makes a Negro . . . puts out the light of intellect, and lights the fires of brutal passions." It followed therefore that "amalgamation simply meant Africanization. . . . You cannot build . . . a nation inside of two antagonistic races."[15]

From this perspective, the mulatto became seen as a particularly dangerous Negro: as natural criminal and rebel because of his inflamed jealousy of whites, and as a natural rapist because especially desirous of sex with white women. These dangerous instincts were said to flow from his combination of black and white blood. In this view, the person of mixed racial ancestry was particularly unstable and volatile because of the internal battle raging between black and white racial instincts. In his or her image the mulatto was a moral degenerate and carrier of sexual diseases, which confirmed the necessity of segregating blacks from whites. Moreover, miscegenation was frequently equated in racist writings with the infection and pollution of white society. In the words of the Southern author, Thomas Nelson Page, "association with an inferior race" led to the dread "peril of contamination."[16]

There is much about this perceptual context to encourage new attention to the era's image of black womanhood. For one thing, as cultural anthropologists have found, pollution images have frequently been associated with the female sex. Moreover, in nineteenth-century America, miscegenation in large part constituted the pairing of the white male with the black woman, who constituted the primary black source of the supposedly menacing mulatto offspring. Indeed, as contemporary scientists observed, "most of the illicit intercourse between whites and coloreds is with mulatto women."[17]

It is difficult to agree with Lawrence Friedman that this intercourse was "rarely mentioned" at a time when the exotic mulatto seductress was a stock character of racist fiction. In turn-of-the-century literature the mulatto woman emerged as a figure as menacing as the stereotypical black male threat to white "purity." In Dixon's novel *The Sins of the Father*, for example, Clio was able to seduce the virtuous Colonel Norton because her white appearance hid the fact that she was a black, "primeval woman." As "a young leopardess from an African jungle looking at him through the lithe graceful form of a Southern woman," this wily temptress had to be fought by poor Norton "as a wounded man . . . fights a beast in the jungle."[18]

It seems difficult to sustain assumptions that the era's virulent sexual racism was not inclusive of black women. As Bell Hooks has suggested:

The horrific nature of violent attacks on black manhood has caused historiographers and sociologists to assume that whites feared unions between white women and black men most. In actuality, they feared legally sanctioned racial mixing on the part of the sexes of either group.[19]

Moreover, as Hooks has pointed out, marriage between black men and white women, representing the union of two subordinate groups, may well have been less threatening to white supremacy than marriage between white men and black women, because the latter liaison can offer real upward mobility as the black woman shares the white man's status and property. In response to this threat, according to Hooks, "white men used psychological warfare . . . the myth of the 'bad,' sexually loose black woman and the myth of the black male rapist." And in her view, this image of black womanhood was a "conscious, deliberate effort on the part of whites to sabotage mounting black female self-confidence and self-respect." It constituted "a calculated method of social control."[20]

Hooks may attribute too much prescience to the era's white supremacists. But it is clear that during the late nineteenth century, sexual racism became more explicit and virulent than ever before. And as Joel Williamson's analysis argues, radical racism was profoundly shaped out of myths of womanhood.

To explain the evolution of radical racism, Williamson has pointed back to the Old South as the time and place where patriarchally prescribed gender roles became particularly rigidified and internalized. Just as the Southern white woman was required to be traditionally feminine, so also the Southern white man had to be the protector of and provider for his family. Similarly, Elizabeth Fox-Genovese has pointed to the Old South's "ideal of the natural division between women and men. . . . Women belonged within families and households under the governance and protection of their men." Central to masculine "honor" was "the protective domination of the father over his family."[21]

However, this Southern family romance was profoundly upset by the Civil War defeat and by the great agricultural depression of the 1880s and 1890s. According to Williamson, unable to provide for his family, the white man turned instead to emphasize his protection of white womanhood from black male violation, "as a kind of psychic compensation." Moreover, in this historian's view, the white man's sense of his own diminished masculinity was fed by the new sexual inaccessibility of black women. Still perceived as sensual creatures who existed to serve the white man's sexual needs, freedwomen were no longer completely vulnerable. Hence, Williamson argues that the white man's rage at the seeming appropriation of these "sexual earth mothers" by black men crystallized into his vision of the "insatiable satyr, specially built . . . for the libidinal women they serve. . . . Thus, black men were lynched for having achieved, seemingly, a sexual liberation that white men wanted but could not achieve without great feelings of guilt."[22]

It may be argued that such contentions regarding the mind of the late nineteenth-century South are speculative. However, to examine racial thinking in the late nineteenth-century North is to come to similar conclusions: that there too myths of race and gender flourished together.

For Northerners, the sense of mounting disorder was greatly intensified by changing gender roles. Middle-class women moved increasingly into the public sphere, in particular in pursuit of the vote, and asserted their right to share in the making of public policy. As well, female assertion of reproductive self-control was evidenced in the shrinking size of the middle-class family, at a time when Social Darwinism was identifying the ability of white Americans to reproduce themselves as the majority with their survival as the fittest race. In this context, as Charles Rosenberg and Carroll Smith-Rosenberg have shown, the challenge to traditional definitions of gender produced pervasive sexual strains which were projected onto the arena of race.[23]

Certainly, late nineteenth-century scientists found new rationalizations confirming that women belonged in "woman's place." For example, combining evolutionary theory with the physical law of the conservation of energy, Herbert Spencer pointed to an "earlier arrest of individual evolution in women than in men, necessitated by the reservation of vital power to meet the cost of reproduction."[24]

Blacks, too, were believed to experience a state of arrested development which left them a "child race." After reaching adolescence, in the words of James Ford Rhodes, they suffered "a diminution and often a cessation of their mental development." But during this era women were also cast as a "race type"—distinctively maternal because supposedly selected by the evolutionary process to serve as the procreators, conservers, and elevators of mankind.[25]

Eugenicists now argued that deviation from traditional femininity promoted white racial suicide. Either women would lead "healthy" lives, or they would damage their reproductive capacity and their offspring and cause national disaster. Therefore, the birthrate of white Americans became a crucial indicator of the nation's health, equated with racial vigor and fitness. From these roots sprang the "black peril" scare of the 1880s, in which the society's designated experts led in fomenting that panic in a way that emphasized the menacing sexuality of Afro-American womanhood.[26]

The "black peril" panic began when the 1880 census appeared to show that the rate of black population increase was vastly outstripping that of whites. The resulting predictions by statisticians and scientists of the looming racial cataclysm of an America dominated by blacks promoted avid interest in the fecundity of Afro-American women. Their reproductive capacity became no longer, as in the Old South, cause for celebration. Instead, it was presented as cause for alarm at a time when white women were seen as failing to fulfill their reproductive duties.

As Charles Rosenberg and Carroll Smith-Rosenberg have pointed out, it was "America's potential mothers" who were cast as "responsible for the impending social cataclysm." These historians have shown that while the "black peril" reflected and served to justify demands for the return of white women to true womanhood, as well, these sexual tensions fueled Northern racism.[27]

In sum, it becomes apparent that during the turn-of-the-century decades, throughout the nation sexism and racism became intensely interrelated by the same search for order that the professionalization of scholarship was to address. Accordingly, it is well worth asking how black womanhood figured in the literature of fact which, in Williamson's words, "lent sophistication, credibility, and integrity to Radical thought."[28]

It becomes crucial to examine how Afro-American women figured in the historiography molded during an era when, as Newby has pointed out, historians played a major role in providing "an intellectual rationale to justify policies of discrimination." While not radical racists, their "endorsement of orderly and paternalistic segregation made the American public more receptive to such extremes." And the historians who came of age in turn-of-the-century America would remain influential long after radical racism had itself faded away. In Van Deburg's words, "a generation of historians . . . proceeded to revitalize preexisting misrepresentations of Africans."[29]

However, in reconstructing the turmoil from which the black women emerged in the story of American history, one further element must be clarified, and this is late nineteenth-century white-authored historiography's love affair with slavery. As John David Smith has demonstrated, during this era slavery became a topic of immense interest to many contemporary Americans. Given the anxieties about modernization and disorder, Northerners as well as Southerners looked back with nostalgia to the Old South, romanticized as a model of social and racial harmony and order. Old South slavery provided a metaphor which functioned to justify the contemporary struggle to impose social and racial control throughout the nation. In this context, as Smith has found, "a vast spectrum of writers contributed a vast literature, polemic as well as historical, on the subject of slavery."[30]

This discourse revived the Old South defense of slavery as a humane institution, which promoted black contentment because it protected and "civilized" the enslaved. As Smith has found, historians assumed a major role in endorsing this updated version of the proslavery argument which said, in effect, that the races could live together harmoniously only when blacks were firmly controlled.

Proslavery historiography therefore played a major role in providing the intellectual foundations supporting the construction of Jim Crow segregation. Clothed in their new garb as the scientists of the past, which defined them as the experts on slavery and race, historians in effect promoted the newly nationalized proslavery consensus by authoritatively recasting blacks as natural slaves. They agreed in assuming that blacks were inherently slavish figures who did not suffer from enslavement as whites would have done. In Smith's words, "their writings contributed, albeit unwittingly, to the racist caricature of blacks that became the norm among almost all whites in the age of Jim Crow."[31]

However, it is time to turn now to examine how Afro-American women figured in this story of slavery, during the radical racist era and throughout the Age of Jim Crow. It is time to acknowledge that the contemporary love affair with slavery was underpinned by the engagement of racism and sexism in a way that by no means left black women invisible.

NOTES

1. Gerda Lerner, ed., *Black Women in White America* (New York: Vintage Books, 1973), xvii.

2. Herbert Aptheker, *Afro-American History: The Modern Era* (New York: The Citadel Press, 1971), 9, 80.

3. Van Deburg, *Slavery and Race*, 13; I. A. Newby, *Jim Crow's Defense: Anti-Negro Thought in America, 1900–1930* (Baton Rouge: Louisiana State University Press, 1973). The origins of the term "Jim Crow" are obscure. However, a song and dance called "Jim Crow" was written in 1838 (by Thomas D. Rice), and "Jim Crow" minstrel shows became popular during the antebellum era. During the 1890s the term became commonly used as an adjective in contemporary references to the segregation of Negroes from whites by legislation and practices institutionalizing the separation of the races in virtually all public facilities and public life.

4. See, for example, E. N. Saveth, *American History and the Social Sciences* (New York: Collier-Macmillan Ltd., 1964).

5. R. H. Wiebe, *The Search for Order* (New York: Hill and Wang, 1967). See also, Richard Hofstadter, *Social Darwinism in American Thought* (Philadelphia: University of Pennsylvania Press, 1944); Rayford Logan, *The Betrayal of the Negro from Rutherford Hayes to Woodrow Wilson* (New York: Collier Books, 1965); and George W. Stocking, Jr., *Race, Culture, and Evolution* (New York: Free Press, 1968).

6. On the relationship between the search for order, professionalization, and racial control, see esp. John Stanfield, *Philanthropy and Jim Crow in American Social Science* (Westport, Conn.: Greenwood Press, 1985).

7. Joel Williamson, *A Rage for Order* (New York: Oxford University Press, 1986). See also Lawrence Friedman, *The White Savage: Racial Fantasies in the Postbellum South* (Englewood Cliffs, N.J.: Prentice-Hall, 1970); and George Fredrickson, *The Black Image in the White Mind: The Debate on the Afro-American Character and Destiny, 1817–1914* (New York: Harper & Row Publishers, 1971).

8. Newby, *Jim Crow's Defense*, 67.

9. Allan Nevins, ed., *History of the United States* (Chicago: University of Chicago Press, 1966), xv; James Ford Rhodes, *History of the United States from the Compromise of 1850*, vol. 6 (Port Washington, N.Y.: Kennikat Press, 1906), 41. On Rhodes see John David Smith, *An Old Creed*, 113–14, 122.

10. Quoted in Newby, *Jim Crow's Defense*, 66, 67.

11. See Vernon J. Williams, Jr., *From a Caste to a Minority: Changing Attitudes of American Sociologists Toward Afro-Americans, 1896–1945* (Westport, Conn.: Greenwood Press, 1989), 40–41.

12. Joel Williamson, *The Crucible of Race: Black-White Relations in the American South since Emancipation* (New York: Oxford University Press, 1984).

13. Newby, *Jim Crow's Defense*, 135–36.

14. Ibid., 136; Friedman, *The White Savage*, 142.

15. Thomas Dixon, *The Sins of the Father: A Romance of the South* (New York: D. Appleton and Company, 1912), 403; Thomas Dixon, *The Leopard's Spots: A Romance of the White Man's Burden* (New York: Grosset & Dunlap Publishers, 1902), 242, 386–87.

16. Thomas Nelson Page, *The Old South* (Chautauqua, N.Y.: The Chautauqua Press, 1919; orig. pub. 1892), 280, 284, 291.

17. Quoted in John Mencke, *Mulattoes and Race Mixture* (New York: UMI Research Press, 1976), 52.

18. Dixon, *Sins of the Father*, 43, 25, 152.

19. Hooks, *Ain't I a Woman*, 61.

20. Ibid., 62, 59, 60.

21. Elizabeth Fox-Genovese, *Within the Plantation Household*, 195, 63.

22. Williamson, *Rage for Order*, 82; Williamson, *Crucible of Race*, 307–8.

23. Carroll Smith-Rosenberg and Charles Rosenberg, "The Female Animal: Medical and Biological Views of Woman and Her Role in Nineteenth-Century America," *Journal of American History* 60 (1973–74): 322–56.

24. In Jill Conway, "Stereotypes of Femininity in a Theory of Sexual Evolution," in Martha Vicinus, ed., *Suffer and Be Still: Women in the Victorian Age* (Bloomington: Indiana University Press, 1972), 141.

25. Rhodes, *History of the United States* 6: 41; Flavia Alaya, "Victorian Science and the 'Genius' of Woman," *Journal of the History of Ideas* 38 (1977): 261–80.

26. Carroll Smith-Rosenberg, "Beauty, the Beast, and the Militant Woman: A Case Study in Sex Roles and Social Stress in Jacksonian America," *American Quarterly* 23 (1971): 562–84; Smith-Rosenberg and Rosenberg, "The Female Animal," 322–56.

27. Smith-Rosenberg and Rosenberg, "The Female Animal," 352. See also George Fredrickson, *The Black Image*, 239–55.

28. Williamson, *Crucible of Race*, 124.

29. Newby, *Jim Crow's Defense*, 18, 69; Van Deburg, *Slavery and Race*, 79.

30. Smith, *An Old Creed*, 5.

31. Ibid., 105.

3

The Age of Jim Crow: White and Black Stories of Slave Women

During the segregationist era white-authored history integrated female figures into its caricatured portrait of slaves. This chapter will explore that literature thematically, with attention to its primary female stock characters singly and as a cast who worked together. It hopes thereby to illuminate what black-authored historiography was up against in struggling, in the words of William Van Deburg, to infuse "the black past with dignity and pride." As Van Deburg has observed, black writers countered the pejorative portraits of black inferiority "through the creation and promotion of literature which declared an alternative slave imagery."[1] However, in this chapter I propose to delineate more fully how the slave woman figured in history.

WHITE-AUTHORED HISTORIOGRAPHY

The late nineteenth-century doctrine of Negro regressionism points to how black women figured in white-authored history during the Age of Jim Crow. According to this conceptualization, freed from slavery's controls, the ex-slaves naturally reverted to type; that is, they regressed to the barbarism of their African ancestors. The Dunning school of historiography, which emphasized the horrors of "Black Reconstruction," seemed to substantiate this Negro decline, while also endorsing its symbolization by the figure of the rapacious "black brute." But black women also figured in retrogressive thinking.

The doctrine grew in concert with the black peril panic of the 1880s. Notions that the postslavery Negro reverted to type were furthered by social scientists as well as by historians, as statisticians pointed to census figures that seemed to show a menacing black population increase. But the vision of inherent Negro barbarism actually alleviated white anxieties by suggesting that this population increase would be stopped in its tracks; that is, as blacks reverted to type, their moral degeneracy would promote increasing promiscuity, sexual diseases, sterility, and crime. Their moral decline would then promote their population decline and, some radical racists hoped, their eventual extinction.

The 1890 census seemed to confirm that the black mortality rate had already increased. According to the statistician Frederick L. Hoffman, this demonstrated that the Negro was not fit to survive. Contemporary social scientists such as Hoffman and Walter F. Willcox appeared, from racist perspectives, to provide a reassuring picture of the postslavery Negro's decline. In an odd way it could be comforting from such perspectives to believe that, in the words of Paul B. Barringer, "If you scratch a negro, you will find a savage."[2]

Certainly historians were not alone in pointing to the ex-slaves' degeneration. However, the historian Phillip Alexander Bruce was a major architect and popularizer of retrogressionism. Bruce pointed influentially to the Negro family and what he cast as fundamentally "bad" black womanhood, as central to Negro decline after slavery's abolition. In his 1889 book, *The Plantation Negro as a Freeman*, this Southern historian presented such supposed evidence of the ex-slaves' degeneracy as the prevalence of bestial black rape of white women. According to Bruce, however, it was actually in large part because of the ex-slave woman's now uncontrolled "wantonness" that the black man turned from her in disgust to pursue women of the white race—and thus to the horrible crime of rape.

The freedwoman's depravity was presented as a taproot of the freedman's sexual savagery. As well, according to Bruce's story, lacking the moralizing influence of contact with whites which slavery had provided, the ex-slave mother socialized her children only in her own unrestrained licentiousness. Therefore, sexual promiscuity was rampant, "the procreative instinct being the most passionate that nature has implanted" in Negroes. Because it was the Negro woman who "really molded the institution of marriage among the plantation negroes, to them its present degradation is chiefly ascribable." So, "lasciviousness . . . more than all the other vices of the plantation negro" promoted the freedpersons' degeneracy.[3]

Bruce was a gentleman scholar, and by profession a lawyer. However, while not a professional historian, his work was respected by contemporaries. *Plantation Negro* enjoyed an enthusiastic reception, acclaimed as "unprejudiced and impartial," and as "a book every American should read." As Herbert Gutman has pointed out, this book penetrated the mind of the public and led the way to the Negro decline thesis that would be presented during the following decades by a host of "scientific" works.[4] Through this body of literature, too, the linked images of black familial decrepitude and of the "bad black woman" would increasingly become embedded as factual in the scholarship of Jim Crow America.

Indeed, during the segregationist decades a host of social scientists would emphasize the decline of the black family as the linchpin of Negro depravity.[5] It is not surprising that when sociology turned in the early twentieth century to examine the "Negro Problem," it was quick to equate the problem with black familial failure and licentious black womanhood. The stories the historians had told pointed to this premise and also served as historical evidence for the scientists who studied the present.

In turn-of-the-century white-authored historiography, as slaves and as ex-slaves, black Americans figured largely in terms of their sexual lives. And the "bad black mother" was, in effect, written back from "Black Reconstruction" into the slavery past in a way that circled back to the Old South's Jezebel image.

James Ford Rhodes, for example, included an eighty-page chapter on slavery in the first volume of his *History of the United States*. Published in 1892, this volume informed readers that slave women had welcomed sex with their masters, while "the negro husband felt little or no displeasure when the fancy of the master chanced to light upon his wife." Miscegenation, Rhodes said, was an offense to the "noble and refined women" of the white race. But it was encouraged by black women devoid "of chaste sentiment." Indeed, "the negress felt only pride at bearing offspring that had an admixture of the blood of the ruling class."[6]

As Rhodes noted, the master's behavior was not to be condoned, but female "mixed-bloods" were particularly beguiling and miscegenation came without marital strings attached. In contrast, outside of the South the white man avoided making "the negress the transient companion of his pleasure" because, "as she may legally become his wife, he shrinks from her with a kind of horror." Subsequent volumes of this prestigious history carried these images into the postslavery period, commencing with Rhodes's presentation of black women during the Civil War as so depraved that in their thronging after Unionist soldiers they abandoned their own children by the wayside.[7]

As John David Smith has pointed out, "a later degeneration of scholars" would "sharpen the focus of Rhodes' vision of the unstable, disjointed black family."[8] However, what needs to be added to Smith's observation is the repetition of Rhodes's Jezebel, slave women caricatures by a generation of historians.

A handful of white-authored histories did seem likely to be somewhat more sympathetic to the slave woman's plight. Albert Bushnell Hart, for example, revealed his abolitionist ancestry in his 1906 book, *Slavery and Abolition*. This work looked critically at the master's "breeding" of slaves as epitomizing the brutality of slavery.

Hart was an influential professional historian, on the faculty of Harvard

University from 1882 to 1926. But like his friend Rhodes, Hart also pointed to blacks as devoid of monogamous family instincts. According to him, even Mammy "was not always a person whose moral character influenced for good the children for whom she cared." And Hart's slave woman emerged at best as an overworked brood mare, cast as a subhuman brute, for example, in his citation of Frederick Law Olmsted's portrayal of slave women as "clumsy, awkward, gross, elephantine . . . pouting, grinning and leering . . . sensual, and shameless."[9]

Ironically, during the turn-of-the-century decades antislavery perspectives tended to lead some white historians to emphasize the most derogatory images of the behavior of slavemen and women. For example, Arthur Calhoun's *A Social History of the American Family* pointed to economic exploitation of blacks as the taproot of the slave family's decrepitude, since "the family is the creature of economic conditions." But in emphasizing the damaged slave family, Calhoun portrayed the sexual behavior of slaves as that of "irresponsible cattle."[10]

The master's "right of rape" and "negro-breeding" were said by Calhoun to have "wiped out female honor." Hence, the "negress" manifested the "spontaneous sensuality" and "promiscuities of chatteldom." And while pointing to the influence of sexual oppression, Calhoun pointed again to inherent African barbarism. In his words, given "the persistence of African mores . . . it is not to be wondered at that a large proportion of women of color were of easy virtue." As well he claimed that slavery had destroyed "maternal solicitude," and the slave mother's attachment to her offspring was "short-lived." In short, in his story "the blacks were gross and bestial," and "slavery almost universally debauched slave-women."[11]

Besides, according to Calhoun, it was especially the sexual allure of the "hybrid woman" which led to the "debauchery of Southern manhood." Referring to contemporary sources labeling the black woman as "the white man's burden," Calhoun simultaneously pointed to white exploitation as promoting her moral depravity, and yet also seemed to endorse studies which proclaimed that "the heaviest part of the white racial burden was the African woman, of strong instincts and devoid of a sexual conscience at the white man's door." These "dusky rivals" presented a "personal affront" to the Southern white woman. This historian even reiterated the Old South dichotomizing of women into white ladies and black whores-cum-female brutes. Overall, his intended illumination of black victimization was both portrayed through and drowned in a sea of dehumanizing images.[12]

Similar images pervaded white-authored history throughout the segregationist era. However, most Jim Crow historians presented unequivocal proslavery portraits in which the enslaved were by no means victims. On the contrary, as U. B. Phillips emphasized most influentially, they were well cared for and fortunate—lazy, improvident, and content.

The reign of this Southern historian and former student of William A.

Dunning represented the triumph of explicit proslavery historiography. Phillips's racism was masked by his impressive research and posture as a scientific historian. Author of nine books and a host of articles, his portrayal of slaves as childish, happy-go-lucky Sambos presided over by fatherly white masters won acclaim from white Southerners and Northerners alike. His portrayal dominated American historiography until it was definitively challenged during the civil rights era.[13]

According to Phillips, slavery was a benevolent, paternalistic institution, not a profitable economic system. Downplaying the Southern slave trade and denying the prevalence of slave "breeding" by masters, in support of his arguments Phillips presented the slave woman as a natural "breeder" and brood mare. For example, according to his 1929 book, *Life and Labor in the Old South*, the "good breeder" sold for

little more than a barren sister and not so much as a man of her age. This was for the same reason that a mare commonly sells for no more than a gelding. Her service was worth far more than her future progeny and her fruitfulness as a mother must automatically diminish her performance of work during pregnancy and the nursing period.[14]

Like Phillips's writings, throughout the Jim Crow decades white-authored historiography continued largely to reiterate the most dehumanizing, defeminizing, and demeaning images as simple matters of fact. Black women figured in this body of literature almost uniformly in terms of a set of pejorative slave-women stock characters. While these often overlapped, they may be identified singly as the brood mare, the Jezebel, the bad black mother, and the Mammy—the sole emblem of "good" black womanhood. The slight variations from source to source were only in terms of how these images were used.

In some sources, the slave woman was not very successful in performing her brood-mare role. Her failure to be a good "breeder" emerged in some histories as necessitating the South's slave trade. For example, according to Samuel Eliot Morison's acclaimed 1927 text, the *Oxford History of the United States*, "Negro wenches on cotton plantations were such poor breeders that the labor supply had to be replenished by purchase."[15]

While the brood-mare image remained constant, it could be used to support various arguments. Frances Butler Simkins, for example, pointed to the slave woman's natural fecundity in support of his arguments that for masters to breed slaves was rare. That the slave mother gave birth to so many offspring, this historian wrote, was simply because of her natural, though "offensive," promiscuity and "sexual familiarities." Unfortunately, however, her "uninhibited passions" and free offering of "bodily favors" corrupted the white man, promoting his preference for "the fellowship of dusky women." Hence, his ladylike wife paid the price for practicing "the Victorian virtues to a greater degree than other women."[16]

Simkins's 1947 history, *The South*, also went beyond slavery to introduce the freedwomen, whom he cast in a comical light. The female ex-slaves were apparently attempting to become "ladies of leisure." They retired from the cotton fields and even called each other "Mrs." and "Miss." More sad, according to this book, was the decay of the postslavery family, with its "barbaric" treatment of children, "whipped until they bled, confined to the house all day while their mothers worked." In this context Simkins put the leisured black woman back to work. Then, moving on to his own era—and toward the image of matriarchy—he noted as "a reality common in Negro society, the black woman who grows masterful after the desertion of her husband." Fortunately, he wrote, the Southern white woman remained "a creature who . . . could be feminine and decorative."[17] Thus, Simkins's defeminized image of black womanhood highlighted the feminine virtues of white womanhood.

In fact, more explicitly than most Jim Crow historians, Simkins articulated the message of sexism-racism. In his book patriarchal and racial order were explicately linked together as Simkins pointed to the tragicomic results of deviation both from "woman's place" and from the Negro's proper place:

The Negro in revolt against the tyranny of the white man was caught in the same trap as the feminist in rebellion against the despotism of man. . . . Their passions for reform led them to imitate that from which they were attempting to revolt.

In this way, the Negro was said to become "pathological" in his abortive attempt to imitate whites "just as the feminist leader became more masculine"; that is, both were abnormal and sick.[18]

Generally, however, Jim Crow historiography avoided such theorizing and simply trotted out the old slave woman caricatures as facts which spoke for themselves. These images showed a striking continuity, although symbolizations of black males showed some change. With the decline of radical racism and with white supremacy securely established by the 1920s, the rapacious black brute symbolization of Negro menace became increasingly rare. Instead, the black man-cum-slave man reemerged largely in the image of Sambo—docile and content, as in Morison's 1927 *Oxford History*: "As for Sambo . . . he suffered less than any other class in the South from its 'peculiar institution' . . . adequately fed, well cared for, and apparently happy."[19]

In contrast, the black woman in her image continued to be depicted as aggressively hypersexed in Jim Crow historiography. Figuring in terms of unrestrained passions and animal instincts, she seemed to serve as a symbol of the racial disorder controlled by the color line. Indeed, the Jezebel image lived on even in Wilbur Cash's 1941 book, *The Mind of the South*, despite Cash's pioneering analysis of the Southern "Lady" as mythical rather than factual.

Cash pointed out regarding the Lady that as "the South's Palladium" she was "the mystic symbol of its nationality in the face of the foe. She was the lily-pure maid." He noted the usefulness of this fiction in rendering the white woman "absolutely inaccessible" to black men. The pedestaled ideal also alleviated the white man's shame at his dalliance with black women: "The (white) woman must be compensated, the revolting suspicion in the male that he might be slipping into bestiality got rid of, by glorifying her." Yet Cash failed similarly to analyze the sexual-savage image of black womanhood as myth. Instead, he simply presented it as fact that

[t]orn from her tribal restraints and taught an easy compliance . . . she was to be had for the taking. . . . For she was natural and could give herself up to passion. . . . [Hence] efforts to build up a taboo against miscegenation made little real progress.[20]

In the same way, the mulatto seductress figure continued to flit through the stories historians told, appearing even in the 1963 edition of Clement Eaton's *The Growth of Southern Civilization*. According to its portraiture of the Old South, mulatto women were largely "crude and promiscuously licentious."[21]

However, by the decades between the Wars, the new scientific orthodoxies increasingly decreed that racial traits should no longer be explained by biological inheritance, but rather by environment and history. Yet Jezebel could also be used to support this new thesis. For example, when reference was made to the black male's reputed history of rapacious pursuit of white women, this reemerged in historical writing as cast by Phillip Alexander Bruce as promoted by black female depravity. Simkins's 1947 history therefore pointed back to lynching as what had been considered a necessary response to Negro rapaciousness, noting that the black male had seemed prone to such "impulsive" behavior. But this was not explained by Simkins in terms of innate racial traits. Instead, the black man's "jealousy was aroused by the conduct of his women."[22] And so, still cast as Jezebel, the black woman was assigned responsibility for the supposed sins of black as well as white men.

Similarly, throughout the Jim Crow decades the old slave Mammy was trotted out repeatedly in this body of literature—but in a much more approving light. As it worked its way into Jim Crow historiography, the Mammy image and its functions may best be introduced by Thomas Nelson Page's 1892 book, *The Old South*.

Page was a popular turn-of-the-century writer who presented himself as a historian. Although by no means a trained historian, he fully voiced the views of professionals that the historian must never diverge "from the absolute and inexorable facts. . . . He must know and tell the truth." However, Page's work was pervaded by racism. The brother-in-law of Philip Alexander Bruce, this Southerner was a popularizer of the myth of the Negro rapist. Lynching was openly and explicitly justified in his writings as the natural determination of whites "to put an end to the ravishing of their people by an inferior race."[23]

In *The Old South*, Page echoed the perceptions of his society that the "Negro question" was "ever-menacing, ever-growing." Pointing to the special peril of miscegenation, he warned that this inferior and "hostile" race posed the horrible threat that "the nation will become hopelessly Africanized and American civilization . . . perish." In this context, he presented slavery nostalgically as a model of the racial order which must be restored, characterizing his romanticized rendering of the Southern past as the South's "true history."[24]

Cast in a romantic light, Mammy and her kin figured in Page's book as emblems of the happy lot of blacks under slavery, but always emblems presented as "facts." Female field hands were not to be seen at work. Indeed, no one seemed really to work. Instead, "there passed young negro girls . . . bearing messages; or older women moving at a statelier pace, doing with deliberation the little jobs which were their 'work.' " From the slave quarters came "the laughter of women and the shrill, joyous voices of children." In the context of this happy-go-lucky, "banjo-playing life" Mammy figured prominently.[25]

Mammy emerged first as a woman of leisure, to be found "in the shade . . . with her little charge in her arms, sleeping in her ample lap." But she was also a model of black industriousness as a labor of love to whites, in her assistance to the plantation mistress, especially in raising the master's children. Clearly, in this book, she regarded her own family with indifference at best. Her harshness to her own offspring contrasted with her tenderness to the white children. But she found ample reward for loyalty and devotion to "her" white family: "the young masters and mistress were her 'children' long after they had children of their own." In addition, she was "an honored member" of the master's family, "universally beloved, universally cared for." Her role in the Big House provided her with "authority . . . second only to that of the mistress and the master."[26]

Similarly, Page presented the idealized Southern Lady as fact: "Her life was one long act of devotion . . . to God, devotion to her husband . . . children . . . servants . . . and to all humanity." This "superior being" was "born a lady." Because of her "innate virtue, piety and womanliness" she grew naturally from a "delicate" and "dainty" belle to "this gentle, classic, serious mother among her tall sons and radiant daughters."[27]

Page's presentation of the Mammy and Lady bears out today's recognition that these were twinned images of Old South mythology. Moreover, his writing confirms Catherine Clinton's observation that, shaped by "the combined romantic imaginations of the contemporary southern idealogue" and the South's historians, Mammy was "not merely a stereotype."[28] Indeed, by the decades around the turn of the century she had truly become a legend. Evoking an entire romanticized story of the Southern past and also a vision of an idealized present, she had become a fully mythical creature. And because her symbolic value was immense, she became a major pillar of Jim Crow white supremacy.

For one thing, Mammy signified the right to rule of the Southern elite. Providing the stamp of historical legitimation, as sociologist John Dollard observed in the 1930s, "the mammy tradition" had become "a criterion of upper-class membership." And as J. W. Johnson pointed out, "the 'sine qua non' of a background of family of good breeding and social prestige in the South is the Black Mammy."[29]

Moreover, she signified the white supremacist vision of rightful racial order based upon black accommodation to Jim Crow. Her value as a symbol in this sense becomes evident, for example, in the "Black Mammy Memorial Association" established in Georgia in 1910. This was to solicit support for a vocational school modeled after Booker T. Washington's Tuskegee Institute and philosophy; that is, essentially that the Negro should be trained to perform the menial and domestic jobs assigned to blacks, and through service, industriousness, and self-help, gradually win a better place in a segregated society.[30]

According to this major black leader, progress toward racial equality could better be forwarded by gradualism and patience than by confrontations and militancy. Not surprisingly, Washington's Tuskegee model was popular among white Southerners. Thus, the "Black Mammy Memorial Institute" was intended to train the Negro "in the arts and industries that made the 'old Black Mammy' valuable and worthy... where men and women learn to work... and to love their work." Black women were to receive the "moral training" that would inculcate in them Mammy's "industry, purity and fidelity" and her "spirit of service." As the Association's pamphlet asked, hypothetically but apparently appealingly, "Did you not have an 'Old Black Mammy' who loved and cared for you?"[31]

Mammy was a major symbol of the idealization of Jim Crow segregation, like slavery, as an institution promoting racial intimacy and harmony. Her image epitomized the linked romanticization and legitimation of both institutions. Thus, during the turn-of-the-century decades, she became virtually a cult figure—the subject of a widespread Southern movement to construct monuments and institutions in her name. Throughout the Jim Crow era she lived on in the stories historians told of the Southern past. But as in Page's *The Old South*, their Mammy was never presented as fiction, but rather as fact.

Indeed, cast over and over again in this light, Mammy emerged as a taken-for-granted truth for which no substantiating evidence whatsoever was necessary, despite the professional historian's emphasis upon the objective and careful documentation of "fact." Instead, as in U. B. Phillips's 1918 history, *American Negro Slavery*, Mammy was herself provided as evidence of the "intertwined" lives of whites and blacks: "If any special link were needed, the children supplied it. The white ones, hardly knowing their mothers from their mammies, had the freedom of the kitchen and the cabins."[32]

In echoing this point, subsequent histories simply recycled Mammy, embellishing her image in various ways as in Simkins's *The South*, which noted that "white children were suckled by black mammies and played indiscriminately with pickaninnies." This picture appeared unchanged even in the revised, 1963 edition of Simkins's history of the South.[33]

Mammy was perhaps a particularly useful prop in the romanticization of Southern history because of her gender. That sexual racism continued especially to taboo the coupling of black male and white female made it less practicable to present black male symbolizations of racial intimacy under slavery. Such explanations of the use of the Mammy as the primary symbol of white-black intimacy may be ventured from the perspective of today. But it is equally important to recognize that according to Jim Crow historiography, Mammy was not merely a symbol, but a historical reality, and indeed, too self-evidently a true character to require even footnoting.

It was not until the post–World War II decades that the reliability or respectability of such conventional academic wisdom became less certain, as indicated by the revision of at least some old historical texts. For example, in his 1927 *Oxford History of the United States* Morison had noted that "there was no physical repulsion from color in the South. White children were suckled by black mammies and played promiscuously with the pickaninnies." But according to the 1964 edition, "there was no physical repulsion from color in the South. White children were suckled by black 'mammies' and played with their children." The extent of such revision need not be commented upon, except to note that while Morison's use of quotation marks did not indicate the close of the Mammy legend, in the civil rights era generally the enclosure of this old-time figure by quotation marks signaled the new stigma that she took on with the liberal attack on, and demolition of, legal Jim Crow segregation during the 1960s.[34]

In sum, commencing in the late nineteenth century and throughout the age of Jim Crow, in white-authored historiography Mammy and her kin figured essentially as taken-for-granted facts. And this cast of female stock characters had more in common than slave-rooted origins. All except Mammy had profoundly derogatory, dehumanizing characterizations. None of them signified traditional, true womanhood in the sense of fragility, passivity, and dependency. Instead, viewed singly and together, these women constituted a profoundly defeminized image of the black woman's historical identity. If the female slave suffered at all in this picture, it was only as the overworked workhorse and brutish brood mare.

This woman was not cast as a *female* victim. On the contrary, she asserted herself so unrestrainedly that she seemingly could overpower the white man's will to resist her allure. Her overpowering sexual licentiousness apparently even drove the black man away in disgust to pursue white womanhood instead. Cast in the image of Eve, the black woman was assigned responsibility for the downfall of the manhood of both races. And as the "bad black mother," she apparently fertilized the seeds of savagery in generations of black children, while also neglecting and abusing them.

In short, the black woman emerged from the stories these historians told as a woman who even sabotaged her own people and yet, while they fell in her wake, lived on to do still more damage. Her singular female power was presented as a liability for her race. And in this composite portrait of a strikingly powerful creature, it was only Mammy, who used her strength in the service of whites, who emerged as a positive image of the black woman in American history.

In this sense, Michele Wallace's "superwoman mythology" does aptly describe the nature of the "hell of a history" thereby assigned to Afro-American women. It also becomes clear that their dual personification of both racial and sexual deviation from the white American norm constituted their double serviceability to Jim Crow historians. In their imagery, they could readily serve as symbols of both racial and sexual order and disorder. They could simultaneously figure as examples of deviant, unwomanly women and as emblems of black inferiority.

It remained for sociologists to link explicitly these conceptualizations of gender and race as cause and effect. However, the stories the historians told provided apparent solid historical foundations for the social science theorizing that purported to explain the "Negro Problem" of the present. Ironically, the black woman's double vulnerability as black and female would long continue to underpin the use and abuse of her history, which cast her as the opposite of vulnerable.

BLACK-AUTHORED HISTORIOGRAPHY

According to some recent studies, black-authored historiography was early to present a very different reconstruction of slavery and the enslaved. It provided interpretations that, in William Van Deburg's words, "varied so greatly from white norms that they might best be described as counter-visions of the black condition under slavery." In his view, Afro-American writers have consistently challenged "misinformation, and racism," countering the "cultural stereotypes."[35] Yet this historian has treated cultural imagery as if it is gender-neutral. It remains to be seen if black-authored interpretations were entirely free of stereotypes of black womanhood.

It has often been assumed that the myths of black womanhood have been entirely white-authored. For example, according to Bell Hooks, the matriarchal mythology was "formulated" by "white sociologists." These "white male scholars . . . were educated in . . . institutions that were both racist and sexist."[36] Yet it should not be assumed that black male scholars were not educated in similarly sexist institutions, or that black sociologists and historians did not play any role in shaping the image of black matriarchy.

To examine the black woman's image in Afro-American oppositional discourse may be to make discoveries that are unexpected and perhaps even unwanted. But these must be understood in the context of the struggle against racism, and against racial images so pervasive that, as Gunnar Myrdal found, they could even cross the color line.

This sociologist's study of American race relations, undertaken for the Carnegie Foundation, was published in 1944 as *An American Dilemma*. Arguing that in a democratic nation the persistence of racial prejudice and discrimination posed an immense contradiction, this book came as the crowning achievement of the era's racially liberal research. Illuminating the way in which the culture's images of race acted as continuing perceptual blinders to objective reality, Myrdal pointed out that the scholar, "too, is part of the culture in which he lives." As he wrote, "observing the prevalent opinions in the dominant white group," it might be expected that "even the scientific biases run against the Negroes most of the time. This expectation has been confirmed in the course of our study."[37] Myrdal found that an anti-Negro bias was apparent in social science and "in the writing of history," in Northern as well as Southern white-authored scholarship. But he also found that

public and academic opinion in the dominant majority group, the Negro scientists' desire to lean backwards and be strictly scientific, and other reasons, may often cause even the Negro scientist to interpret the facts in a way which is actually biased against his own people.[38]

However, it may also be that images that crossed the color line were among the shaping forces of Afro-American scholarship, inclusive of the historical writing that struggled to create an alternative vision of slavery and race.

As S. P. Fullinwider has observed, "The Negro's first efforts in America toward scholarship were, in large part, shaped by his reaction to the literature of white racial apologists . . . during the last two decades of the nineteenth century."[39] This means that early black historians sought both to demonstrate the damaging effects of racism and also to counter pejorative stereotypes by emphasizing the black capacity for progress. And black historians would long seek, as John Hope Franklin observed in 1957, "to establish a secure and respectable place for the Negro in the evolution of the American social order."[40] This means too that until recently, Afro-American historiography has been, in the words of Robert Harris, "dominated by an effort to achieve the notice and respect of white America."[41] Thus, black historians have long been fundamentally bound, according to Saunders Redding, to "the angle of vision, the perceptions, and the interpretations . . . of white historians and chroniclers."[42]

It is clear that early black historians strove to create an alternative vision of slavery. As John David Smith has found, during the late nineteenth century a host of black writers, including newspaper editors, clergymen, and teachers, joined the small group of professionally trained Afro-American historians who were challenging the proslavery consensus. And by the decades around the turn of the century, "the slavery theme, more than any other, dominated black historical writing." But Smith has also discovered that this writing was characterized by "a maze of inconsistencies and contradictions," revealing disagreement even on the question of whether blacks were inherently inferior to whites.[43]

Around the turn of the century, the black intelligensia was influenced by the accommodationist philosophy of Booker T. Washington. While not a professional historian, Washington shared the era's interest in slavery. However, while pointing to this institution as a sin, in Washington's interpretation slavery also emerged as forwarding the technical skills and work-ethic values important to Negro progress after emancipation. As Smith has pointed out, such interpretations "played into the hands of... white racists." Noting a similar ambivalence elsewhere in Afro-American historiography, Smith argues:

The paucity of professionally trained historians goes a long way toward explaining the inconsistencies and weaknesses in the bulk of the work of the pioneer black writers. Few blacks studied slavery in a systematic manner, ... they presented slavery in a defensive, biased, partisan and moralistic tone.[44]

While Smith's explanation is insightful, what needs to be added is attention to constructions of gender which crossed the division between racist and antiracist discourse. Attention must also be brought to the influence of the antislavery tradition on the shaping of black historical writing by casting blacks as a "feminine race."

The antebellum abolitionist movement left a legacy of resistance to slavery in which myths of gender and race were oddly blended together. As David Levy has found, the Old South's proslavery emblem of Sambo and antislavery images of race were in some ways very similar. Both sets of images portrayed the Negro as patient, docile, affectionate, and childlike. However, abolitionist writers reinterpreted these supposed racial qualities, presenting them as virtues associated with the Negro as a natural Christian martyr: pious, long-suffering, forgiving, and loving, on the model of Uncle Tom of Harriet Beecher Stowe's best-selling novel. They thereby presented the virtuous slave as dependent upon and deserving of the help of whites. As Van Deburg has noted, the Negro was thus portrayed as "a Man almost unman'd" by friends as well as oppressors.[45]

From antebellum antislavery perspectives, however, this feminization of the Negro was to do him a favor. It appealed to white paternalism and also reflected what was seen as racial reality. As George Fredrickson has shown, the abolitionists' romantic racialism assigned virtually identical attributes to blacks and women, equating femininity with moral superiority, and blacks with femininity. In the words of a contemporary antislavery leader, "The negro race is the feminine race of the world . . . because of his social and affectionate nature . . . because he possesses that strange moral instinct that belongs more to women than to men." From this perspective it followed that "the negro is superior to the white man—equal to the white woman."[46]

After slavery's abolition, however, the equation of race and gender devolved from a culturally positive to a negative image of blacks. During the radical racist era the "soft," feminine image of the Negro was largely supplanted by the "hard" racist imagery of aggressive Negro menace, epitomized by the stereotypical rapacious "black brute."

In this context, to provide an alternative imagery and countervision of race might well involve reiteration of the "feminine race" mythology, in conjunction with the messianism that, as Wilson Moses has found, pervaded Afro-American thinking on race. His book, *Black Messiahs and Uncle Toms*, has shown that black Americans have long embraced a missionary mythology in which they figured in some ways much like the old Uncle Tom. From messianic perspectives, they were a people of long-suffering Christian martyrs bearing a redemptive message for humanity, which sprang from the special, humanizing qualities associated with their historical oppression. Indeed, early black historians inherited a legacy that included this messianic image of race, and that associated the Negro with qualities traditionally attributed to women—equating both women and blacks with achieving moral superiority through their very victimization.[47]

But among the forces shaping early black historiography were also white definitions of virtue. As black Americans joined the march toward scholarly professionalization, they did so in a context that could encourage their adoption of white perspectives. Many of the black intelligentsia were members of the American Negro Academy, an institution that reflected the elitist philosophy associated with its first president, the clergyman and historian Alexander Crummell. According to this outlook, the elevation of the Negro was to be achieved especially by the educated black intelligentsia. This "talented tenth"—named thus by the Academy leader, W.E.B. Du Bois—was to lead the race up from cultural "primitiveness" to "civilization." Convictions of the necessity of "civilizing" the black masses were central to this "missionary paternalism." And as Alfred Moss has observed, "civilizationism" involved commitment to at least a "selective imitation of white Western culture."[48]

Imitation of white, Western culture need not entail adoption of its definitions of gender. According to Rosalyn Terborg-Penn, nineteenth-century "black male leaders were more supportive of women's rights than white male leaders." On the other hand, according to Bell Hooks, "nineteenth-century black male leaders . . . did not support social equality between the sexes. They were, in fact, adamant in their support of patriarchal rule."[49]

Bess Beatty's study of the Afro-American press from 1865 to 1900 may help to illustrate the prevailing cultural milieu. As she has found, the black-authored press overwhelmingly proclaimed that the black woman's "highest mission was caring for her home and children, serving as her husband's helpmate and maintaining the highest standards of morality." According to Beatty's findings, this vision of woman's place was essentially the same as in the white-authored press's idealization of true womanhood. Black newspapers were pervaded by the same "stereotypes of woman's unique nature and restricted role."[50]

As well, Michele Wallace has pointed to a turn-of-the-century Afro-American cult of the "black lady" which attempted "to uplift the black woman to the white woman's level." And according to Lawrence Friedman, the black lady cult flourished because it "helped black males to eliminate white competition for black females." Emphasizing that the black woman must be chaste and sexually loyal to her race, the black lady ideal reinforced Afro-American males' "guardianship over 'their woman.' " Thus, in Friedman's view, "white Southern racists and black activists looked at women in similar terms . . . as a second sex with distinctly limited privileges."[51]

These interpretations warn us that racial oppression has not necessarily inured Afro-American men to the dominant society's patriarchal norms. But to turn to the writings of William Wells Brown may even suggest that at least this early black historian shared the dominant society's most negative views of black womanhood.

William Wells Brown is perhaps most often remembered as a novelist. However, while he was by no means a professional historian, he was seen by contemporaries as a pioneering black historian. According to him, in Africa, the black woman was the sexual slave of polygamy. She had rarely aspired "to anything higher than merely to gratify the passions of her husband." In Brown's writings, as a slave in America the black woman figured as "impassioned and voluptuous," and "despised by whites and blacks alike." While her licentiousness flourished because "no inducement [was] held out to slave women to be pure and chaste," it was clear that "the greater portion of the colored women, in the days of slavery, had no greater aspiration than of becoming the finely-dressed mistress of some white man." At least, so William Wells Brown told his readers in *The Rising Son* and *My Southern Home*, published respectively in 1873 and 1880.[52]

On closer inspection, however, it becomes clear that these negative images were intended to support Brown's rejection of white views of slavery as civilizing the benighted African. Instead, he was arguing that slavery's oppression had exacerbated African backwardness and degradation, including the degradation of Afro-American women. Unfortunately, his image of black womanhood thereby emerged in a most pejorative light. This extended to his portrait of the freedwomen after emancipation as pursuing a mad passion for gaudy ornaments and dresses so that "their husbands have little or no control over them, and are obliged ... to see most of their hard-earnings squandered." Echoing the society's sexual double standard in his portrait of the ex-slaves, Brown advised that it was "bad enough for men to lapse into habits of drunkenness. . . . But a drunken girl—a drunken wife—a drunken mother—is there for women a deeper depth? Home made hideous—children disgraced, neglected, and maltreated."[53]

In retrospect, it is easy to see how such images could play into the hands of racists. Certainly, Brown's account of the past was well-received. In the view of the *Boston Evening Transcript*, for example, *The Rising Son* deserved acclaim as "a well-written resume of the history of the dark-hued people."[54]

However, it should be noted that Brown did present flattering images of some black women. But it was largely mulatto women whom he admired. And it was only Afro-American women who approximated white "ladies" in their appearance and behavior who were included in his sketches in *The Black Man* of "notable" black Americans. Describing over fifty such historical and contemporary success stories, he included only three women, who epitomized the culture's definitions of true womanhood. In *The Rising Son*, expanding his "Representative Men and Women" to respectively, seventy-four and seven, Brown made it even more clear that admirable black women were "cultivated," "sensitive," "frail," "chaste," and "childlike."[55]

In short, in Brown's writings the Afro-American woman's identity emerged as dichotomized between the depraved and degraded slave-woman figure, and the elevated, whitish, black lady. While the former symbolized the evil effects of slavery and the latter the Negro's capacity for racial uplift, both sets of images endorsed traditional definitions of true womanhood.

Brown's bifurcated imagery and his use of black female symbols for antislavery and antiracist ends may have influenced, and certainly foreshadowed, how Afro-American women figured in the stories told by Afro-American historians during the turn-of-the-century decades. For example, the historical writings of Alexander Crummell presented much the same portraiture. As John David Smith has observed, although a "critic of slavery, Crummell's contradictory statements are still apt to confuse."[56]

Crummell's slave woman was essentially a dehumanized brute. In his writings, her history emerged as one of endless sexual exploitation, forced labor, and ruined motherhood as she was compelled to abandon even her newborn infant for work in the cotton fields. In his view, her maternal and familial proclivities were lastingly damaged. Her negative attitudes to family and motherhood lived on after emancipation, perpetuated by the continuation of oppression. Hence, according to this historian, the black family remained an institution in ruins long after slavery itself was dead and gone. Accordingly, Crummell's image of the freedwoman remained as dematernalized, demoralized, and unidimensional, signifying his views of the benightedness of the black masses.

The combination of Crummell's hatred of slavery and his views that black

Americans could and must be elevated to the level of Western civilization shaped his portraiture of the black woman's past. In his writings the middle-class black woman emerged in the image of a lady as respectable, refined, and admirable. Her role was to serve as exemplar for and uplifter of her degraded sisters and brothers.[57]

Much the same images figured as well in the writings of George Washington Williams. Williams was a skilled historian who spent seven years researching his 1883 *History of the Negro Race in America*, which emphasized the cruelties of slavery. Yet in this book the African woman remained reduced by polygamy to "the merest abject slave" of her husband's "unholy passions." Readers might learn, too, that she was "stupid, sulky and phlegmatic." However, it becomes clear that Williams intended to show that the Negro even in Africa was not beyond the influences of "civilization" and "Christianization." So, he recast the African man in the abolitionist image of the Negro as the feminine race: as sensitive, gentle, and delicate. The African man was said to be characterized by the same "intuition" and "nervous imagination" that characterized "cultivated women." Williams quoted as a "fair account" a book entitled *Savage Africa* which proclaimed that "if the women of Africa are brutal, the men of Africa are feminine. Their faces are smooth, their breasts . . . full. . . . The men have gracefully moulded limbs, and always after a feminine type." This feminized image complemented what Williams meant as a positive casting of the Negro in America. By reiterating the abolitionist image of the Negro as "gentle, affectionate and faithful," he was, in effect, challenging contemporary stereotyping of the black man as a natural criminal and rapist.[58]

That postslavery black Americans did not always act "gentle, affectionate and faithful" was presented by Williams as evidence of the damage of racial oppression. The damage, he claimed, was especially to Negro familial values and norms. The black family's destruction by slavery had left it the source of continuing sexual promiscuity and moral depravity. In this context, in Williams's story, the postslavery black mother emerged with major responsibility for the uplift of her race through her restoration of the "pleasant home" and "the influence of books and papers, and the blessings of a preached gospel." Without explaining how the impoverished Afro-American woman was to achieve such blessings, Williams assured his readers that

wives and mothers are doing much to elevate the tone of the race and its home. Great care must be given to the education of the colored women in America, for virtuous, intelligent, educated, cultivated, and pious wives and mothers are the hope of the Negro race. Without them educated, colored men and the miraculous results of emancipation will go for nothing.[59]

In sum, Williams's image of black woman was again unidimensional and dichotomized. As a slave woman figure, her defeminized depravity emphasized the evil effects of white oppression. And as an emblem of the posts-lavery black capacity for progress, she was cast in the image of true womanhood.

Yet it should be noted that Williams did thereby provide a striking alternative imagery of the black condition, in the context of the retrogressive vision of the Negro's reversion to savagery. The black male, in Africa and in America, was redefined from a rapacious sexual savage to a reassuring, feminized figure. And Williams's postslavery "good" black mother countered racist depictions of the freedwoman as the taproot of Negro familial decline and moral degeneracy. Early black historians such as Williams were writing black demoralization and familial destruction back into time, as the casualties of slavery. They were emphasizing that freedom facilitated black progress toward adoption of "civilized" values and norms. Ironically, however, the result was that their slave-woman images did not differ much from the pejorative caricatures of racist writings.

Actually, the Afro-American historian often had little more interest than his white counterpart in discovering the real historical experience and role of the Afro-American woman. Instead, he was largely interested in her as a "type." And to present her as a positive type, he was especially interested in introducing black female "notables." Therefore, like William Wells Brown, George Washington Williams also included some women among his portraits of "Representative Colored Men." Fanny M. Jackson, for example, was admired for her "pure and womanly influence." For her work with Negro orphans, Louise de Mortie was admired as having "a genuine Christian heart." Williams emphasized that such notable black women provided examples of "race pride, industry, enthusiasm, and nobility of character." But they also became refeminized exemplars of black womanhood, cast like the early black poetess, Phyllis Wheatley, as "charming": refined in manners, sensitive, delicate, and always "modest" in demeanor.[60]

It may be that in this historiography, black men did emerge as more multidimensional, fully human individuals. At least, Smith argues that while white-authored writings merely caricatured the slave as an "unperson," "blacks portrayed him as a real person with mature emotions and human sensitivities."[61] However, my findings suggest that black men often figured too in this literature as types, as black-authored writings attempted to re-type both ex-slave men and women into the society's vision of appropriate gender roles.

For example, in a society that emphasized rugged masculinity, Williams expressed some criticism of the natural, Christian, Uncle Tom image of the black man as too "lamb-like" and obsequious: "He lacks the elements of an endangered manhood." Yet a page later his portrayal became refeminized, describing the postslavery Negro as becoming increasingly admirable in character by characterizing him as "gentle in manners, confiding, hopeful, enduring in affection, and benevolent to a fault."[62]

But it is precisely in such ambivalence that the immensity of the task confronting early black historians emerges, in the face of a mystification of race all the more powerful because spun out of the complementary mystification of gender. In this context, the presence and role of black female symbols in this antiracist historiography become more comprehensible. To counter the radical racist vision of aggressive Negro menace by restoring the Negro as a reassuringly feminine race pointed to female symbolization.

Yet by the late nineteenth century the preferred Afro-American image of black men was beginning to move away from the feminized abolitionist vision toward the reconstruction of manliness. In this context, to portray manly resistance to slavery while also emphasizing the damage of slavery pointed to an emphasis on female, rather than male, victims of oppression. Hence, the damage to the slave family and the slaves' supposed moral depravity were largely conveyed through images of exploited, damaged slave-women.

By the same token, to reshape the ex-slave women into the patriarchal image of true womanhood was in effect to revise the black male from Uncle Tom and Sambo to the culture's image of true masculinity. For example, Williams emphasized the black man's masculine involvement with the man's world of action and military prowess in his pioneering study, *A History of the Negro Troops in the War of the Rebellion*. Similarly, the manly black man emerged in Edward Johnson's *A School History of the Negro Race*: "As a soldier and citizen he has always been faithful to his country's flag." While black masculinity could thus be shaped in the image of patriotism, it was also restored in the public world of work, and economic and professional achievement. In Johnson's words: "He has been a legislator, a judge, a lawyer, a juror, a shrewd business man."[63]

However, this emphasis on restoring black men to a man's world revealed traditional perspectives on gender that, in black historiography, left the roles of black women almost entirely invisible in the world of work and public activity. Indeed, in the reconstruction of postabolition Afro-American history as the story of progress and racial uplift, black women virtually never figured as workers, although most were very much in the labor force. However, they generally emerged only in such mention as was provided by Carter Woodson and Charles Wesley in their 1935 history, *The Story of the Negro Retold*: "Thousands of faithful spend weary nights at the ironing-board and wash-tub in order to get money to help their children obtain an education."[64]

In part this exclusion also reflected the reality that the work of black women, long after slavery, remained largely as menial and low in status as ever, and was therefore contradictory to the black historian's story of racial uplift and progress. Moreover, it is not surprising that black American's spokesmen, recognizing the black woman's special vulnerability as a domestic servant to sexual exploitation by white male employers, called for her restoration to the home. Their vision of what she should be, and also of what she *had historically been*, is revealed by an anthology entitled *The United Negro: His*

Progress and Prospects. Published in 1902, it contained the addresses and proceedings of the Negro Young People's Christian and Educational Congress, and despite its title, it had a good deal to say about the Afro-American woman.

Contributors to this anthology emphasized that her place was in the home, in which she was to mold "the character of the statesmen . . . the clergymen . . . the educators . . . and the women who have mothered the world. Women have been the civilizers of mankind." In the home lay "her greatest responsibility . . . to sustain, nourish, train, and educate the future man." The "pure and chaste" woman set a good example for her man. But while boys would naturally "sow their wild oats," and "a pure motherhood" was "the basis of racial integrity" and uplift, "women are the weaker sex and are much influenced by men." As a result, contributors lamented that, vulnerable and exposed to worldly temptations, working black women became bad women and bad mothers. Laboring "over the wash-tubs and ironing-boards" they failed to guide their children righteously. What resulted was "the great flood-tide of impurity that rushes down upon our boys and girls."

Moreover, according to a female contributor, "we must own to our shame that no race or people is too low for the Negro woman to stoop." By her "slatternly" behavior the Negro woman was said to invite white sexual overtures and even Jim Crow segregation itself: "Such conduct is largely responsible for the restrictions we now face." Accordingly, the black woman was exhorted to be a lady. She was warned to keep only "pure literature" in the home, "avoid dressing your children in low-necked gowns," and to "separate your boys and girls."[65]

Such admonitions ignored the impoverished living conditions of the vast majority of contemporary black Americans and their reliance upon the black woman's work outside the home. But in this book Nannie Burroughs was unique in her call for an end to Negro antagonism to "working girls." While calling for better wages and improved working conditions, especially for female domestics, she argued that the industriousness and thrift of the "servant woman" were more praiseworthy than scores of "parlor ornaments."[66]

Otherwise, however, Afro-American women figured in this anthology only in terms of the dichotomized identification of "bad" and "good" womanhood. This dichotomy was reinforced by the slave woman's image as "bad." This was presented as what the black woman had historically been. Contributors presented as taken-for-granted facts that the slave mother was de-maternalized, slaves had "no homes," and the slave woman's sexual depravity had "crushed the moral nature of the race."[67]

Indeed, by the early twentieth century this story of the black woman's slave-rooted history had virtually become conventional academic wisdom. And ironically, the black-authored story of history had contributed to its acceptance as fact. Symbolizing the damage of slavery to the black family and sexual morality, the slave woman figured in a largely negative light even, and perhaps especially, in the most outraged portraits of black suffering under slavery. For example, Frances Hunter presented as tragically factual in the *Journal of Negro History* in 1922 that the slave had no family life, the Negro woman's "maternal instincts" had been "crushed," and "the usual love between mother and child was absent." Hunter provided as her only evidence that a slave woman was said, when on her death bed, to have been asked how she felt about leaving her children. Supposedly her answer was, "I don't mind them."[68]

At the same time, almost paradoxically, in the black-authored story of history the slave mother often figured as the sole force holding the slave family together. Actually, however, the paradox is nonexistent, given the consensus that such a family was not a real family. That the slave family's existence was mother-centered was the evidence of its ruination. As Frederick Douglass had explained in his 1881 narrative of his own history as a slave, "Slavery had no recognition of fathers, as none of families." However, the writings of this major advocate of both black and women's rights were unusual in presenting the crucial role of slave mothers as an asset, not as a liability. As Douglass recalled, from his grandmother and mother "I learned . . . I was . . . somebody's child. I was grander upon my mother's knee than a king upon his throne."[69] By the early twentieth century, however, such a positive vision had been largely submerged by the overwhelmingly negative portrait of slave womanhood that pervaded the black-authored story of history.

Some did question the prevailing consensus. For example, *The Negro in Our History*, jointly authored by Carter Woodson and Charles Wesley in 1922, argued that the black American had inherited a strong familial tradition from Africa regarding "fatherhood, motherhood, and childhood." Furthermore, according to these Afro-American historians, in Africa there were "no loose women. . . . Every woman has her own marital connections." Although those African values and norms were severely tested by American slavery, it was

a gross violation of the truth . . . when they try to make it appear that the Negro family was non-existent except in so far as being held together by the mother who became attached to first one man and then another. The moral sense of the imported Negro African rebelled against any such promiscuity.[70]

By the "they" who violated the truth, Woodson and Wesley meant white writers who as "pseudo-historians" had "prostituted modern historiography."[71] In contrast, they referred admiringly to such black historians as William Wells Brown and George Washington Williams. But the images and vision of the past that they were striving to revise had been shaped and endorsed by black- as well as white-authored history. The difference is that black historians employed these images to emphasize the damage of racial oppression in a slavery history recast as tragic. But in this context, antiracist

goals had involved the presentation of stereotypical images of slave womanhood, which remained unsubstantiated by research.

As well, the ex-slave woman remained unrestored to history as a full human
being. Just as the freedwoman's place figured in domesticity, so also the
black female public activist remained largely invisible in Afro-American historiography. For example, while Carter Woodson's 1928 book, *Negro Makers
of History*, discussed the early twentieth-century antilynching movement, it
made no mention of the movement's black female leader, Ida Barnett-Wells.
In such texts Sojourner Truth was given some recognition as an antebellum
abolitionist leader, but was generally identified by her "quaint language"
and "heavy voice," as an atypical woman.[72]

However, it is also of interest that included among those omissions were
some of the major stock characters of white-authored historical discourse.
These included the stereotypical exotic mulatto temptress who invited the
white man's attentions. Instead, as Carter Woodson forcefully argued in a
1918 article in the *Journal of Negro History*, white-black sexual relations resulted from white rape of slave women.[73]

In particular, Mammy was noticeably left out—an absolute nonentity of
the past, and thus also of the present. Thus, Carter Woodson was virtually
alone in questioning the invisibility of the Mammy. Indeed, Woodson perhaps best deserves the title of "father of black history," not only because
of his own impressive scholarly outpourings, and as founder and first editor
of the major historical periodical, the *Journal of Negro History*, but also because
his work raised questions about conventional orthodoxies.

Woodson dared even to argue that in her continuing Mammy roles as a
domestic worker for whites, the Afro-American woman had been done a
disservice by her exclusion from the black-authored story of history. Even
more unusual was his keen recognition that black-authored scholarship could
be restricted by the racist myths of the past. In particular, he pointed to the
spell of the Mammy legend.

As Woodson pointed out, in 1930 it remained the case that practically
nothing was known of the vast group of black women who had historically
labored and who continued to labor as domestics in service to whites. In
explanation of their invisibility, he pointed to the stigma attached by black
Americans to the Mammy because of the legend that cast her as the historical
collaborator with whites. Hostility to this white supremacist and slave-rooted
image, he observed, had led Afro-American scholars to ignore such Mammy-
like figures as the ubiquitous black washerwoman. He argued that instead,
these women deserved recognition and respect.

And in Woodson's 1930 article in the *Journal of Negro History* Mammy
reemerged, but not as in white-authored history. Instead, she was the slave
who labored for a "despotic mistress" during the day, and then at night for
her own family as a labor of love. While agreeing that slavery promoted the
mother's centrality to the black family, Woodson pointed out that after

abolition she often became the sole family breadwinner, as her husband was barred from employment. So, through her Mammy-like service to whites, she labored valiantly to help her man and "bore her losses like a heroine in a great crisis." She could be counted upon to provide for the children and impart to her home "the aspect of a civilized life." At the same time, she worked for the school, the church, and a host of black self-help organizations. In short, according to Woodson, despite the stigmatized image of Mammy, these female domestics were "the true and tried coworkers in the rehabilitation of the race along economic lines." And "in no other figure in the Negro group can be found a type measuring up to the level of this philanthropic spirit in unselfish service." Woodson's reconstruction showed that what racist discourse had made of the Mammy need not determine what Afro-American scholarship could discover about Afro-American women.[74]

Yet, in the black-authored scholarship of Jim Crow America, Mammy remained conspicuous by her absence. As the white sociologist, John Dollard, observed during the 1930s, the Mammy tradition continued to be "a point which whites like to remember and Negroes to forget."[75] Similarly, Jessie Parkhurst pointed out in a 1938 article in the *Journal of Negro History* that "because the 'Black Mammy' originated in and came out of the period of bondage, she is an acceptable symbol to whites and an unacceptable one to Negroes." As this study noted, "she became an imaginary figure . . . for in order to be recognized as belonging to the aristocracy of the Old South it was necessary to be able to say that one had been tended by a 'Black Mammy' in youth."[76]

Parkhurst's own attempt to separate fiction and fact was rare, and not very successful, casting Mammy largely in the familiar image of being completely devoted to her white family and having a "sense of identification with the group who owned her." Parkhurst referred both to U. B. Phillips and to Thomas Nelson Page as reliable sources on the Mammy, but provided no substantiating evidence for their and his generalizations. The significant point raised in this study was left undeveloped: that the Mammy legend itself attributed qualities to black women, as "strong, just . . . quick-witted, capable, thrifty, proud, regal, courageous," that were entirely "denied to slave women as a group." But such positive slave-woman images were generally as rare in black as in white historiography. It seems fair to conclude that in turn-of-the-century America, and throughout the age of Jim Crow, black-authored historiography resembled white-authored historiography in one respect; that is, it too revealed more about its vision of race and gender than about the historical experience of Afro-American women.

Afro-American historiography did provide a counterimage of black womanhood in the sense that its slave women figured as *victimized* into degradation, and its freedwomen were *progressing* and uplifting their race. The latter were, however, achieving this progress in their image virtually only, in the words of George Washington Williams, as "virtuous . . . wives and mothers."[77]

It is not surprising that the postslavery black woman was thus reshaped into the image of patriarchally prescribed femininity. In a patriarchal America this reshaping did represent a positive image that not only rejected the racist's "bad black woman," but also reflected the desire to emphasize Negro progress toward "civilization." By the same token, to point to the damage done to the slave woman, and in particular to slave motherhood, emphasized that these were suffering female victims—not Jezebels who deserved what they got.

By reshaping black women into the image of true womanhood, black historians did provide an alternate vision to that of a literature and society that treated these women as if they were not women at all. That this oppositional discourse did not challenge the dominant culture's vision of gender, and instead tried to reshape the black woman's story in this patriarchal light, can be interpreted as part and parcel of its creation of a counterview of race.

On the other hand, it must be acknowledged that the vision of damaged slave womanhood could readily play into the hands of racists, and also that the "black lady" vision could raise irrational expectations of impoverished Afro-American women. This alternative imagery was a dangerous, double-edged sword. And when social scientists turned to examine the "Negro Problem," they could find in both white and black stories of the past materials upon which to construct theories about the present that, more explicitly and authoritatively than ever, equated race and gender in a negative sense.

But what could be reconstructed out of even the most positive vision of black womanhood becomes clear in what was made of the legacy of W.E.B. Du Bois, to whose work I now turn to examine his "mother-idea."

NOTES

1. Van Deburg, *Slavery and Race*, 51, 50.

2. Quoted in Mencke, *Mulattoes and Race Mixture*, 119. For discussion of the Negro decline thesis see also Vernon J. Williams, Jr., *From a Caste to a Minority*, 21; and Fredrickson, *The Black Image*, 250–51.

3. Quoted in Herbert G. Gutman, *The Black Family in Slavery and Freedom, 1750–1925* (New York: Vintage Books/Random House, 1977), 534–36. See also Smith, *An Old Creed*, 173–77.

4. Gutman, *The Black Family*, 538.

5. Ibid., 533.

6. Rhodes, *History*, vol. 1: 336, 335.

7. Rhodes, *History*, vol. 1: 311; Rhodes, *History*, vol. 5: 26.

8. Smith, *An Old Creed*, 122.

9. Albert Bushnell Hart, *Slavery and Abolition, 1831–1841* (New York: Harper & Brothers Pub., 1906), 98, 93. See also Smith, *An Old Creed*, 126–27.

10. Arthur Calhoun, *A Social History of the American Family*, vol. 1 (New York: Barnes & Noble, Inc., 1960; orig. pub. 1917), 329; vol. 2 (orig. pub. 1918), 243.

11. Ibid., 243, 246, 292, 264, 243, 290.

12. Ibid., 295, 294, 309, 310.

13. Smith, *An Old Creed*, 239, 264.

14. U. B. Phillips, *Life and Labor in the Old South* (Boston: Little, Brown & Co., 1963; orig. pub. 1929), 174.

15. Samuel Eliot Morison, *Oxford History of the United States*, vol. 2 (New York: Oxford University Press, 1927), 7.

16. Frances Butler Simkins, *The South, Old and New: A History, 1820–1947* (New York: Alfred A. Knopf, 1947), 65.

17. Ibid., 210, 211, 212, 350, 292.

18. Ibid., 421.

19. Morison, *Oxford History*, vol. 2: 7.

20. Wilbur J. Cash, *The Mind of the South* (New York: Alfred A. Knopf, 1962; orig. pub. 1941), 86, 84.

21. Clement Eaton, *The Growth of Southern Civilization, 1790–1860* (New York: Harper and Row, 1963), 145.

22. Simkins, *The South, Old and New*, 408.

23. Quoted from Thomas Nelson Page, *The Negro: The Southerner's Problem*, in Fredrickson, *The Black Image*, 275.

24. Thomas Nelson Page, *The Old South*, 280, 284, 291, 320, 342, 273.

25. Ibid., 149, 116.

26. Ibid., 149, 165, 156.

27. Ibid., 155, 157, 162–64, 161.

28. Clinton, *Plantation Mistress*, 201.

29. John Dollard, *Caste and Class in a Southern Town* (New York: Doubleday Anchor Books, 1957; orig. pub. 1937), 82; J. W. Johnson, *Hang This Way* (New York: The Viking Press, 1933), 10.

30. For discussion of recent interpretations of Washington's thinking and role, see Smith, *An Old Creed*, 201–3.

31. June O. Patton, "The 'Black Mammy Memorial' Institute," *Journal of Negro History* 65 (1980): 153–54.

32. Ulrich B. Phillips, *American Negro Slavery: A Survey of the Supply, Employment and Control of Negro Labor as Determined by the Plantation Regime* (New York: D. Appleton and Co., 1918), 313.

33. Simkins, *The South, Old and New* (1947), 63, 45; Simkins, *A History of the South*, 3d and revised edition (New York: Alfred A. Knopf, 1963), 126.

34. Morison, *Oxford History of the United States* (1927), 8; Morison, *Oxford History of the American People*, revised edition (New York: Oxford University Press, 1964), 5–6.

35. Van Deburg, *Slavery and Race*, 51, 50.

36. Hooks, *Ain't I a Woman*, 71, 72, 73, 75.

37. Gunnar Myrdal, *An American Dilemma*, 2 vols., vol. 2 (New York: McGraw-Hill Co., 1964; orig. pub. 1944), 1035.

38. Ibid., 1037.

39. S. P. Fullinwider, *The Mind and Mood of Black America: 20th Century Thought* (Homewood, Ill.: The Dorsey Press, 1969), 3.

40. John Hope Franklin, "The New Negro History," *Journal of Negro History* 43 (1957): 89.

41. Robert Harris, "Coming of Age: The Transformation of Afro-American Historiography," *Journal of Negro History* 67 (1982): 107.

42. Saunders Redding quoted in Harris, "Coming of Age," 107.

43. Smith, *An Old Creed*, 197, 199, 200.

44. Ibid., 201, 227.

45. David W. Levy, "Racial Stereotypes in Antislavery Fiction," *Phylon* 30 (1970): 265–79; Van Deburg, *Slavery and Race*, 13.

46. Fredrickson, *The Black Image*, 114.

47. Wilson Jeremiah Moses, *Black Messiahs and Uncle Toms: Social and Literary Manipulations of a Religious Myth* (University Park, Pa.: Pennsylvania State University Press, 1982).

48. Alfred A. Moss, Jr., *The American Negro Academy: Voice of the Talented Tenth* (Baton Rouge: Louisiana State University Press, 1981), 299; see also 248–67.

49. Rosalyn Terborg-Penn, "Black American Perspectives on the Nineteenth-Century Woman," in Sharon Harley and Rosalyn Terborg-Penn, eds., *The Afro-American Woman: Struggles and Images* (Port Washington, N.Y.: Kennikat Press, 1979), 28; Bell Hooks, *Ain't I a Woman*, 91.

50. Bess Beatty, "Black Perspectives on American Women: The View from Black Newspapers, 1865–1900," *The Maryland Historian* 9 (1978): 47, 39.

51. Wallace, *Black Macho*, 222, 42; Friedman, *The White Savage*, 141, 142.

52. William Wells Brown, *The Rising Son: The Antecedents and Advancements of the Colored Race* (Boston: A. G. Brown and Company, 1874; Johnson Reprint Co., 1970), 109; Brown, *My Southern Home: The South and Its People* (New York: Negro Universities Press reprint, 1969; orig. pub. 1880), 218, 203, 218.

53. Brown, *My Southern Home*, 170, 240.

54. William Edward Farrison, *William Wells Brown: Author and Reformer* (Chicago: University of Chicago Press, 1969), 443.

55. William Wells Brown, *The Black Man: His Antecedents, His Genius, and His Achievements* (Miami: Mnemosyne Pub. Inc., 1969; orig. pub. 1865), for example, 231; Brown, *The Rising Son*, esp. 418–540.

56. Smith, *An Old Creed*, 227.

57. See for example, Alexander Crummell, "The Black Woman of the South: Her Neglects and Her Needs," in Crummell, *Africa and America: Addresses and Discourses* (Springfield, Mass.: Houghton Mifflin Co., 1914; orig. pub. 1891).

58. George Washington Williams, *History of the Negro Race in America, from 1619 to 1880* (New York: Arno Press and the *New York Times*, 1968; orig. pub. 1883), 60–61, 415.

59. Ibid., 548, 415, 417–18, 451.

60. Williams, *History of the Negro Race*, 448–50, 197–99.

61. Smith, *An Old Creed*, 218.

62. Ibid., 547, 548.

63. Edward A. Johnson, *A School History of the Negro Race in America from 1619 to 1890*, revised edition (New York: AMS Press Inc., 1911), 196.

64. Carter G. Woodson and Charles H. Wesley, *The Story of the Negro Retold* (Washington, D.C.: Associated Publishers, Inc., 1959; orig. pub. 1935), 160.

65. I. Garland Penn and J.W.E. Bowen, eds., *The United Negro: His Progress and Prospects* (New York: Negro Universities Press, 1969; orig. pub. 1902), 186, 433–35, 439–400, 450, 454–55.

66. Ibid., 327–29.

67. Ibid., 449–50.

68. Frances L. Hunter, "Slave Society on the Southern Plantation," *Journal of Negro History* 7 (1922): 6–7.

69. Frederick Douglass, *Life and Times of Frederick Douglass* (London: Collier-Macmillan Ltd., 1969; orig. pub. 1881), 36.

70. Woodson and Wesley, *The Story of the Negro Retold*, 29, 209–11.

71. Ibid., 475, 408.

72. Carter Woodson, *Negro Makers of History* (Washington, D.C.: The Associated Publishers, Inc., 1928); Woodson and Wesley, *The Story of the Negro Retold*, 135.

73. Quoted in Smith, *An Old Creed*, 221.

74. Carter G. Woodson, "The Negro Washerwoman, a Vanishing Figure," *Journal of Negro History* 25 (1930): 270, 273, 275, 277.

75. John Dollard, *Caste and Class in a Southern Town* (New York: Doubleday Anchor Books, 1957; orig. pub. 1937), 82.

76. Jessie W. Parkhurst, "The Role of the Black Mammy in the Plantation Household," *Journal of Negro History* 23 (1938): 349, 351.

77. Williams, *The Negro Race*, 451.

4

The All-Mother Vision of W.E.B. Du Bois

Any exploration of the historiography of slavery must devote careful attention to the writings of W.E.B. Du Bois. As John David Smith has observed, he was the most "important black student of slavery in the pre–World War I period," and "led the black assault" on the dominant proslavery historiography.[1] Yet how black women figured in Du Bois's historical writings must also be understood in the context of his analysis of contemporary race relations and his racial activism. Indeed, Du Bois was preeminent among those who rejected the accommodationist racial philosophy of Booker T. Washington.

As Bettina Aptheker has observed, Du Bois was "a pivotal figure in the struggle of human rights and, consistent with this humanitarian impulse, he was strikingly advanced in his views on women." She has observed that he both recognized the immense power of "sexual myths and stereotypes" to divide the races, and "expressed many of the modern themes of the feminist movement."[2]

W. E. Burghardt Du Bois was a steady, vocal, and activist advocate of the rights of women and of blacks. In his words, "the race question is at bottom simply a matter of the ownership of women; white men want the right to own and use all women, colored and white, and they resent any intrusion of colored men into this domain."[3] Moreover, he wrote much more about black women than did any other contemporary; his vision of black womanhood is significant from several perspectives.

As a primary spokesman and shaper of the Afro-American intellectual tradition, Du Bois helps to illuminate the dilemmas of black scholarship in a racist society. As well, he was both a sociologist and a historian, and in wearing these two hats together, sometimes uncomfortably, he demonstrates in his writings the mixing and mingling of these disciplines of present and past, which characterized the scholarship of race during the Jim Crow era. From this brew in his work stemmed images of black womanhood both old and new. Many of these were undeniably mythic, although Du Bois was very much a professional scholar.

While receiving his Ph.D. in history, he was also educated during the late nineteenth century as a sociologist. At a time when sociology was becoming a professional discipline, he emphasized that, like history, this field too must be free from moralism and bias to discover objective reality. As well, he was ahead of many contemporaries in adopting the environmentalist theories of the social anthropologist, Franz Boas, that challenged the prevailing belief in hereditary racial characteristics. Yet his racial thinking was ambivalent.[4]

Du Bois sometimes extolled the culture and "soul" of the black masses, emphasizing the Negro mission to bring the race's special qualities to America to humanize the nation. In this context he referred to an inherent "race spirit." At other times he referred to race as a social construct shaped by experience and environment. Calling for the elevation of the black masses by the educated black intelligentsia, he voiced his "talented tenth" philosophy. Indeed, as August Meier has observed, Du Bois "becomes the epitome of the paradoxes in American Negro thought."[5]

One way of approaching the enigma of Du Bois is by examining his personal experience of paradox as the essence of Afro-American life. Born in 1868 in New England, while of both white and black ancestry, by society's definitions Du Bois was a Negro. He was thus irrevocably excluded from the white world to which he belonged by culture. Perhaps he had especially compelling personal reasons for recognizing the dilemma of identifying with an America that rejected the Negro as an American. Certain he most eloquently expressed this perception in 1903: "One ever feels his twoness,— an American, a Negro; . . . two warring souls in one dark body."[6] As Du Bois's own recollections suggest, his awareness of the color line came initially at the hands of the white woman.

His first recognition of the "vast veil" of racial prejudice came in childhood, when a white girl rejected his friendship "peremptorily with a glance." He seems as well to have resented the white woman for the racial etiquette requiring that the black man must scrupulously avoid any physical contact with her. For example, he recalled "brushing by accident against a white woman on the street. Politely and eagerly I raised my hat to apologize. . . . From that day to this I have never knowingly raised my hat to a Southern white woman." In the view of Wilson Jeremiah Moses, at times Du Bois's attitudes to white American women bordered on contempt.[7]

In contrast, Du Bois consistently expressed the highest admiration for black women and outrage at their oppression. As editor from 1910 to 1934 of *The Crisis*, the journal of the National Association for the Advancement of Colored People, he used his pen for a host of feminist as well as Afro-American causes. But in particular he exposed and condemned America's

abuse of black women—economic and sexual, psychological and physical—
revealing that not only black men but also black women were victims of the
horror of the lynch mob. And as Arnold Rampersad has found, in his fictional
writings Du Bois was especially admiring of the black woman, often presenting her as morally and intellectually superior to the black man.[8]

Some studies suggest that Du Bois's vision of black womanhood stemmed
from his relationship with his mother and from his personal psychohistory.[9]
But while this may or may not be the case, it is clear that his discourse was
shaped by the black intellectual tradition, which provided both idealized
and ambivalent images of black women.

As August Meier has pointed out, Du Bois articulated "most of the threads
of Negro thought at that time."[10] This included the tradition of messianism;
that is, the missionary mythology portraying black Americans as bearing a
special message for their society and even for humankind, which stemmed
from the redemptive power of suffering. As Wilson Jeremiah Moses has
pointed out, messianism originates as a mechanism by which an oppressed
people finds something of value in oppression itself. For black Americans
to make, in effect, a virtue out of necessity was to find a means of retaining
self-respect.[11]

"Uncle Tom" continued to live on in Afro-American messianism. In the
context of the antebellum antislavery conceptualization of the Negro as the
natural Christian, Uncle Tom was a problack emblem symbolizing the abolitionists' emphasis on the patient martyrdom and virtuous "feminine" traits
of the Negro race. And as Moses has found, in black-authored writings Uncle
Tom survived in this positive light long after the slavery era. In fact, black
historians ranging from Alexander Crummell to Booker T. Washington often
portrayed the Negro in this light. But according to S. P. Fullinwider, Du
Bois converted this image into a mythology of the "Black Christ."[12]

It has often been pointed out that in spite of his impressive professional
credentials and skills, Du Bois's writings often included elements of myth.
But his work is best seen in the context of an era when, in the words of
John Barker, "racist mythologies were at their peak."[13] In this context Du
Bois challenged racist images of Negro inferiority not only with facts, but
also with counterimages of race. Moreover, it is clear that Du Bois regarded
history as having special value as a tool of racial protest and for promoting
a proud black self-identity. In this sense, as Herbert Aptheker has pointed
out, "what interested Du Bois as a maker of history helped determine what
he wrote, and what he wrote helped make history."[14]

Yet, during the turn-of-the-century decades, wearing the mantle of sociologist, Du Bois's own research seemed to support the most pessimistic
conclusions about the limited capacities of black Americans for progress.
Especially in his early sociological writings, he fleshed out his theories regarding the present with a portraiture casting black American history as one
long tale of degradation and damage. In this context, familiar slave-women

figures emerged in his work together with profoundly negative images of contemporary black womanhood. But this was not because he accepted the black woman's story as portrayed in racist historiography.

Associated with the depths of black servility, the slave-rooted past had long inspired ambivalent responses among black historians themselves. According to Alexander Crummell, for example, slaves were "ignorant, benighted, besotted and filthy." As Sterling Stuckey has pointed out, from black-authored scholarship emerged some of the most "gloomy," "devastating," and "stereotypical portraits of black humanity."[15] Du Bois drew heavily from the historical research of others, since as John Barker has noted, given "his many concerns and commitments, his histories were often hastily produced and inclined to be superficial."[16]

Often unable to do his own research, Du Bois treated as reliably factual the histories provided by scholars whom he respected. But recognizing the racism that pervaded the white-authored story of the past, he relied extensively upon the work of early black historians, including George Washington Williams. And as Wilson J. Moses has found, Alexander Crummell was a major influence upon Du Bois's views of the past. Therefore, it is not surprising that in his sociological writings, commencing with *The Philadelphia Negro* in 1899, Du Bois endorsed black-authored history's antislavery emphasis on the damage of slavery by reiterating that the Negro family was "destroyed by slavery." And he reiterated the equation of this ruination with the slave father who had no power and who "sank to a position of male guest in the house."[17]

As well, in his early sociological publications the slave woman figured largely in negative terms, as the depraved mother and brutalized sex object degraded into promiscuity. In his role as a scientist of the present, Du Bois argued that it followed from the slave's "lack of respect for the marriage bond [that] sexual looseness" had resulted. And it followed that "the point where the Negro American is furthest behind modern civilization is in his sexual mores." According to this reading of the past, for the contemporary Negro the family actually constituted "a new social institution."[18]

In concert with these assumptions, Du Bois's early sociological research focused heavily upon the contemporary black woman's sexual behavior. He pointed, for example, to the high rate of illegitimate births as what "represents the unchastity of large numbers of women," arguing that their historically "lax morality" had been compounded by the dislocation associated with recent black migration to the city. Thus, while articulating an environmentalist interpretation of racial behavior, Du Bois also reiterated denigrating images of black womanhood. His apparent objective presentation of fact often masked the moralistic perspective underpinning these images. For example, notwithstanding his recognition of the effects of discrimination and impoverishment, and in spite of the necessity of the participation of black females in the labor force, he advised that "leaving their children unattended, working mothers contributed to their poor morals." The poor personal hygiene and lack of cleanliness of black mothers was assessed by him as a major cause of the high rate of black infant mortality.[19]

The Philadelphia Negro, in particular, revealed the perspectives of a judgmental, sexual puritanism. In this, Du Bois advised, for example, that the "colored girl" had too much freedom, and what she needed was a strict home life. It was "the duty of Negroes" to "solve" the problem of female "unchastity" by "keeping little girls off the street at night, stopping the escorting of unchaperoned young ladies to church and elsewhere."[20]

Published in 1909, *The Negro American Family* was also pervaded by moralism, but it was somewhat more optimistic about Negro progress, finding "more female purity, more male continence, and a healthier home life today than ever before." Female "purity" remained essential in this study, as the primary measuring rod of Negro progress through the "various stages of moral, intellectual and industrial evolution." But motherhood out of wedlock was presented in a less disapproving light, as Du Bois observed that this did not indicate that these women were licentious and promiscuous, but instead reflected their high valuation of children: "The Negro mother-love and family instinct is strong." Moreover, in this text he even suggested that "the Negro woman, with her strong desire for motherhood, may teach modern civilization that virginity, save as a means of healthy motherhood, is an evil,and not a divine attribute." Yet this book also warned that while "the tendencies are hopeful, still . . . sexual immorality is probably the greatest single plague spot among Negro Americans." The "greatest cause" of this was said to be slavery, and continuing "disregard of a black woman's virtue."[21]

Thus, Du Bois reiterated the emphasis of black historians on the tragic damage done by slavery, and also emphasized the lasting, crippling results. Responsible for "crushing out . . . African clan and family life," slavery had left black Americans "raped of their own sex customs and provided with no binding new ones."[22]

As we shall see in a later chapter, today's historians have rejected the old portrayals of slaves' sexual depravity, ruined homes, and lastingly crippled Afro-Americans. However, given his own cultural resources, and challenging the dominant contemporary historiography, which cast slavery as a civilizing institution and slaves as contented and happy-go-lucky, Du Bois had good reason to accept and endorse the antislavery story told by contemporary black historians.

Yet Du Bois's portrayal of contemporary black womanhood became increasingly laudatory. As S. P. Fullinwider has observed, his *Morals and Manners among Negro Americans* "was a paean to the 'strength of purpose' and 'purity of life' of Negro mothers." But according to Fullinwider, this 1914 book "revealed a Du Bois in whom all scientific objectivity had stepped aside for mysticism. . . . It was propaganda, not sociology." In Fullinwider's view, Du Bois's newly laudatory image of black womanhood grew from his

"Black Christ" mythology, because "to complete the imagery implied by his central image (the Black Christ) a black madonna was needed."[23]

According to Fullinwider's analysis, Du Bois's "Black Christ" was an "invidious" image of black superiority that reflected Du Bois's hostility to whites and was the basis for the subsequent growth of a ghetto culture equating "soul" with black racism. By this reading, Du Bois's "Black Christ" even evolved into black idealization of "the con man . . . who defies social convention."[24] Yet Fullinwider's analysis reveals elements of self-contradiction. In particular, on the one hand it interprets the "Black Madonna" as a spin-off from the "Black Christ" mythology. But on the other hand, it argues that Du Bois's "mother-idea" implanted the "seed that would blossom . . . into the invidious Black Christ image."[25]

However, to assess the validity of this analysis it is necessary to turn to Du Bois's historical writings in order to develop a more comprehensive understanding of his vision of race and gender.

To examine Du Bois's historical writings is to confirm that he took considerable poetic license in reconstructing the past. However, this was an era when, as Carter Woodson and Charles Wesley observed, American historiography served largely as "propaganda in justification of domination and exploitation of the weak by the strong."[26] For Du Bois, history was a major vehicle for his creation of an oppositional discourse that shaped, in Rampersad's words, "profound and enduring myths about the life of the people."[27] In his historical writings, Du Bois demonstrated a keen awareness that pride in the history of black women as well as black men was crucial to Afro-American self-respect.

Moreover, as a historian Du Bois revealed the increasing discomfiture with which he wore the dispassionate mantle of sociologist, decrying that "while sociologists gleefully count his bastards and his prostitutes, the very soul of the toiling, sweating black man is darkened by . . . a vast despair." Indeed, in his historical writings Du Bois discovered black womanhood in a very different light than he did as a scientist of the present.[28]

In his 1924 book, *The Gift of Black Folk: The Negroes in the Making of America*, Du Bois brought a keen attention to black women in American history. He rejected the "stain of bastardy which two centuries of systematic legal defilement of Negro women" had stamped upon the race. And he found new meaning even in the slave woman-cum-Jezebel, as a figure both "painful" and "beautiful." Regarding her concubinage to the white man, he advised, "let us regard it dispassionately, remembering that the concubine is as old as the world." Moreover, "whatever judgment we may pass . . . the fact remains that the colored slave woman became the medium through which two great races were united in America." And in his 1921 book, *Darkwater*, Du Bois even revised the meaning of black "promiscuity," reinterpreting this as the "innate decency" that had led "black women to choose irregular and temporary sexual relations with men they liked rather than to sell themselves to strangers."[29]

Nor did Du Bois leave the black woman's Mammy-like work invisible. Instead, he presented the black female worker as the archetype of female liberation. That the slave woman had proved herself as economically productive as any man, in his view, placed her in the vanguard of a widened and richer femininity. That the black woman "could and did replace the white man as laborer, artisan and servant, showed the possibility of white women doing the same thing, and led to it."[30]

Moreover, that her labor-force participation was essential to Afro-American economic survival was no cause for shame. Instead Du Bois emphasized that it was praiseworthy, that in the absence of male providers it was her wages that supported the children. He lauded Sojourner Truth's call for recognition that female productivity and strength were fully womanly. Praising this early black women's rights leader and abolitionist as "an Amazon," he wrote equally admiringly of such powerful female figures as Harriet Tubman, the escaped slave who assisted so many others to escape from the confines of slavery. Such women finally emerged in Du Bois's story as exemplars of black resistance and as historical heroines.[31]

Nonetheless, it should be noted that Du Bois's special veneration seemed reserved for "a not more worthy, but a finer type of black woman." In this "type" he found "that delicate sense of beauty and striving for self-realization which is as characteristic of the Negro soul as is its quaint strength and sweet laughter." And like other Afro-American historians, in *Darkwater* Du Bois wrote especially admiringly of the delicate poetess, Phyllis Wheatley. He also praised Mary Shadd—as a refined, mulatto woman of "ravishing dream-born beauty," whose "sympathy and sacrifice" were "characteristics of Negro womanhood."[32]

In actuality, Mary Shadd was also a very strong-willed, independent, and highly intelligent woman, and an antislavery leader who was noted for her public feuds with contemporary abolitionists.[33] There is much more that can be said about her and other notables who figured in Du Bois's historical discourse. Certainly, Du Bois by no means transcended the practice of casting black women as "types." Rather, he presented a much wider and richer range of types than did any other contemporary. But most significantly, he drew from virtually any and all images of historical black womanhood, however demeaning and disempowering, transfiguring these into emblems of worth. Indeed, even Mammy reemerged in this light.

Unlike most of his peers, Du Bois was able to reject the white-authored Mammy legend without rejecting the Mammy. Instead, he reshaped her into an image of black Christian martyrdom. Thus, he juxtaposed the old, slave Mammy to the white man, presenting these two figures on the day of slavery's abolition:

the one ... with hate in his eyes;—and the other, a form hovering dark and mother-like, ... had aforetime quailed at that white master's command, had bent in love over the cradles of his sons and daughters ... had laid herself low to his lust, and borne a tawny man-child to the world, only to see her dark boy's limbs scattered to the winds by midnight marauders.[34]

Thus, Du Bois's image of Mammy symbolized what he presented as the race's special spiritual qualities of forgiveness, patience, and love, as "one of the most pitiful of the world's Christs ... crucified on the cross of their own neglected children for the sake of the children of masters."[35]

Nonetheless, while emerging in Du Bois's discourse in a new light, Mammy did not emerge as a real living woman of history. It must also be acknowledged that in his major work of historical research, *Black Reconstruction*, women figured hardly at all. In this 1935 history, Du Bois often seemed most concerned to challenge the dominant historiography's diminishment of black men as men. He decried: "The whole history of Reconstruction has with few exceptions been written by passionate believers in the inferiority of the Negro," while "one fact and one alone explains the attitude of most recent writers toward Reconstruction; they cannot conceive Negroes as men."[36]

Nevertheless, even in *Black Reconstruction*, black women figured in more humanized shapes than elsewhere. For example, we may contrast Rhodes's depiction of depraved female creatures thronging after the Unionist troops, abandoning their infants by the wayside, to Du Bois's portraiture of the black woman's response to emancipation: "Slim dark girls ... wept silently; young women ... lifted shivering hands, and old and broken mothers ... raised great voices and shouted to God."[37]

It is true that Mammy and her kin still emerged in this discourse more as images than in substance. Moreover, it becomes clear that for Du Bois, femininity was particularly identifiable with motherhood. Equating the black woman above all with motherhood, in his historical vision she reemerged as the most feminine, and also empowered, of women. In this image she transcended slavery and emerged as

the primal black All-mother of men down through the ghostly throng of mighty womanhood ... down to our own day and our own land. ... All the way back ... it is mothers ... who seem to count, while fathers are shadowy memories.[38]

In short, this historian significantly transfigured the primacy of black mothers from a liability into an asset. He also shaped his "mother idea" into an image shaping and endorsing the identity of the Negro as the feminine race—which, it should be noted, remained in his thought, a very positive vision of race. In his words,

the child of the mother is and was Africa ... the spell of the African mother pervades her land. ... Nor does this seem to be solely a survival of the historic matriarchate through which all nations pass—it appears to be more than this—as if the great black race . . . gave the world . . . the mother-idea.[39]

Du Bois's "mother-idea" should not be confused with the "black matriarchy" thesis that much later would crystallize into the 1965 Moynihan Report. Instead, it was both a mystical concept and also referred to the very close bonding of mother and child that Du Bois presented as central to the real vitality and strength of African family life, thereby rejecting racist images of African barbarism. In his view, the mother-idea lived on in America in the sense that it continued to impart to Afro-Americans "that deep, emotional nature which turns instinctively towards the supernatural." Hence, for him the Negro race in America remained integrally identified with its women: "To no modern race does its women mean so much as to the Negro, nor come so near to the fulfillment of its meaning."[40] In sum, while presenting the black woman's history of oppression in America as a trial by fire, Du Bois strikingly reinterpreted the results as creating "an efficient womanhood."[41]

In light of Du Bois's emphasis on the primacy of women—as epitomized by his "all mother" idea—and in light of his frequently feminized symbolization of the virtues he attributed to the Negro race, it seems a great mistake to interpret his work as creating some "Black Christ" mythology which underpinned a later era's cult of black machismo and antiwhite racism.

Du Bois's "all-mother" was both the controlling metaphor of his vision of black womanhood, and also was central to his mystique of race. Fullinwider appears quite mistaken in viewing the "Mother idea" as "but a small fragment in the pattern of all-encompassing mosaic—a mosaic patterned around the Christ-like myth and its mission ideology."[42] On the contrary, Du Bois's empowering vision of historical black womanhood was central to, and greatly illuminated, his vision of race.

Moreover, it becomes clear that for Du Bois, it was history that revealed the inadequacies and errors of the sociological analysis that explained the contemporary "Negro Problem" as largely the legacy of history, and therefore likely to continue for the foreseeable future. For him, instead, history provided a legacy of survival and strength of which the Afro-American woman was the taproot, epitomizing and nurturing the ability of her race to move ahead into the future. He wrote: "For this, their promise, and for their hard past, I honor the women of my race."[43]

Du Bois did not reconstruct black women as full human beings *in* history. But he did point the way to discovering their diverse realities in a transfigured light, by reinterpreting even the most disempowering, demeaning images in a positive, empowering light.

In the decades which followed, the all-mother image would itself be transfigured, from perspectives leading ultimately to crystallization of the "Black Matriarchy" as a central and profoundly disempowering image of American racial mythology. But to read history backward in a way that assigns Du Bois responsibility in some sense for what others made of his vision would be a great mistake.

In his own era Du Bois was a pioneer in the transformation of even the most dehumanizing images of black womanhood into empowering symbols of worth. And as he wrote, "to save from the past the shreds and vestiges of self-respect has been a terrible task."[44] Du Bois might well have been referring to his role as historian. But he was referring to the historical achievement of Afro-American women.

NOTES

1. Smith, *An Old Creed*, 209.

2. Bettina Aptheker, "On 'The Damnation of Women': W.E.B. Du Bois and a Theory for Woman's Emancipation," in Bettina Aptheker, *Woman's Legacy: Essays on Race, Sex, and Class in American History* (Amherst: The University of Massachusetts Press, 1982), 78, 86, 79.

3. Quoted in Irene Diggs, "Du Bois and Women. A Short Story of Black Women, 1910–1934," *A Current Bibliography on African Affairs* 7, no. 3 (1974): 1.

4. Williams, *From a Caste to a Minority*, 28.

5. August Meier, "Washington and Du Bois," in Seth M. Scheiner and Tilden G. Edelstein, eds., *The Black Americans: Interpretive Readings* (New York: Robert E. Krieger Pub. Co., 1975), 321.

6. W.E.B. Du Bois, *The Souls of Black Folk* (Greenwich, Conn.: Fawcett Publications, Inc./Crest Reprint, 1961; orig. pub. 1903), 17.

7. W.E.B. Du Bois, *The Souls of Black Folk*, 2; W.E.B. Du Bois, *Darkwater: Voices from Within the Veil* (Millwood, N.Y.: Kraus-Thomson Org. Ltd., 1975; orig. pub. 1921), 14; Moses, *Black Messiahs*, 130.

8. Jean Fagan Yellin, "Du Bois' 'Crisis' and Woman's Suffrage," *Massachusetts Review* 14 (1973): 365–75; Arnold Rampersad, *The Art and Imagination of W.E.B. Du Bois* (Cambridge, Mass.: Harvard University Press, 1966).

9. See for example, Jack B. Moore, *W.E.B. Du Bois* (New York: G. K. Hall & Co., 1981).

10. Meier, "Washington and Du Bois," 321.

11. Moses, *Black Messiahs*.

12. Moses, *Black Messiahs*, esp. x–xii, 53, 61, 62, 114, 154; Fullinwider, *Mind and Mood*.

13. John Barker, *The Superhistorians: Makers of Our Past* (New York: Charles Scribner & Sons, 1982), 242, 250.

14. Herbert Aptheker, *Afro-American History*, 47.

15. Crummell and Stuckey quoted in Moses, *Black Messiahs*, 52.

16. Barker, *Superhistorians*, 255.

17. W.E.B. Du Bois, *The Philadelphia Negro: A Sociological Study* (New York: University of Pennsylvania Press/Benjamin Blom, Inc., 1967; orig. pub. 1899), 196; W.E.B. Du Bois, *The Negro American Family* (Westport, Conn.: Negro Universities Press, 1970; orig. pub. 1908), 49. Regarding Crummell's influence upon Du Bois, see

Wilson J. Moses, "Civilizing Missionary: A Study of Alexander Crummell," *Journal of Negro History* 60 (1975): 229–51.

18. Du Bois, *Philadelphia Negro*, 72, 71; *The Negro American Family*, 37.

19. Du Bois, *Philadelphia Negro*, 67, 70, 194, 163.

20. Ibid., 72, 389–93.

21. Du Bois, *Negro American Family*, 39, 42, 41.

22. Ibid., 21–22.

23. Fullinwider, *Black America*, 51, 52.

24. Ibid., 46, 52, viii, 194–206.

25. Ibid., 52.

26. Woodson and Wesley, *The Story of the Negro Retold*, 443.

27. Rampersad, *Art and Imagination of Du Bois*, 88.

28. Rampersad, *Art and Imagination of Du Bois*, 88; Du Bois, *Souls of Black Folk*, 20.

29. W.E.B. Du Bois, *The Gift of Black Folk: The Negroes in the Making of America* (Boston: The Stratford Co., Publishers, 1924), 265, 268; *Darkwater*, 116.

30. Du Bois, *Darkwater*, 262.

31. Ibid., 183; *Gift of Black Folk*, 263, 272.

32. Du Bois, *Darkwater*, 177.

33. See, for example, Jim Bearden and Linda Jean Butler, *Shadd: The Life and Times of Mary Shadd Cary* (Toronto: N C Press, 1977).

34. Du Bois, *Souls of Black Folk*, 34.

35. Du Bois, *Gift of Black Folk*, 337.

36. W.E.B. Du Bois, *Black Reconstruction in America: An Essay Toward a History of the Past Which Black Folk Played in the Attempt to Reconstruct Democracy in America, 1860–1880* (New York: Russell & Russell, 1956; orig. pub. 1935), 381, 726.

37. Ibid., 124.

38. Du Bois, *Darkwater*, 166, 168.

39. Ibid., 166.

40. Ibid., 172; for the "mother-idea" see also *Darkwater*, 169, and *The Negro American Family*, 19–25.

41. *Darkwater*, 172.

42. Fullinwider, *Black America*, 51.

43. Du Bois, *Darkwater*, 185.

44. Ibid., 71.

5

Slave Women of the Sociological Imagination

As W.E.B. Du Bois observed in *Black Reconstruction*, "In propaganda against the Negro . . . we face one of the most stupendous efforts the world ever saw to discredit human beings, an effort involving universities, history, science, social life and religion."[1] Yet according to J. P. Fullinwider it was Du Bois who was a major mythmaker, and Du Bois's scholarship became problack propaganda. In Fullinwider's view, while "myth has constantly dragged Negro ideology in the direction of the irrational," "the sociological imagination has constantly worked to pull it back."[2] But upon investigation of how Afro-American women figured in American sociology during the Jim Crow era, this laudatory view of the "sociological imagination" becomes difficult to sustain.

Indeed, derogatory slave-woman stereotypes pervaded social-science studies of race during the segregationist decades. In sociological literature in particular, the spinning together of past and present shaped enduring myths of black womanhood that were constructed as factual.

To understand the mixing and mingling of past and present, and its results in the scholarship of race, it should be noted first that like history, sociology also became a professional discipline during the decades around the turn of the century. Thus, it too was midwifed by the nation's search for order, which in large part reflected the anxieties of middle-class Americans of British ancestry. Sociologists were, in effect, designated as the experts who would alleviate these anxieties by discovering the causes of and solutions to the problem of disorder.

During the early twentieth century, to the perceived problems of social and industrial conflict and the influx of southern and eastern European immigrants, was added the swelling migration of black Southerners to the

North. In this context, what had been seen as merely the South's "Negro Problem" became nationalized. Northern social scientists came to share the South's attention to race.

As sociologists throughout the nation turned to examine the "Negro Problem," they professed to bring empirical, objective, entirely "scientific" perspectives to their studies. However, in actuality their findings included presuppositions and value judgments, as they also drew from contemporary cultural and intellectual resources. These resources included the prevailing doctrines of racial determinism and the contemporary ranking of human cultures into savagery, barbarism, and civilization that, in effect, defined white American society as the pinnacle of civilization.

The prevailing white supremacist conviction of inherent Negro inferiority was, by the early twentieth century, challenged by the revisionist thinking led by Franz Boas. This German-educated American anthropologist was a pioneer in emphasizing that environment and experience shaped racial differences—not inherited biological determinants. As Vernon J. Williams has found, the challenge to racial determinism had some influence by the 1920s. Nonetheless, most sociologists still believed that black Americans were dominated by peculiar "race characteristics" which rendered them unassimilable into the American mainstream. However, these racial "traits" were now presented as resulting from nurture rather than nature. Thenceforth, American sociologists moved forward toward a racial liberalism which by World War II emphasized the capacity of black Americans for progress and assimilation—defining progress in terms of adoption of white norms.

At least, this is Williams's thesis, that "despite a capitulation before 1911 to the forces of racism and reaction, sociologists . . . transformed their discipline into one of the most forward-looking of all social science disciplines."[3] On the other hand, in John Stanfield's view, the interwar decades were by no means a golden age of race-relations research, and American social scientists continued to be "gate keepers" of racial conservatism.[4]

Stanfield has pointed out that throughout the segregationist era American scholars remained fundamentally dependent upon the support of institutions that perceived the "Negro Problem" as an issue of social control. From the perspective of these institutions, the primary goal was to forward Negro adjustment to the color line and adoption of the norms defined as desirable by white culture. Any scholar, white or black, who worked outside of this accommodationist framework found it very difficult to find funding and institutional facilities. In this way, social scientists practiced a selective, accommodative empiricism which served to legitimate rather than to challenge white racial biases.

In short, Stanfield's findings argue that the scholarship of race tended to update rather than to challenge racist ideology. While it became less acceptable to explain Negro "backwardness" and inequality in terms of inherited racial traits, it was instead increasingly explained by the new thesis of Negro cultural inferiority. That is, black culture was said to be inferior to white culture because of the black experience of history. But to understand this thesis fully, including its implications for how black women figured in this body of literature, it is important to remember that among the resources drawn upon by social science was the historiography of slavery and race.

Because of their early interest in slavery and Reconstruction, historians had a head start in terms of research on racial matters. When sociologists turned to the "Negro Problem" to understand and explain the present, they frequently turned to the evidence regarding the past that they found in history. Moreover, the disciplines of sociology and history were linked by a shared historicism that pointed to the supposed patterns and "laws" of the pats as relevant to current social realities. Accordingly, the often indiscriminate mixing and mingling of these disciplines were foundations for the developing sociology of race. In the early twentieth century this blending process was promoted by the doctrine of retrogressionism which cast the postslavery Negro as reverting to barbarism.

According to Joseph A. Tillinghast's 1902 text, *The Negro in Africa and America*, people of African descent were characterized by unrestrained "sexual proclivities," since the process of natural selection in Africa had promoted "exceptionally strong reproductive powers." Thus, according to this Southern sociologist, while blacks in America had benefited from the civilizing restraints of slavery, after the institution's abolition they naturally reverted to barbarism.[5]

Similarly, Jerome Dowd cast African societies as "retrogressive," to explain why the Negro's "passions and natural impulses are exceptionally potent and his inhibiting power exceptionally feeble." He also reiterated the familiar proslavery story that ended with the horrors of "Black Reconstruction." So, these leading early twentieth-century Southern sociologists brought sexual racism and history not only to the support of racial segregation, but also into contemporary sociology. As Williams has pointed out, despite their "slipshod work," they were highly respected by distinguished Northern as well as Southern scholars.[6]

Retrogressionist images of the Negro would continue to bolster American scholarship long after the doctrine of the inherent barbarism of the race had been discredited. The persistent combination of past and present shaped American sociology in a way that perpetuated attention to slavery and to supposed black sexual degeneracy. Moreover, in the scholarship of race these themes became integrally spun together in a way that eventually promoted special attention to the supposed flaws of the contemporary Negro family.

What linked these themes in particular was the new doctrine of "Negro pathology" that underpinned the thesis of black cultural inferiority. This thesis reflected the growing emphasis on environment and history as the shaping forces of race. In this context, the Negro's historical experience of oppression and what was termed "deprivation" were said to be responsible for his continuing cultural inferiority. From this inferiority rooted in history seemingly sprang what was called "Negro pathology"; that is, as blacks strove and failed to imitate white culture, this process was said to promote their self-contempt.

In more technical terms, Afro-Americans' reaction formations to racism led to self-hatred and psychic illness. This syndrome was said to explain their antisocial, deviant, and fundamentally immoral behavior. Social scientists pointed to a self-perpetuating cycle that rendered Negro pathology the core of the "Negro Problem." It followed that reform of Negro morality was essential to forward Negro "adjustment" and perhaps eventual assimilation into American society. Or at least, so Americans were told by the social scientists associated with the University of Chicago.

This university had become by the 1920s the primary center for the American study of sociology. And it was this university's leading sociologist, Robert E. Park, and his students who were most influential in developing the thesis of Negro pathology. It is important to note that while Park was, in the context of this era, a white racial liberal, he still believed that races were characterized by distinctive "temperamental qualities" or "traits." And in his view, "the negro is, by natural disposition . . . primarily an artist, loving life for its own sake. His metier is expression rather than action. He is, so to speak, the lady among the races."[7]

Park reiterated a conceptualization that, as we have seen, dated back at least to antebellum antislavery—that the Negro was the feminine race. And this old-time analogue of race and gender deeply pervaded the formulation of the Negro pathology thesis.

In Park's words: "Man has got what he wanted by tackling things; going at them directly. The Negro and the woman have got them by manipulating the individual in control. Women and Negroes have required the machinery of rapid and delicate adjustment to the words and temper of men."[8] It followed, in this view, that for both blacks and women, outwardly accommodating behavior led to repressed frustration projected into self-contempt. Then, this damaged psyche promoted the damaging behavior that perpetuated Negro pathology.

This was a circular argument that in effect made black failure to adjust to a racist society the cause of continuing black cultural inferiority and racial inequality. Nonetheless, it was apparently persuasive to contemporaries, while the doctrine of Negro pathology became integrally supported by studies that seemed to show that the Negro family was in a chaotic state. But as Eleanor Engram has found of contemporary research on the Afro-American family, this was a body of literature steeped in the mythology of race. Engram's findings help to clarify the peculiarly linked conceptualizations of race and gender that came to underpin scholarly interpretation of the "Negro Problem."

As Engram has pointed out, the culture's traditional conceptualization of male/female dichotomies defined masculinity as independent, instrumental, and aggressive, and femininity as dependent, expressive, and passive. From these perspectives, the paradigm of gender relations was female subordination and accommodation to male dominance. Similarly, America's paradigm of race relations has assumed black subordination and accommodation to white supremacy. And Engram's findings argue that in research on the black family these paradigms became intricately spun together.[9]

That black sexual norms and familial life did not conform to the traditional gender paradigm was interpreted in this research as Negro familial "disorganization" and sexual *immorality*. And this supposed Negro moral depravity became equated with black familial *decrepitude*, as cause and effect. This supposed syndrome was presented as the key to continuing Afro-American pathology and cultural inferiority. In sum, the departure of black gender relations and sexual behavior from prescribed gender norms became identified as largely responsible for continuing racial inequality.

But it is by examining how black women figured in the sociology of race that it becomes clear that what Engram has identified as the myths of the Afro-American family both forwarded and also sprang from presuppositions about Afro-American womanhood. Moreover, it becomes clear that these presuppositions originated in slave-woman images.

During the age of Jim Crow, sociologists drew heavily from the slave-woman portraiture endorsed by the stories historians told. They also embellished and updated that portraiture. From the promiscuous mix of history and sociology, the black woman emerged, in past and present alike, as the linchpin of Negro pathology and cultural inferiority.

The mixing process promoting this result may best be discovered in the work of Edward Byron Reuter, a sociologist trained at the University of Chicago under Robert E. Park. Complementing their interest in Negro pathology, Park and his students were interested in examining what they saw as the problematic identity of the mulatto. From their perspective, the American of black and white ancestry was the personification of Negro pathology because mulatto "superiority" demanded but was denied recognition by the dominant society. Thus the mulatto was what Park called the "marginal man."[10]

This thesis of mulatto marginalization became the conventional academic wisdom by the interwar decades, and Reuter was a pioneering scholar in the field. His interest was in establishing the causes of mulatto leadership in racial activism; that is, in what he called mulatto "superiority." Examining this question in the early twentieth century, during a time when scholarly views still remained in flux as to whether race was genetically inherited or the product of environment and culture, Reuter wavered between both views. But despite Williams's recent attempt to fit Reuter into his thesis that sociology was in the vanguard of racial liberalism, Reuter's explanation of mulatto "superiority" reflected presuppositions regarding Afro-American women that were fundamentally racist.[11]

Indeed, in Reuter's theorizing, the familiar, racist images of slave women cast as licentious Jezebels and exotic mulatto seductresses become strikingly visible as evidence for his conclusions. One suspects that in large part they constituted his premises. Reuter's reasoning was that historically in America mulattoes were largely the product of miscegenation between white men and black women. Today's historians would not necessarily agree with his further observation that white-black sexual relations historically involved largely lower-class, "dissolute" white males: "The class of white men who have intercourse with coloured women, are, as a rule, of an inferior type."[12] However, Reuter could not find the explanation of mulatto "superiority" in paternal origins. Therefore, arguing that this must stem from the Negro side of miscegenation, he turned instead to the mulatto's maternal origins, and here his reasoning became dominated by familiar slave-woman caricatures.

According to Reuter's 1918 book, *The Mulatto in the United States*, "the women of the lower races . . . desire, seek, feel honoured by the attention of the higher class men." Moreover, according to Reuter, history showed that "the [Negro] race never has shown any hesitancy about crossing with other races in any time or country. Their women have mixed with every race and people with whom they have come in contact." As he noted (ignoring black-authored historiography), American history showed that during the slavery era concubinage "was not in any sense a forced role on the part of the Negress; on the contrary, it was a role to which . . . [she] aspired as the highest honor and privilege." As well, history was said to have demonstrated that "wherever the Union armies went in the South, they were besieged by an army of Negro women." For this social scientist, history proved that "the Negro woman never has objected to, and has generally courted the relationship. . . . The amount of intermixture is limited only by the self-respect of the white man."[13]

Given the supposed nonparticipation in miscegenation of self-respecting "good white men," mulatto "superiority" had to be explicable in terms of "superior" maternal ancestry. Reuter drew from a version of social Darwinism to argue that from the supposed sexual competition among black women for white men, in concert with the working of natural selection, the fittest— that is, what he termed the "choicest"—slave women won out and became the mothers of mulattoes. By "choicest" he meant the most nearly white women. According to him, over time white American males had repeatedly selected as sexual partners

the choicest females of the black group. . . . The female off-spring of these mixed unions become chosen in turn to serve the pleasure of the superior group. By this process of repeated selection of the choicer girls of the black and mulatto groups . . .

there has been a constant force making for the production of a choicer type of female. . . . [Hence] the mulattoes, from one side of their ancestry, at least, have tended to produce a superior type.[14]

As Reuter noted, this explanation assumed that "a correlation maintains between physical perfection and mental superiority," and that "such superiority is a heritable thing."[15] He did not also recognize his own presuppositions regarding the superior physical attractiveness of women who looked more "white" than their sisters. And in sum, his work reiterated and endorsed the familiar caricatures of the mulatto seductress and the licentious slave Jezebel. John David Smith is correct that Reuter's work "rivaled even the crudest proslavery tract in its racist poison."[16]

Reuter's work helps to show how the mingling of sociology and history was both fed by and in turn fed symbolizations of sexual racism that were fully inclusive of black womanhood. In fact, while in Reuter's writings the black man was virtually invisible, slave-woman figures were predominant. And Reuter's work by no means confirms that the "sociological imagination" challenged the power of myth in American scholarship.

Certainly the era's white social scientists claimed to know the Negro race. For Howard Odum, for example, the Negro in his family life "is filthy, careless and indecent. He is as destitute of morals as any of the lower animals." And contemporary historians had written and were writing this picture of sexual depravity back into the past, confirming that, in the words of the historian Arthur Calhoun, "primitive traits and the heritage of slavery are slow to be eliminated. . . . At the opening of the twentieth century, the point where the Negro American was furthest behind modern civilization was in his sexual mores."[17]

Given the snowball effect whereby each scholar drew from and cited his predecessors to build and substantiate his own analysis, history and sociology worked closely together to confirm that the Negro's "backwardness" was due to what he did and did not learn in the Negro home. It came to be the consensus of a vast body of scholarship that the taproot of racial inequality was the historically inherited sexual immorality of blacks, which was perpetuated in the demoralized Negro home. Central to this consensus was the notion that the decrepitude of the black family was the cause as well as the effect of Negro pathology, and in turn that the linchpin of this was the inadequacy of Negro women as women.

The evolution of this story may be seen at work, for example, in John Dollard's 1937 study, *Caste and Color in a Southern Town*. This social psychologist set out to test what he perhaps euphemistically called the "hypothesis" that Negro behavior was rooted in self-hatred, that is, the pathology thesis. Convinced that "sex is at the heart of many problems in the racial field," much of what he saw himself as discovering about Negro pathology related to the black woman's sexual behavior. Dollard did bring an apparent questioning attitude to her image as hypersexual. He suggested, for example, that her seductress image in part reflected the wish-fulfillment fantasies of white men. As well, he suggested that for the white male the sexual "conquest" of Negro women was more than a matter of lust; it was also a political weapon asserting his supremacy over the black male.[18]

However, Dollard also pointed to what he claimed was the "very common delusion of black women that they were white." According to him, rejecting their own racial identity they readily traded their bodies for association with the white race. The Negro woman who responded "permissively" to white male overtures might also be acting out her "wishes for transitory gratification." However, the evidence Dollard provided largely supported the thesis that her licentious sexual behavior was a manifestation of pathological Negro responses to white supremacy.[19]

In Dollard's portrait, the black woman's behavior epitomized the sexual depravity of lower-class black Americans, and the source of their promiscuity was the mother-led Negro family. Citing the research of E. Franklin Frazier—of whom more will be said in this chapter—Dollard pointed to the Negro husband's inability to control his own wife. Her work role outside the family was said to make her uncontrollable by him and hence, sexually independent and often dominant in the black family. In short, in Dollard's view, the mother-led family promoted Negro sexual promiscuity, and thus also intraracial jealousies, violence, and other antisocial behavior.[20]

Nonetheless, ending on a somewhat more cheerful note, Dollard suggested that the black woman's sexual freedom gave her an opportunity denied to the white woman for sexual gratification outside as well as within her own race. Moreover, in her economic independence and central familial role, she was said to have escaped the factors depressing the status of "American" women.[21]

How the black woman saw her status and her experience did not emerge in this book. Her sexual behavior was of primary interest, and of interest primarily as evidence of black pathology and familial demoralization. And during the interwar decades a vast body of social science literature came to identify the mother-led family—which was variously called the "maternally organized" or, sometimes, the "matriarchal" black family—as central to the "Negro Problem." This analysis pervaded racially liberal sociological research, both white- and black-authored.

In these studies, since psychic health was identified with the adjustment of the individual to the social group, black maladjustment to Jim Crow was identified in terms of pathology. Contemporary social scientists sought, in the words of the black sociologist, Charles Johnson, to "define the conditions under which identification with the dominant cultural group is achieved."[22] The consensus grew that this "healthy" identification was especially undermined by the historically "weak," "matriarchal" Negro family, that is, the black family was defined as weak because matriarchal.

Johnson was himself a distinguished exponent of this swelling consensus. A former student of Robert E. Park, in 1928 he became chairman of Fisk University's social sciences department and later became the university's president. It should be noted that he firmly rejected racial determinism, pointing instead to black progress as forwarded by modernizing forces such as education and urbanization. However, Johnson pointed also to the persistence of Negro pathology.[23]

According to his 1941 book, *Growing Up in the Black Belt: Negro Youth in the Rural South*, the problems of the Negro family constituted a pattern inherited from history. Familial ill health was a "carryover" from slavery, perpetuated by the "independence" of Negro women and, therefore, the "irresponsibility" of Negro men. Because "reproduction had no value to the slave, but free sex was followed as an end in itself," promiscuity and illegitimacy had become self-perpetuating manifestations of Negro pathology. In a similar way, according to *The Personality Development of Negro Youth in the Urban South* authored by Allison Davis and John Dollard, these "emotional snarls" continued to cripple the personality development of Negro young people.[24]

Identifying psychocultural health by applying what were essentially white, middle-class standards to selected empirical data, these studies agreed that sexual behavior was, in Johnson's words, "one of the most vital indices of Negro family organization and cultural advancement."[25] Any empirical evidence that Afro-Americans might have their own standards of morality, and that black Americans were "adjusted" to their own culturally defined norms, was readily reshaped into white-defined categories of cultural progress.

Hylan Lewis's findings, for example, argued that among blacks themselves the "respectable" Negro mother was not defined by her marital status. Rather, she was the woman admired for her maturity and involvement in church and community work. Lewis noted that, as identified by blacks, the "non-respectable" woman was unethical and one who drank to excess. Nonetheless, from Lewis's perspective, as revealed in his 1955 book, *Blackways of Kent*, Negro respectability was identifiable in terms of the marital status of mothers, that is, in terms of rates of illegitimate births. Because these were higher among blacks than among whites, he identified Negro "subculture" as de facto nonrespectable and pathological.[26] By such definitions, the black woman could not be respectable and "good" on her own terms.

To review this literature is to recognize that data which did not substantiate the pathology thesis was of little interest unless it could be retranslated into evidence substantiating this thesis. For example, in examining the occupational aspirations of rural black teenagers, Johnson found that both boys and girls, but especially girls, hoped to enter the trades and professions to escape the fate of being locked into farming. However, he interpreted these ambitions as further evidence of Negro pathology, demonstrating "a pronounced psychology of escape in the occupations selected." Johnson was somewhat more hopeful about evidence of the desire of these girls to find a husband "who will support me." This aspiration, he noted, suggested a growing rejection of the black woman's principal role in the family. And this was a good sign, because it was the consensus of this body of scholarship that the adoption of patriarchal norms and values was essential to Negro adjustment and well-being. The "matriarchal" Negro family was cast as profoundly damaging to the "wholesome integration of personality and the social world."[27]

As the scholarship of race became pervaded by these intermeshed premises and conclusions, in effect, it also continued and embellished the race-gender analogue that identified racial "traits" and sexual identity as two sides of the same coin. By blending the image of "matriarchy" into the Negro pathology thesis, black departures from patriarchal gender relations and white-defined sexual norms became equated with the Negro's cultural inferiority and there-fore, inequality. Rolling this analogue forward was the snowball process in which scholars fed and built upon each other's work. But in particular, by the 1940s the sociology of race both drew heavily from and also seemed to confirm the theories of the major Afro-American scholar, E. Franklin Frazier.

E. FRANKLIN FRAZIER

Another former student of Robert E. Park, by the mid-1930s Frazier was chairman of Howard University's sociology department. In recognition of his major contributions to family and race relations research, in 1946 he was elected president of the American Sociological Society. Emphasizing that race was a social and cultural construction, he was in Williams's words "per-haps the most influential scholar to persistently challenge racism" during the 1930s and 1940s.[28]

On the other hand, to discover how black women figured in Frazier's writings does not entirely confirm this characterization. Moreover, while highly skilled as a sociologist, Frazier frequently put on the historian's man-tle, perpetuating the mingling of these fields in a way that authoritatively forwarded the thesis of "black matriarchy."

As some have acknowledged, Daniel Patrick Moynihan's "Black Matriar-chy" thesis was by no means single-handedly created by Moynihan. Instead, in large part the 1965 Moynihan Report, in Deborah White's words, "echoed Frazier's sentiments."[29]

Opponents of the Moynihan thesis have not wished to discover any black American as its father. Yet while a leading opponent, Herbert Gutman has acknowledged that Frazier in his 1939 book, *The Negro Family in the United States*, led to the Moynihan thesis through "nearly all other standard works on this important subject that rest heavily upon this influential book." Sim-ilarly, Shepard Krech III has pointed out that it was Frazier's characterizations of the Negro family as mother-led, and thereby disorganized and unstable, that stood behind much of the 1940s sociology of race, and that were restated by Moynihan's *The Negro Family*. Therefore, critics of the Black Matriarchy thesis have often attempted, in effect, to defend E. Franklin Frazier.[30]

Gutman, for example, in noting his "misdirected emphasis," quickly added that "Frazier of course, was not a racist" but a vigorous opponent of racism. And Eleanor Engram has insisted that his work was "misread" by others, and that he has been unjustly blamed for fathering the matriarchy mythology. However, such defenses reveal a lack of attention to how black women actually figured in Frazier's work. As well, they treat Frazier as if he were isolated from the scholarship of his era.[31]

The enigma of Frazier can in part be addressed by recognizing that the Afro-American intellectual tradition itself provided a legacy of slave-woman images that could readily be molded into the shape of matriarchy. As we have found, mothers had emerged in black-authored historiography as central to the slave home. Yet slave mothers had largely emerged as female failures in the work of such historians as Alexander Crummell. And as Wilson J. Moses has pointed out, Crummell was one who anticipated Frazier's Black Matriarchy thesis by many decades.

Emphasizing the continuity of the Afro-American intellectual tradition, Moses has suggested that Du Bois was the primary organ of transmission of Crummell's ideas to Frazier. Indeed, Du Bois's sociological publications had reiterated the black woman's centrality in the Afro-American family, although as historian he had recast the "mother-idea" into a story emphasizing the black woman's immense contribution to her race. But more often, her familial centrality was interpreted in this historiography as evidence of slavery's damage to black femininity and the family.[32]

Certainly, in *The Negro Family in the United States* Frazier suggested his debt to Afro-American scholarship, paying particular tribute in his introduction to Du Bois's research on the contemporary Negro family. However, Frazier's citations of sources indicate that he also relied upon white-authored histories for his understanding of the past. While he assessed some research as racist, often he accepted the data and arguments of his sources—including the work of Edward Byron Reuter—without attention to their racial bias.

In this 1939 book, Frazier's focus began essentially where Du Bois's had appeared to end: with the high rate of illegitimate births among contemporary black Americans. Viewing Negro motherhood out of wedlock as a most "serious economic and social problem," Frazier focused on the Afro-American family in search of explanations. This institution, he argued, was the primary key "to the problem of the assimilation of the Negro and his adjustment to modern civilization." His intention in *The Negro Family* was "to apply the tools and concepts of modern sociological analysis to the study of this problem in the North."[33] But it was in large part the stories historians told that he brought to, and endorsed, in this study.

It is true that Frazier had much to say about the contemporary "Negro

Problem." In particular, he found associated with urbanization "the problem
of unmarried mothers." In Negro children lacking in monogamic role models
and left alone by working mothers, Frazier pointed to sons who became
juvenile delinquents and fathers who deserted their own children, while
daughters grew up to imitate "the loose behavior of their mothers." He
argued that "loose sex behavior" and "disorganized family life" had become
a destructive, self-sustaining pattern of motherhood out of wedlock and
mother-led households.[34]

Frazier recognized the damaging effects of contemporary racial discrimination and poverty. Nonetheless, in presenting the "maternally organized"
family as the linchpin of the problems contemporary Negroes faced, his book
presented this as in large part the legacy of history. In particular, he reiterated
that slavery had ruined the black family. And in his story of slavery, the
slave woman emerged as a composite figure consisting of familiar racist
caricatures as well as black-authored images.

Beginning with his 1930 article, "The Negro Slave Family," Frazier detailed the destruction of this institution. Citing Du Bois, for example, he
repeated that slaves were "raped of their sex customs." Miscegenation had
corrupted their sense of morality. On the other hand, he also proclaimed
that "in many instances men of the master race did not meet much resistance." In this context, Frazier reiterated white-authored images of slave
women who sought by sex to gain favors and prestige from association with
white men, or who submitted "out of animal feeling" and "mutual
attraction."[35]

Miscegenation had a positive side, according to Frazier. From the slave
woman's concubinage stemmed "enduring affections" that "paved the way
for assimilation." The mulatto offspring of these unions adopted the norms
and ambitions of their white fathers. Similarly their mothers benefited from
their association "with the cultured classes of the South." In this context,
Frazier portrayed a happy picture of the "family groups consisting mainly
of slave mother and mulatto offspring." According to him, it was their descendants who went on to become the most advanced class of Afro-Americans, characterized by stable, two-parent families that adopted white norms
and patriarchy together.[36]

By contrast, according to Frazier by far the most prevalent type of slave
family was mother-led. It was this type that in his book epitomized the most
damaging results of "motherhood in bondage." According to Frazier's story,
because of the trauma of the slave ship Middle Passage, "the last spark of
maternal feeling was probably smothered." In America, forced to breed like
animals, bondswomen developed "a distinct antipathy toward their offspring." Forced away from her infants and back to the fields, "it was not
unnatural that the slave mother often showed little attachment to her
offspring."[37]

For this story of dematernalized slave motherhood, Frazier's empirical evidence was very scanty, heavily reliant upon secondary sources, and at times explicitly drawn from white-authored stereotypes and myths. Mammy, for example, was recycled as evidence and as a historical "fact" so self-evidently true as to need no substantiation at all. Frazier noted regarding her well-known reputation that "there is plenty of evidence to give a solid background to the familiar picture-stories of cold, and often inhuman, indifference toward her own offspring, and undying devotion to the children of the master race." Thus, he found it unnecessary to provide any evidence of the objective reality of such mammies.[38]

Frazier's story of slave womanhood, however, was beset by contradictions. He clearly agreed with the consensus of Afro-American historiography that what remained of the slave family revolved around the slave mother. But in this context, she sometimes reemerged as a more maternalized figure. According to Frazier, "only the bond between the mother and the child" survived slavery's damage, and "under all conditions of slavery, the Negro mother remained the most dependable and important figure in the family." In this context, "in the slave cabin, where she was generally mistress . . . the mother could give full reign to her tender feelings," and demonstrate "deep and permanent love" for her children.[39]

What was clear in Frazier's story was the slave woman's familial dominance. Hearkening back to Du Bois's casting of her as "the head of the family," while the black man "sank to a position of male guest in the house, without respect or responsibility," Frazier agreed that "the father was the visitor often to the home presided over by the mother." Her familial dominance was supported by her economic role, since "as a worker and free agent . . . she developed a spirit of independence and a keen sense of her personal rights."[40]

Recognizing no incongruity in designating the slave woman as a "free agent," Frazier then pursued the path which led him away from Du Bois's empowering "mother-idea." In Frazier's story, the "dominating position of the mother" and "timid" character of the father became two sides of the same coin, and the correspondence of female strength to male weakness took on explicit explanatory value as the basis of continuing Negro inequality.[41]

For the father to assume the "aggressive role" was essential to Negro success in Frazier's view. According to his story some slave families were not "demoralized" and "had achieved a fair degree of organization," by which Frazier meant male dominance. In these families after slavery's abolition, the freedman's paternal authority remained firmly established, "and the woman in the role of mother and wife fitted into the pattern of the patriarchal household. . . . The father became the chief, if not the sole bread-winner." In these "well-organized" families, male "responsibility for the maintenance of the family and direction of property" was passed down from father to son, and the adjustment to freedom was smooth and successful.

Unfortunately, most of the ex-slaves had no patriarchal tradition, and according to Frazier, after slavery's abolition "promiscuous sexual relations and constant changing of spouses became the rule with the demoralized elements in the freed Negro population." After emancipation "the drifting masses were left without any restraint upon their vagrant impulses and wild desires."[42]

In contrast, it is the consensus of today's historians that in the aftermath of slavery the freedpersons thronged to legalize their marriages. It is now the consensus that their "drifting" was most often in search of loved ones and family members from whom they had been separated by slavery, as well as in search of work away from the home plantation. However, for this story of the freedpersons, Frazier relied heavily upon the "facts" provided by Phillip Bruce, the late nineteenth-century architect of the doctrine of the Negro's reversion to savagery with the lifting of slavery's restraints. Frazier went on to argue that, freed from institutional controls and deserted by her man, the freedwoman fell into an "unfetterd motherhood" in which she continued to play "the dominant role."[43]

"Unfettered motherhood" meant motherhood out of wedlock to Frazier. According to his findings, the high rate of illegitimate births became further endorsed by black female attitudes, which valued procreation and children in any context, promoting premarital and extramarital sex. Moreover, the freedwoman's schooling by slavery in "self-reliance and self-sufficiency" continued to undermine her "spirit of subordination to masculine authority." Hence, "with each generation of women following in the footsteps of their mothers," what this book titled "the Matriarchate" became a self-perpetuating institution.[44]

According to Frazier's findings, by 1930 up to twenty-five percent of the South's rural black households were female-led. But his term "Matriarchate" involved more than matrifocality. It meant extended female households in which mother and children continued to live with the grandmother. The "granny' was a most influential person in the rural black community and a role model for young women. They looked forward to being "elevated" to her status. In turn, the granny supported her daughters and their offspring. According to Frazier, she discouraged them from marrying, perpetuating the "maternal family organization." In his book, the Matriarchate became not an asset, but a liability, particularly as Southern blacks migrated from the countryside to the city.[45]

Frazier found that urbanization undermined the values and mores that had, in the countryside, reinforced the maternal family tradition. It was in the city that Afro-American women emerged in *The Negro Family* in an overwhelmingly negative light, as brutalized, "painted and powdered . . . with lustful songs upon their lips." There, the mother-led family became an institution which transmitted "loose sex behaviour" and "moral degeneracy" from one generation to the next. In this way, motherhood out of wedlock—

"unfettered motherhood"—emerged as a great curse, as the black mother left her own offspring uncared for and even murdered "her unwanted child by throwing it in the garbage can." So, "unfettered motherhood" became "outlawed motherhood."[46]

As Frazier recognized, what he called "outlawed motherhood" was associated with urban black impoverishment. But his references to the roles of racial discrimination, job exploitation, and poverty were scanty. The thrust of both his arguments and images was to emphasize the problematic persistence of historically inherited "rural folkways concerning unmarried motherhood." In fact, this book's depiction of the "Matriarchate" converted what Du Bois had termed as the "mother-idea" into a major perpetuator of slavery's damaging legacy. However, it was especially Frazier's 1949 history, *The Negro in the United States*, which cast Afro-American womanhood itself as fundamentally damaged, in the countryside as well as the city.[47]

In this book, even bleaker images emerged. For example, hearkening back to Rhodes's portrayal, Frazier repeated that civil-war-era black mothers "often" left "their exhausted and dying children by the roadside. In some cases the mothers put their children to death." The freedwomen were similarly portrayed as continuing in this depraved way. Frazier's sources for such "facts" were the late nineteenth-century white-authored histories of the "Black Reconstruction" school, together with more recent racist scholarship such as W. D. Weatherford's *The Negro from Africa to America* (1924), and Jerome Dowd's *The Negro in American Life* (1926). And in *The Negro in the United States*, black women figured almost entirely in terms of their sexual behavior and supposed familial dominance, while the "maternally organized" family became explicitly labeled as "matriarchal." The slave father was said to have been "compelled" to accept the mother's dominance, while after slavery the tradition of matriarchy persisted in a most damaging way.[48]

But in *The Negro in the United States* Frazier clarified that he was by no means pessimistic about the prospects of Afro-American progress, despite the crippling legacy of history. In his view the dislocation of urbanization was a kind of necessary evil that did away with the matriarchal tradition, paving the way for black modernization, assimilation, and progress. For Frazier, assimilation was progress, and he never questioned the necessity of patriarchy for either race. Instead, he applauded all signs that Afro-Americans were embracing this, as the father became "the chief breadwinner and assumed a responsible place in the family." Thence, in his view, "the gains in civilization which result from participation in the white world will in the future as in the past be transmitted to future generations through the family." Frazier argued, essentially, that to challenge racial inequality, black Americans must adopt the society's sexual inequality and patriarchal gender relations and roles.[49]

Certainly in Frazier's writings gender and race became ever more tightly and authoritatively spun together into the equation of supposed black female familial dominance with the persistence of black inequality. The message was that "good" womanhood adhered to traditional prescriptions of femininity. Frazier's black woman therefore emerged as largely defeminized and problematic, because she departed from "woman's place." He thereby presented an image of Afro-American womanhood that, in Gutman's words regarding his portrayal of black Americans in general, "paradoxically fed the racist scholarship he attacked."[50]

Moreover, in Frazier's 1957 book, *Black Bourgeoisie*, the most uniformly negative vision of Afro-American womanhood crystallized. Focusing on middle-class black Americans, this text detailed how their abortive imitation of white culture led to pervasive self-hatred and contempt for the Negro race among blacks themselves.

In the context of this full-blown pathology thesis, the middle-class black woman emerged in the book as an entirely frivolous creature, whose charitable and club work only manifested her selfish status seeking. If she worked outside of the home, it was only to escape her fear of being alone with herself and her frustrating lack of sexual fulfillment. Furthermore, according to Frazier, her spouse's sexual failings were largely her own fault. While the black male remained excluded by a racist society from normal channels of masculine self-assertion and power, his emasculation was said to be inherent in the "subordinate role" assigned to him by the "tradition of female dominance, which is widely established among Negroes." He was said to cultivate his personal attributes like a woman. And so, Frazier reiterated that the Negro was "the lady among the races." But in Frazier's paradigm of race and gender, that the Negro was the feminine race was by no means, as in the earlier black intellectual tradition, a positive image.[51]

Frazier's image of blacks as a feminine race signified his view of pathological black male emasculation and flawed femininity. According to him, "the middle-class Negro woman's fear of the competition of white women is based often upon the fact that she senses her own inadequacies and shortcomings." Said to focus obsessively for satisfaction upon her offspring, she spoiled her children and made them unfit for life in a competitive world. Sexually frustrated, she turned for personal fulfillment to cards and social climbing. For her, Frazier noted, a win at poker could amount to a sexual orgasm. Meanwhile, "the husband is likely to play a pitiful role." As a "slave" to his wife and to "all her extravagances and vanities," many a black male apparently sat "at home alone, impotent physically and socially . . . a pathetic picture."[52]

In short, Frazier's Negro pathology thesis focused clearly upon black male-female relations and sexual identity as if these were racial traits, albeit presented as the legacy of history. He cast black masculinity and femininity as profoundly flawed. Therefore, it becomes difficult to deny that this major Afro-American scholar reinforced rather than challenged the historical pattern in which, as observed by Barbara Christian, American racism has been integrally associated with the assault upon the black person's sexual identity as male or female.[53]

In historical imagery, Frazier's black men and women figured largely as emasculated Sambos and defeminized matriarchs, respectively. Furthermore, Frazier's interpretation of history was integral to his analysis of the present. Unfortunately, he fleshed out the black tradition's antiracist account of slavery as tragedy by bringing its most ambivalent images of slaves, together with white-authored caricatures of them, to the aid of the story he told. The result, for his version of black women's history, was, indeed, tragic.

Frazier was by no means alone in shaping what a later era would see as the myth of the Black Matriarchy. Instead, the snowball process of decades of American scholarship had converted slave-rooted images into this symbolization of Negro pathology-cum-cultural inferiority. However, Frazier's particularly detailed attention to history, together with his scholarly stature, did provide a most influential updating of Mammy and her kin into the image of a domineering, emasculating black matriarchy. Frazier's story of past and present disparaged black women and men alike. A counterview of race could not possibly be fashioned from this fabric.

As Vernon Williams has pointed out, Frazier prided himself on his own objectivity and was actually pleased at black criticism of his failure to present "Negro women as martyrs in the relations with southern white men."[54] However, in actuality, Frazier's perspectives were pervaded by patriarchal and assimilationist values, which denied the possibility of both sexual and racial pluralism.

In conclusion, what needs to be added to Herbert Gutman's observation that Frazier accepted "a printed historical record heavily colored by racial and class conceptions and biases," is that this was a record equally colored by sexual and sexist biases. In this context, it becomes at least more understandable that Frazier, in effect, endorsed and furthered the hellish repute of black women's history.[55]

NOTES

1. Du Bois, *Black Reconstruction*, 727. See also his discussion of scholarly "propaganda," pp. 711–29.
2. Fullinwider, *Mood of Black America*, vii–viii.
3. Williams, *From a Caste to a Minority*, 1.
4. Stanfield, *Jim Crow in American Social Science*, 191, 194.
5. As quoted in Williams, *From a Caste to a Minority*, 36, 37.
6. Ibid., 38, 34.
7. Quoted in Williams, *From a Caste to a Minority*, 86.
8. Quoted in Stanfield, *American Social Science*, 53.

9. Eleanor Engram, *Myth, Science, Reality: The Black Family in One-Half Century of Research* (Westport, Conn.: Greenwood Press, 1982).

10. Robert E. Park, "Human Migration and the Marginal Man," *American Journal of Sociology* 33 (1928): 881–93; Robert E. Park, "Mentality of Racial Hybrids," *American Journal of Sociology* 36 (1931): 534–51.

11. Williams, *From a Caste to a Minority*, 88. See also Mencke, *Mulattoes*, 79.

12. Edward Byron Reuter, *The Mulatto in the United States* (New York: Negro Universities Press, 1969; orig. pub. 1918), 137.

13. Ibid., 93, 128, 40, 161, 163.

14. Edward Byron Reuter, "The Superiority of the Mulatto," *American Journal of Sociology* 23 (1917): 98–99; see also Reuter, *The Mulatto*, 94, 164.

15. Reuter, "The Superiority of the Mulatto," 99.

16. Smith, *An Old Creed*, 88.

17. Odum and Calhoun quoted in Gutman, *The Black Family*, 459.

18. Dollard, *Caste and Color in a Southern Town*, 135, 136, 144, 160, 165.

19. Ibid., 71, 152.

20. Ibid., 152–53, 83, 275, 397.

21. Ibid., 393, 396–408, 414.

22. Charles S. Johnson, *Growing Up in the Black Belt: Negro Youth in the Rural South* (Washington, D.C.: American Council on Education, 1941), xvii.

23. Williams, *From a Caste to a Minority*, 167–68.

24. Johnson, *Growing Up in the Black Belt*, 58–59, 225; Allison Davis and John Dollard, *The Personality Development of Negro Youth in the Urban South* (Washington, D.C.: American Youth Commission, 1962; orig. pub. 1940), 101.

25. Johnson, *Growing Up in the Black Belt*, 225.

26. Hylan Lewis, *Blackways of Kent* (Chapel Hill: University of North Carolina Press, 1955), 4, 82–113.

27. Johnson, *Growing Up in the Black Belt*, 196, 223, 236, xvii, 58.

28. Williams, *From a Caste to a Minority*, 153.

29. Deborah White, *Ar'n't I a Woman?*, 166.

30. Herbert Gutman, *The Black Family*, xvii–xviii; Shepard Krech III, "Black Family Organization in the Nineteenth Century: An Ethnological Perspective," *Journal of Interdisciplinary History* 12 (1982): 429–52.

31. Gutman, *The Black Family*, 9; Engram, *Science, Myth, Reality*, 11.

32. Moses, "Civilizing Missionary: A Study of Alexander Crummell," 229–52.

33. E. Franklin Frazier, *The Negro Family in the United States* (Chicago: University of Chicago Press, 1947; orig. pub. 1939), xix.

34. Ibid., 355, 331, 326.

35. Frazier, "The Negro Slave Family," *Journal of Negro History* 40 (1930): 197, 236; *The Negro Family*, 67, 68, 85.

36. Frazier, *The Negro Family*, 75, 81, 62.

37. Ibid., 44, 47, 51, 49.

38. Ibid., 42; see also 49–50.

39. Ibid., 58, 41, 52, 61.

40. Ibid., 57–58; Du Bois, *The Negro American Family*, 57, 49.

41. Frazier, *The Negro Family*, 58.

42. Ibid., 59, 106, 67, 97, 95.

43. For revisionist perspectives on slavery's aftermath and the freedpersons, see,

for example, Gutman, *The Black Family*, 363–447; and David G. Sansing, ed., *What Was Freedom's Price?* (Jackson: University Press of Mississippi, 1978). Frazier, *The Negro Family*, 96, 107, 108.

44. Frazier, *The Negro Family*, 107, 108, 115, 125.

45. Ibid., 126, 153, 144, 143.

46. Ibid., 299, 354; see also, for example, 329, 347.

47. Ibid., 354, 353, 357.

48. E. Franklin Frazier, *The Negro in the United States* (New York: The Macmillan Company, 1964; orig. pub. 1949), 625, 11, 309.

49. Ibid., 487, 488.

50. Gutman, *The Black Family*, 9.

51. E. Franklin Frazier, *Black Bourgeoisie* (New York: The Free Press, 1966; orig. pub. 1957), 220.

52. Ibid., 218, 223, 222, 221.

53. Christian, *Black Women Novelists*, 252.

54. Williams, *From a Caste to a Minority*, 159.

55. Gutman, *The Black Family*, 182.

6

Prefabricated Women of the Mid-Twentieth Century

By the middle of the twentieth century perhaps no other American woman had received so much scholarly attention and yet remained so fundamentally mysterious as the Afro-American woman. As Ralph Ellison observed in 1952 in *The Invisible Man*, "prefabricated Negroes are sketched on sheets of paper and superimposed upon the Negro community."[1] This was surely the case with black women.

However, prefabricated Negroes took on a new air of implausibility after World War II, in the aftermath of the struggle against Nazi racism and the substantial black American contribution to that struggle. While racial liberalism grew from several roots, at the same time sexual conservatism set in as the men returned home from the war and demanded that women return to the home. The rightfulness of true womanhood was rediscovered with a vengeance. As those of us raised in that era well recall, it was very clear that women were either "good" or "bad"—virgins or "damaged goods." Our sexuality was firmly assigned to "woman's place" in the home where we were to be perfect wives and mothers. In this revival of Victorianism, the prefabricated, flawed, and defeminized black woman became increasingly woven into American scholarship as an emblem and the source of Afro-American pathology and failure.

During the 1950s American scholarship turned more than ever to history, as Dwight Hoover noted, to find an explanation for the Negro's continued "failure to be fully accepted into American life." According to Hoover's 1968 text, *Understanding Negro History*, the central question was why the Negro was not assimilating, and "the major problem in Negro history, then, is how to explain failure."[2]

When the question was thus posed as, in effect, why did blacks remain losers in a nation of winners, the thesis of historic, familial failure which had crystallized especially into E. Franklin Frazier's story of history seemed very persuasive. It explained Negro failure in liberal, environmental terms, and yet pointed to eventual assimilation and "progress" as blacks became more like whites, and as whites were educated regarding the "American dilemma." Liberal scholarship set out to facilitate this education by revealing the historically crippling effects of oppression on black Americans.

In this context, Frazier's thesis became ever more deeply embedded as factual, and also embellished in a vast body of historical and sociological literature. Its early postwar evolution can be found, for example, in Maurice Davie's 1949 sociology text, *Negroes in American Society*. Referring to Frazier's research, Davie presented it as established fact that the "maternal family" was the "heritage of slavery." He reiterated that "the family... of the Africans was practically destroyed by slavery" and that the slave mother was central to what remained of the slave family, emphasizing her dominance and the slave man's subordination to her:

When the father did live with the family, he usually possessed little authority.... The cabin was hers. The weekly rations... were issued to her.... The children were listed on the plantation records as belonging to her.... She had the privilege of naming the children and the responsibility for their care and discipline.... Around the house he was an appendage. In fact, so dependent upon the women were the men of the plantation that they regarded freedom from female domination as one of the gains of emancipation.[3]

That Frazier had not ever found or discussed such supposed views of the freedmen was immaterial to the postwar discourse, which increasingly cast black womanhood as not only damaged, but also as *damaging* to black masculinity. Providing no empirical evidence for such views, Davie went on to emphasize the postslavery continuation of this damaging black female dominance. Citing the work of Charles Johnson, for example, he emphasized "the matriarchal nature of the Negro family"; in nearly one out of four families "a woman is the head, in contrast to one out of seven among the whites." From this apparently followed an illegitimacy rate "from five to ten times as high as among whites," as "part of the general disorganization of the family." Pointing to the "dominant position" of the woman "among the great mass of lower-class Negroes," Davie detailed how this supposedly led to loose sexual behavior and conflict. Moreover, the black woman's economic "independence" was said to perpetuate "laziness" and "lack of responsibility" among Negro men, and to make her "sharp-tongued, bitter, and resentful." Such households were presented as breeding juvenile delinquency and "Negro Criminality."[4]

Davie noted that "Negroes are affected by substandard housing, unsanitary conditions... and similar conditions." However, rather than encouraging reform of these material conditions, he began and ended by assuming that their moral reform was crucial: "The development and strengthening of the family institution are basic to further Negro advancement."[5]

In 1951 *The Mark of Oppression*, by Abram Kardiner and Lionel Ovesey, forwarded the same interpretation, from professed liberal perspectives. The authors worried that their findings might be misused by others, but pointed out that their premise was that Negro characteristics were not inborn but acquired as the psychological scars comprising "the mark of oppression." Pointing especially to the findings of E. Franklin Frazier, they built upon and embellished his story.[6] As Kardiner and Ovesey observed, the slave woman was valued by whites as a sexual object, as mistress and "breeder," and as "Mammy." Thus, in their view, she was more advantaged than the slave man, who had only utility value. Slavery was said to have been especially hard on black fatherhood. These patterns continued after slavery. The black woman's greater value (to whites) "gave her a head start in relative prestige, while that of the Negro male fell." The weakness of the Negro family brought particular "disparagement" to the black man.[7]

Migration to the city exacerbated this situation. While "actually or potentially economically independent" and continuing to take "the dominant role," tired and poor, "the mother is ill-tempered, imposes severe and rigid discipline, demands immediate obedience, and offers only sporadic affection." For these reasons, the black male child grew up to have "uniformly bad relations... with females on an emotional level," unable to perform sexually. Female dominance continued to undermine his assumption of the masculine role. Thus, his resulting self-contempt undermined his ability to interact and compete normally with others. In the meantime, the black woman was said to scapegoat him for his failures as a man, and to manifest "sexual disorders." Moreover, these marks of oppression were said to be manifest among black men of all classes.[8]

Moving still closer to the Moynihan Report's "Black Matriarchy" was Thomas Pettigrew's 1964 text, *A Profile of the Negro American*, a source cited by that report in support of its thesis. Reiterating the familiar story of the persistence of the mother-dominated black family after slavery, Pettigrew described how the Negro woman's disgust with her financially dependent husband drove him away. Consequently, "embittered" black mothers "perpetuate the mother-centered pattern by taking a greater interest in their daughters than their sons." The father's absence comprised "the scar of slavery upon Negro family life." Lacking a male role model, male children established a feminized sexual identity. As well, their feminine self-image was said to be promoted by the mother's overprotective "smother-love." Indeed, whereas often in other sources she apparently did not love her male children enough, in this book she lavished too much love on them. Compensating for their emasculation, they showed exaggerated masculine behavior and an extreme need for power and dominance. So, these "mother-raised boys" turned to violence, while mother-dominated two-parent families apparently were the cause of sexual impotency, schizophrenia, and other mental illnesses, together with venereal diseases. Certainly these patterns were said to be "common even among intact lower-class Negro families."[9]

Furthermore, the mother-dominated family was said to be self-perpetuating, as daughters were socialized "to assume male as well as female responsibilities." This syndrome was described as what continued to perpetuate the Negro's "devastating personality scars" inherited from slavery. On the other hand, scholars actually advised that given a "stable and complete family" the Negro could survive poverty and discrimination as little more than an "inconvenience."[10]

From such perspectives the supposedly dominant black woman emerged as what made black poverty and discrimination especially "inconvenient." More explicitly than ever before, her strength and ability to take on whatever responsibilities were necessary were being interpreted as racial liability.

In their book *Racism and Psychiatry*, Alexander Thomas and Samuel Sillen have pointed out that *The Mark of Oppression* was based upon interviews with only twenty-five persons, of whom eleven were paid, twelve were paid with psychiatric assistance, and all except one of whom had clear symptoms of psychological disorders. As these authors observed: "Psychoanalytic case studies serve as the model for historical investigation of the black people. The appeal is not to historical evidence but to . . . psychodynamic theory presented as clinical findings."[11] Yet contemporary social science frequently did point to history as evidence for its analysis of the present, and for good reason, since American historiography was and continued to be replete with the images of damaged black womanhood and manhood.

Postwar historiography did take an increasing antislavery stance. Following the lead of black historians in emphasizing the evils of slavery, it reflected the liberal faith that, once educated about the contradictions between the American creed and racial inequality, white America could be morally transformed and liberated from the blinders of racism. And as yet, Afro-American historians shared this faith in the value of educating white Americans in the meaning of democracy. As John Hope Franklin advised in 1957, the purpose of Negro history was "to force America to keep faith with herself."[12]

John Hope Franklin was the major Afro-American historian of the early postwar era and a former student of E. Franklin Frazier. His work drew deeply from Frazier's scholarship and from other black historians such as George Washington Williams, Benjamin Brawley, Carter Woodson, and W.E.B. Du Bois. Like his predecessors, Franklin strove to deromanticize the Old South, showing that "far from being a civilizing force . . . the plantation bred indecency in human relations." In this context, the slave woman figured, when she figured at all, in terms of this indecency, emerging only as a brutalized, dehumanized creature.[13]

Sexually used by the white man, she was unlikely "to care for her husband who had been forced upon her." Nor did she have opportunity to develop "real attachment for her children." Otherwise, there seemed little to say about her. Apart from Franklin's fleeting mention of such "notables" as Harriet Tubman and Sojourner Truth, he cast the slave woman only as one who was done to and damaged, and in no sense as an agent who played some role in shaping her own destiny. Moreover after slavery, according to this book, the black woman remained a passive figure who actually was uninvolved in racial uplift work and protest until the World War I era. In short, in Franklin's reconstruction of Afro-American history, she figured as victim when he was arguing that the nation's treatment of the Negro "is America's greatest scandal," and she became invisible when he was emphasizing the black "struggle for realization of freedom." But while she was thereby profoundly marginalized, it is interesting that Franklin did not cast her in a matriarchal light. Instead, it was predominantly white-authored histories that did so.[14]

Postwar liberal white-authored historiography set out to delete racist myths from the written record of the past, and also to show that black Americans were historically just like other Americans. The desired color blindness was reflected in Kenneth Stampp's observation that "innately Negroes *are*, after all, only white men with black skins, nothing more, nothing less." To demonstrate the human identity of black people, such historians emphasized especially their sufferings as slaves. Presumably to suffer was to be human.[15]

Epitomizing this approach was Stampp's 1956 study of Old South slavery, *The Peculiar Institution*. In this book Stampp drew heavily from black-authored research in rejecting the white historiography hitherto dominated by U. B. Phillips's vision of kindly masters and happy slaves. Stampp's slaves certainly did not figure as happy. But they took on another set of familiar images associated with their brutalization and demoralization by the "peculiar institution."

Slave women emerged considerably often in this book, but almost entirely in the context of sexual brutalization and depravity, and the ruined black family. While figuring as victimized sexual objects, they also acted like Jezebels, since "many whose sexual behavior was altogether promiscuous doubtless gave their favors without restraint to whites and Negroes alike. Others . . . out of sheer opportunism willingly submitted." But in a slave-breeding society "sexual promiscuity brought them rewards." And in light of their general promiscuity "it is certain that few escaped without serious damage to their psyche." Such speculations were presented with little or no empirical substantiation, as self-evident truth.[16]

In this context, the slave family was presented as an institution in ruins, and the slave woman was stripped of maternalism and presented as "a full-time worker for her owner and only incidentally a wife, mother and homemaker" who "often did no cooking or clothes making." Yet a page later, casting the family's decrepitude in a matriarchal light, Stampp restored the slave mother to these same functions as "responsibilities which traditionally belonged to women, such as cleaning house, preparing food, making clothes, and raising children." Thus, she was restored to the home when this historian was arguing that "the typical slave family was matriarchal in form." Stampp reiterated that the father "was not the head of the family, the holder of property, the provider, or the protector. . . . The male slave's only crucial function within the family was that of siring offspring." Apparently the slave family was matriarchal after all, leading to the lack of affection between husbands and wives, the "casual attitude" to sex, and "the indifference with which most fathers and even some mothers regarded their children."[17]

The portrayal in *The Peculiar Institution* of the natural sexual and familial order as turned upside down by slavery underpinned Stampp's emphasis on the crippling effects of oppression on slave culture. According to him, in this "cultural chaos" the enslaved lived "aimlessly in a bleak and narrow world." But in this context, Stampp's slave woman remained cast in terms of prefabricated caricatures, as a symbol of cultural chaos.[18]

Ironically, the dominance of black motherhood in the slave family emerged even in the work of a historian who appeared to leave the black woman almost completely invisible, even in image. But her exclusion from Stanley Elkins's 1959 book, *Slavery*, did not inspire the raging controversy that quickly ensued after its publication. Instead, the controversy was largely focused on the story he told about slave men.

Elkins's *Slavery* was a major influence in two particular ways. First, more than any other contemporary historical source, it provided, for some, clear confirmation that the Afro-American psyche had been severely damaged by slavery. Second, the controversy surrounding it inspired the development of a new, revisionist reconstruction of slavery which recast Afro-American history as an epic story of black heroism-cum-*manliness*. Certainly, as Afro-American nationalism mounted during the 1960s, what was particularly unacceptable to Elkins's critics was his image of blacks as docile Sambos.

Elkins had examined the old stereotype of "Sambo, the typical plantation slave," who was, in image,

docile but irresponsible, loyal but lazy, humble but chronically given to lying and stealing; his behavior was full of infantile silliness. . . . His relationship with his master was one of utter dependence and childlike attachment: it was indeed this childlike quality that was the very key to his being. Although the merest hint of Sambo's "manhood" might fill the Southern breast with scorn, the child . . . could be both exasperating and lovable.[19]

This historian argued that in actuality "Sambo was real . . . a dominant plantation type." This personality type, in Elkins's view, resulted from the American system of slavery, as a "closed" or "total" institution in which the slave was totally dependent upon the master not only physically, but also for his sense of identity. This was because the master was the absolute and only authority and "significant other" in the American slave's life—truly his father figure. Hence, according to Elkins, the American slave was unable to mature into healthy adulthood because he drew his self-portrait only from the master's perception and treatment of him as a perpetual "boy." In sum, drawing from social science theories regarding personality development, this historian argued that the Sambo stereotype was based on the reality that black people were truly infantilized—"Samboized"—by slavery.[20]

Certainly Elkins's thesis was fully in concert with contemporary social science portrayals of the American Negro as emerging from slavery, in the words of Kardiner and Ovesey, with "no intrapsychic defenses—no pride, no group solidarity, no tradition." According to their *Mark of Oppression*, "the marks of his previous status were still upon him—socially, psychologically and emotionally. And from these he has never since freed himself."[21]

It is not surprising that the Elkins thesis seemed to support such contentions, because it was largely based upon his reading of the same secondary sources that emphasized black pathology. But as a historical source, his own book became a new brick supporting the edifice that constructed the image of black psychic and cultural illness. As such, it was referred to by Daniel Patrick Moynihan and Nathan Glazer in *Beyond the Melting Pot*, and in Moynihan's 1965 *The Negro Family: The Case for National Action*. Elkins's *Slavery* therefore was a main support of the conceptual construction which crystallized in the Moynihan Report's "Black Matriarchy," although Elkins had said virtually nothing about black women.

At first reading, *Slavery's* examination of slaves was general, rather than gender-specific. But a closer look reveals that its attention was to Sambo as a man—although "the merest hint of Sambo's 'manhood' might fill the Southern breast with scorn." Elkins's book appeared to confirm Sambo's lack of manliness, as becomes clear if feminine pronouns are substituted for masculine, for example, in the section already quoted. Thus, this would read instead as "*Her* relationship with *her* master was one of utter dependence and childlike attachment, and it was indeed this childlike quality that was the very key to *her* being" (emphasis added). Had Elkins's discourse been feminized in this manner, it would simply have presented a restatement of traditionally prescribed femininity, rather than a thesis of profound damage. The damage he pointed to was thus to the male slave as a man.

The identification of Sambo as male becomes more explicit in the only section of the book that referred to the slave woman. In it, the familiar image of her familial dominance was presented as evidence of the damage to black masculinity. The unmanned male slave, "addressed as 'boy,' " was explicitly associated here with his lack of authority as husband and father, while the mother's role "loomed far larger for the slave child than did that of the father. She controlled those few activities—household care, preparation of food, and rearing of children—that were left to the slave family."[22]

Reiterating this (by then) conventional academic wisdom, Elkins perhaps revealed an Achilles' heel of his argument: that the lack of a role model of parental black authority promoted the slave child's identification of the master as father and internalization of the master's perception of him as a perpetual "boy." Given this book's own reiteration of the slave mother's central activities in the home, it might logically follow that slave children were thereby provided with a parental model from which to discover a self-identity apart from that assigned by the master. Moreover, it would seem logical that because of her familial roles, the slave woman herself could develop an independent sense of identity and self worth. But such possibilities remained unconsidered in this book, it may be speculated, because from traditional perspectives woman's work in the home was viewed as marginal at most, and perhaps as inherently slavish.

In any case, Deborah White has perceptively pointed to Elkins's "subliminal exclusion of black females from the Sambo theory." She asked: "Where were the women?"[23] However, such questions were not raised by the controversy inspired in the 1960s by the Elkins thesis. Rather, at the heart of the controversy lay the question, Where are the men? In other words, the question was, in effect, Where are the manly men?

As editor of *The Debate Over Slavery* (1971), Ann Lane correctly observed that "the critical responses to *Slavery* have been many and varied."[24] But objections to its thesis and much of the revisionist slavery studies that followed revealed a special sense of outrage that black Americans had been stripped by Elkins of a history of manly heroism, and that this must be rediscovered and rescued. Thus, the anger about *Slavery* both reflected and stimulated the first real rejection by American scholarship of the long-established paradigm casting blacks as the "feminine race," and of the complementary images of female dominance and male emasculation.

Despite the fact that Elkins himself did not relate Sambo to modern black America, as Ann Lane pointed out, Moynihan and Charles Silberman, "among others, have used this frame of reference, for which they have frequently received hostile reactions from within the black community."[25] Indeed, Silberman had used, and many might say, abused, Elkins's *Slavery*, in his 1964 book, *Crisis in Black and White*. Elkins was said to have demonstrated that "negroes are not white men with black skins." Silberman contended that "the reality of racial differences" must be recognized; for example, "Negroes *do* display less ambition than whites . . . *do* have 'looser morals . . . 'care less for the family.' " While few might agree, according to Silberman it was not racist to point to the reality of such stereotypes so long as it was not concluded that "they are inherent characteristics. On the contrary, every one of them can be explained by the facts of Negro history in the United States." Pointing to Elkins's story, he noted that black Americans had "been subject to a system designed to destroy ambition, prevent independence, and erode intelligence." It therefore followed in his view that

Sambo "was a reality and to a considerable extent still is. . . . Negroes are still bound by its effects on their minds and spirits." Similarly, Silberman pointed to Frazier's *The Negro Family* as substantiation of his claim that "slavery had emasculated the Negro males, had made them shiftless and irresponsible and promiscuous . . . negating their role as husband and father."[26]

Briefly, spinning the emasculated Sambo more explicitly than ever into the thesis of Negro pathology, Silberman emphasized "the problem of Negro personality" as both rooted history and continuing history. The 1965 Moynihan Report largely expanded upon the same conclusions, specifying and emphasizing that the core of the damage to black masculinity lay in the matriarchal home.

But despite Moynihan's emphasis on the "Black Matriarchy," it was the rejection of Sambo's reality that characterized the era's historiography, enraged as it was by the kind of interpretation that emerged in Silberman's work of Afro-American men as lastingly crippled. From Silberman's perspective, "the Negro will be unable to compete . . . until he really believes . . . that he is a free man. . . . Therefore, only the Negro can solve the Negro problem."[27]

Such contentions, by seeming to blame blacks for their problems in a way that trivialized the continuation of racism and structural discrimination, fueled the rejection of the pathological portrayal of black history. Those who objected to the thesis, in Silberman's words, that "the Negro cannot move into the main stream of American life unless he is able to destroy the image [of Sambo] in his own mind," set out to destroy the idea that Sambo had ever been in the black mind, let alone the typical plantation slave; therefore, in all possible ways they set out to slay this emblem of black male emasculation.[28]

Critics argued especially that Sambo was only a mask worn by the slave to protect himself by duping the master. Sambo-like behavior was merely role-playing, and was said to represent the slaves' "strategies" for survival and resistance. But in Lane's anthology, the only female-authored critique of the Samboization thesis made no mention of the slave woman. Articles such as "Slaves as Inmates, Slaves as Men" by Roy Simon Bryce-Laporte indicated the male-centered focus of this anthology, in attacking "the emasculating . . . and effeminate image of the Black male as a misunderstanding and disservice to the race." Calling for the reevaluation of "slave accommodation and so-called Uncle Tomism," Bryce-Laporte eloquently affirmed in his article that *"Yes (we) Black men are still living! We must search for another scholarly way to lay bare the cruelties of our conditions without further degrading our identity as men—proud, normal, and equal men."*[29]

In short, the suffering, and so the human identity of black Americans could no longer be conveyed by a discourse which feminized them. Certainly the rejection of the thesis of Samboization was a major catalyst for the development of slavery studies into a major field of American historiography, inspiring an explosion of new research. Yet the direction of this was preset, in Deborah White's words, "because Elkins' *Slavery* defined the parameters of the debate." How black women fared in the context of this debate now deserves our attention.[30]

NOTES

1. Ellison quoted in Gutman, *The Black Family*, 474.

2. Dwight W. Hoover, ed., *Understanding Negro History* (Chicago: Quadrangle Books, 1968), 14, 15.

3. Maurice R. Davie, *Negroes in American Society* (New York: McGraw Hill Book Co. Inc., 1949), 206, 207.

4. Ibid., 209–15, 422.

5. Ibid., 216.

6. Abram Kardiner and Lionel Ovesey, *The Mark of Oppression: Explorations in the Personality of the American Negro* (New York: Meridian Books, 1962; orig. pub. 1951), xii–xv.

7. Ibid., 41–47.

8. Ibid., 59, 65, 70, 308, 360, 349, 336.

9. Thomas Pettigrew, *A Profile of the Negro American* (Princeton, N.J.: D. Van Nostrand Co. Inc., 1964), 16–19, 22–26.

10. Pettigrew, *The Negro American*, 22–26, 86–87.

11. Alexander Thomas and Samuel Sillen, *Racism and Psychiatry* (New York: Brunner/Mazel Pub., 1972) 50, 62.

12. John Hope Franklin, "The New Negro History," *Journal of Negro History* 43 (1957): 89.

13. John Hope Franklin, *From Slavery to Freedom* (New York: Alfred A. Knopf, 1964; orig. pub. 1956), 206.

14. Ibid., 202, 548, 603.

15. Kenneth Stampp, *The Peculiar Institution* (New York: Vintage Books, 1956), vii–viii, emphasis added.

16. Ibid., 359–60.

17. Ibid., 343, 344, 346.

18. Ibid., 361.

19. Stanley M. Elkins, *Slavery: A Problem in American Institutional and Intellectual Life* (Chicago: University of Chicago Press, 1968; orig. pub. 1959), 82.

20. Ibid., 82, 84–87, 128–32.

21. Kardiner and Ovesey, *Mark of Oppression*, 384–87.

22. Elkins, *Slavery*, 130.

23. White, *Ar'n't I a Woman?*, 19–20.

24. Ann J. Lane, ed., *The Debate Over Slavery: Stanley Elkins and His Critics* (Chicago: University of Illinois Press, 1971), 8.

25. Lane, ed., *The Debate Over "Slavery,"*, 13.

26. Charles E. Silberman, *Crisis in Black and White* (New York: Random House, 1964), 74, 77, 94, 108. Emphasis added.

27. Ibid., 77.

28. Ibid., 12.

29. Mary Agnes Lewis, "Slavery and Personality," in Lane, *The Debate*, 75–86; Roy Simon Bryce-Laporte, "Slaves as Inmates, Slaves as Men," in ibid., 274, 292. Emphasis in original.

30. White, *Ar'n't I a Woman?*, 18.

7

The Invisible, Shrinking Woman

As the Black Movement promoted a swelling pride in the Afro-American identity, American scholarship took on a new sensitivity to the discourse of race. Leaving behind the old zeal to demonstrate the black "contribution" to America to a white audience, by the 1970s, in the words of Robert Harris, Afro-American historiography was "coming of age."

As Harris pointed out, Afro-American historiography was no longer merely contributionist. Nor did it continue to examine the Negro as a "project" or "problem"—as someone to be acted for or upon. Rather, it became "a distinct area of inquiry . . . with black people as its primary focus to reveal their thoughts and activities over time and place." In this context slavery studies flourished, reinterpreting the slave experience, in the words of William Van Deburg, "as a triumph of the human spirit over adversity." Van Deburg suggested that "since both black and white academics . . . reached this same general conclusion, there was hope that the lingering influence of antebellum stereotypes might at last disappear." Yet, as he also observed, "Uncle Tom and his kin" remained "alive and well" in the popular media.[1]

However, less interested in Aunt Jemima and her kin, Van Deburg did not acknowledge, any more than Harris, that despite its coming of age, the new Afro-American historiography was not inclusive of Afro-American women. Therefore, such scholarship could not fully confront the mythology of race. To fail to address the stereotyping of black women was the Achilles heel of the scholarly attack on the stereotyping of black men.

Certainly the new studies portrayed the enslaved in a striking new light. Slaves emerged as a people who, far from being lastingly damaged and crippled, resisted brutalization and constructed a rich and vital culture.

Framed in this epic way, as Nathan Huggins observed, Afro-American history
spoke to the wish for a prideful historical identity:

> It is claimed that history should . . . contribute to one's sense of identity. . . . Many
> want to find heroes and great men in the past with whom black people . . . can identify.
> . . . Because taught history gives black youngsters few manly and influential ancestors
> to emulate . . . it is human enough for blacks to see an Afro-American history as a
> way to celebrate (and to create) great black men.[2]

Nathan Huggins was critical of the new Afro-American historiography for
constructing new myths of "great" men rather than discovering reality—and
ordinary men. However, he seemed still to equate Afro-American history
with the story of black *men*, great or otherwise. Certainly his critique gave
no notice to the continued exclusion of black women from this historiography
and from the 1971 anthology for which he served as an editor, *Key Issues in
the Afro-American Experience*. No contributor to it discussed the experience
of black women under or after slavery, and while "black people" were
referred to as if gender-neutral, the attention was to black Americans as
males.

Joel Williamson's article, "Black Self-Assertion Before and After Emancipation," exemplifies the perspectives of *Key Issues*. Combating the thesis
that "the black man was a Sambo," Williamson sought to show that "he was
a man like any other." The "self-assertion" Williamson discovered was exclusively male. It was said to have been demonstrated when, after slavery's
abolition, the freedmen spoke for their families in economic and legal matters
and "asserted themselves by insisting that wives spend more time in home
management . . . by demanding that mothers care for their children." In his
words "black families in Reconstruction were father-led rather than mother-
led."[3]

Williamson was early to restore male dominance to the black home. But
his contention foreshadowed a host of 1970s studies that, for the first time
ever in American scholarship, cast the Afro-American family as father-led,
and black culture as historically male-led.

The attack on Sambo became two-pronged. Fueled by Elkins's *Slavery*,
after publication of the 1965 Moynihan Report, in order to slay Mr. Sambo
it seemed increasingly essential to slay Mrs. Matriarch as well—as the other
side of the same coin that disparaged black masculinity. In response to the
Elkins thesis, historians discovered slave docility as a mask and reconstructed
it and other strategies of resistance in demonstration of manly black heroism
and ingenuity. But given the added catalyst of the Moynihan thesis, restoration of black psychic and cultural health to slavery seemed during the 1970s
to require reconstruction of a historically traditional sexual universe and
hence, in effect, to eliminate the power of black women. Or so their new
image in Afro-American historiography suggests.

In exemplification, we may turn first to one of the most powerful black-authored challenges to Sambo, John Blassingame's *The Slave Community*, published in 1972. In this book the slave family was rediscovered as a major pillar of what Blassingame presented as the flourishing slave culture that underpinned black survival of oppression. In the family, slaves played other than only slave roles and found significant others in the black community as their basis for establishing an independent self-identity. Yet, it was essentially the survival and strength of black manliness that was emphasized by Blassingame, while cultural health was equated with patriarchal norms, especially in the original, 1972 edition of the book.

According to the 1972 edition, in Africa the family was said to be "rigidly patriarchal." In America, the slave was confronted with great obstacles in "his efforts to build a strong stable family." Nonetheless, this book described "his" success–having equated success de facto with the slave *man's* family-building role, authority, and masculine initiatives. In contrast, the slave woman figured as passive object, whether acted upon by white or black men. For example, "young slave men pursued their black paramours," and slave men wished "to marry women from another plantation" to avoid having to see their wives being abused. Whether or not the wife preferred her spouse to live elsewhere, her perspectives in general were not of interest. The 1979 edition of this book did add that the slave family was "America's first democratic family . . . where men and women shared authority and responsibility." Otherwise, apparently slave gender relations and roles remained male-dominated.[4]

Action and initiative, from courting and "sexual conquest" to marriage and family building, were all firmly associated with slave men. In the meantime the slave woman figured as a domestic prop to the man-centered action, emerging essentially as good wife and mother. Her work and nonfamilial roles remained obscure. However, she certainly emerged as no matriarch in Blassingame's book. In fact, independent and self-assertive black women did not figure at all. Mammy was mentioned, but in a nurturing role, intended to show that she won the white male child's abiding affection. Blassingame was thereby pointing to the origins of the white man's continuing sexual pursuit of black women. However, this historian said very little else about Mammy, and nothing about what she may have felt, thought, and believed.[5]

Indeed, Mammy was in the process of shrinking to the vanishing point from American historiography. Her portrayal in Earl Thorpe's 1961 text, *The Mind of the Negro*, helps to illuminate the reasons for the stigma which promoted this slave figure's new invisibility. As Thorpe noted, while for white Americans the Mammy had long served as a primary emblem of racial intimacy, for black Americans she symbolized a system in which black men "could not wear the pants in their households." Thorpe pointed to the "domineering proclivities" of contemporary black women as a "heritage from slavery," citing Frazier as his source. As well he pointed to the slave "Auntie" as devoted to whites. Thorpe's image of Mammy complemented his argument that slave women had discouraged the slave man's resistance, encouraging him to be docile because, "as ever has been the case between the sexes, the female among slaves was usually . . . more conservative than the male, ever cautioning him to mind his sassy tongue, to work hard . . . don't run away."[6]

Moreover, this historian reiterated the time-honored identification of the Negro as the feminine race: "Woman has ever been more receptive, patient, adaptive. . . . It is precisely those qualities which enabled the Negro race to survive slavery in America."[7] However, this timeworn image of race was now powerfully contradicted and rejected by the Black Movement, and became unacceptable during the 1960s and 1970s.

In a historiography that emphasized assertive black power and a manly historical identity, the prescribed role of slave women was to be fully supportive of slave masculinity. In this context, the old slave Mammy became an anathema as the archetypal strong black woman who used her strength in the service of whites.

Mammy's ill repute as a race traitor in an era of black nationalism may best be captured in Eldridge Cleaver's casting of her and Aunt Jemima as epitomizing the black woman's supposed collaboration with the enemy. In Cleaver's words in his 1968 book, *Soul on Ice*, she was "the silent ally . . . of the white man. . . . He turned the black woman into a strong self-reliant Amazon and deposited her in his kitchen—that's the secret of Aunt Jemima's bandanna."[8]

By the 1970s only Eugene Genovese dared to present this stigmatized figure as a genuine and prideworthy historical personage. Although recognizing the Mammy's "steadily worsening press," in *Roll, Jordan, Roll* Genovese dared to suggest she was more than just a "white legend," asking "Who were these Mammies? What did they actually do?" In answer, Genovese presented Mammy as a figure of real authority in both the white and black worlds. She did raise and love the white children, but did not therefore disdain her own offspring. She was loyal to "her" white family, but far from "serving" it, she ran the Big House as the plantation mistress's "executive officer or her 'de facto' superior." Her important roles and the white family's devotion to her made her a powerful woman. But according to this historian, she used her power to protect her kinfolk and people, demonstrating "courage, compassion, dignity and self-respect."[9]

To summarize, Genovese's Mammy was no female Uncle Tom. Nor was she reconverted into Du Bois's image of a suffering Christian martyr. However, Genovese was well aware of the "controversy over the ill-fated Moynihan Report . . . according to which slavery had emasculated black men, created a matriarchy, and prevented the emergence of a strong sense of family." And he was a leading critic of the "matriarchy legend." Nonetheless, he reconstructed Mammy as a "tough, worldly-wise, enormously resourceful woman," emphasizing her "strength of character" and "iron will." In this book she was even liberated from the quotation marks that, during the Civil Rights era, had come customarily to surround her fleeting appearances elsewhere, indicating her stigma and falsification as a racist legend.[10]

Genovese's attempted rehabilitation of Mammy was compatible with his thesis that Old South slavery was a paternalistic institution involving a system of reciprocal obligations between master and slave. In his view, the enslaved were able to use paternalism to assert their rights in a way that let them carve out some space to create their own self-identity and culture. Of all slave figures, in Genovese's view it was especially the Mammy who epitomized the workings of paternalism. She linked masters and slaves in a way that underscored and epitomized the struggle of the enslaved to shape their own world.

However, Genovese's portrayal of both slavery and Mammy was profoundly out of step with the passionate racial politics of an era that favored demonstrative black power and nonaccommodative historical heroes and rebels. Thus, he was charged with mistakenly attempting "to strip Ulrich B. Phillips's idea of paternalism from its racism." According to Robert Harris, Genovese still saw slavery "through the slavemasters' lens." Harris pointed to James Anderson "for an incisive critique."[11]

Anderson had disposed of Genovese's "reverence for the Mammy" with alacrity, if not incisiveness. In his "Aunt Jemima in Dialectics" (1976) he argued that Genovese's Mammy comprised a distortion of slavery's coercive basis and denied the slaves' intelligence and political will to resist. According to this critique, in spite of the Black Movement's call for a nonracist construction of the past, "too much work had gone into the making of the Aunt Jemima image for it to disappear." Genovese was accused of changing only the form and not the substance of the old images of slavery and slaves, just as the pancake-box image had been "transfigured by bright and shining colors." In short, Mammy was an absolutely unacceptable emblem of black strength under slavery. In Anderson's view, she epitomized the continuing weaknesses of historiography. According to him, "like Aunt Jemima, American scholarship to a large extent became sugar-coated. . . . Though her complexion had been presumably improved, her heart remained the same."[12]

Indeed, the old slave Mammy had become an absolutely unacceptable emblem at a time when, as David Brion Davis has aptly observed, slavery studies had become "a game of racial dodge-ball." Davis noted: "Postwar historians have not only striven to dissociate themselves from any taint of racism, but have defensively suggested that their own interpretation of slavery is the only one free from racist implications." It is not surprising that Mammy became a casualty of this ongoing warfare.[13]

In this context, as in early black-authored history, the Mammy was virtually deleted from American historiography. She appeared very rarely, and when she did, dismissively. For example, Herbert Gutman's 1976 history, *The*

Black Family in Slavery and Freedom, included her only in a footnote. In it, Gutman observed that after slavery most black female domestics were young, unmarried women who worked to supplement parental incomes. This reality, he noted, should put the lie to the old image of the slave domestic as "an aged 'mammy' who remained in her antebellum place out of loyalty to a white family"—although how a fact of the postslavery era could become evidence of the facts of the slavery era is mysterious. But the new Afro-American history was very much shaped—and delimited—by the very myths which it sought to slay.[14]

The rejection of Sambo, compounded by the rejection of the image of Black Matriarchy, to a large extent set the terms of what was discovered, or discoverable, about slavery. Slave women could be, and most often were restored to the Afro-American family, where they figured as traditional good wives and mothers. Indeed, in *Roll, Jordan, Roll*, in spite of Genovese's empowered Mammy, the slave woman emerged in her image as traditionally feminine.

In that book the slave woman demonstrated her healthy "maternal instincts" by cooking, washing, sewing, raising children, and also, according to Genovese, by her high rate of reproduction. As he observed, her loving mothering against all odds was an achievement of "heroic proportions." Otherwise, however, in such studies heroism was reserved for slave men, while slave women "knew their own dignity required having strong men who could meet their responsibilities," and "wanted their boys to grow up to be men and knew . . . that, to do so, they needed the example of a strong black man."[15]

Genovese was intent upon slaying the modern "Myth of the Absent Family"; that is, "the legends of the matriarchy, the emasculated but brutal male, and the fatherless children." Accordingly, he worked backward from his vision of the present to history: "The slave children, like the ghetto children of later decades, saw a pattern of behavior that implied clear sexual differentiation"; and the enslaved valued "a two-parent, male-centered household."[16]

It is a truism that every generation rewrites its own past. Yet, in David Brion Davis's words, "we must always be wary of presentist influences." As Davis noted of the new slavery historiography, "even the bravest and most honest historians have not been able to escape the coercions of the times." Certainly the experience and perspectives of slave women could not be discovered in this context.[17] On the other hand, as it came of age, Afro-American historiography by no means perpetuated the old myths of black womanhood. And while Mammy vanished, so did the Jezebel.

According to Genovese, slave mothers strove for their daughters to "grow up right," pressed them into early marriages, and hid the sexual facts of life from their children. As he perceptively recognized, the "legend of slave promiscuity" was not focused on black men but on the supposed behavior of slave women. But countering this legend, Genovese emphasized the "Victorianism" of slave women. Indeed, they strove "to carry themselves as women with sensibilities as delicate as those of the finest white ladies."[18]

However, miscegenation may have posed a dilemma for this historian. Contemporary scholarship could not repeat the old story, which cast slave women as encouraging white male sexual attention. Yet Genovese's thesis of the slaveocracy's paternalism made it unlikely that masters would be portrayed in his story as forcing themselves on their female slaves. Instead, he argued that miscegenation was largely tabooed by the master class's Victorian and puritanical values. When it did happen, it usually "occurred with single girls under circumstances that varied from seduction to rape and typically fell between the two." The suggestion that a woman might thus, in effect, be a little bit raped, may well seem implausible. However, black women figured in this literature to make points about slavery and black culture—not in terms of their own perspectives and realities.[19]

In this context, as the survivalism and psychic and cultural health of the enslaved were emphasized, slavery's exploitation of black female sexuality was de-emphasized, sometimes to the point of outright denial. Certainly in their two-volume 1974 study, *Time on the Cross*, Robert Fogel and Stanley Engerman argued that "the belief that slave-breeding, sexual exploitation, and promiscuity destroyed the black family is a myth." Instead, masters were presented as rational managers who encouraged the stability of two-parent slave families as the most efficient way of ensuring the reproduction of their labor force. As well, masters were said to have eschewed miscegenation because it worked against maintaining the distance from slaves that was necessary for efficient labor force control. Moreover, they apparently preferred sex with white women. Evidence for these contentions was found in the low percentage of Southern prostitutes who were black. However, as Peter Kolchin has objected, these historians failed to see an obvious explanation: "There was little need for black prostitutes since so many black women could be taken without charge."[20]

But *Time on the Cross* reflected the consensus that rehabilitated the slave woman's image as "good," in effect moving her close to the turn-of-the-century "black lady." According to Fogel and Engerman, slave sexual mores were "not promiscuous but prudish." Evidence for this was found, for example, in statistics arguing that on average, slave women did not give birth to their first child until married and about twenty-two years of age. As well, evidence of the slave woman's devotion to motherhood was found in the slave mother's breast-feeding of infants for an entire year, although in Peter Kolchin's view it was "embarrassing to read such statements by authors capable of such sophisticated technical analysis."[21]

However, for the most part, what inspired controversy about *Time on the Cross* was its authors' use of quantitative, econometric methodology to recast slavery as a rational, economic institution in which the masters promoted productivity and profits by providing incentives and material well-being to the labor force, that is, to the slaves.

Fogel and Engerman argued that the past could be reconstructed with much more certainty on the basis of computation of statistics and quantifiable data than by traditional historiography's reliance upon literary sources and written records, which were inherently subjective and biased. Proclaiming the superiority of their "new history" over the "old," they pointed to Kenneth Stampp's *The Peculiar Institution* in demonstration of the flaws of the latter. In their view, he and others had done the Afro-American reputation great harm by presenting slavery as a harsh system that stripped blacks of the norms and work ethic necessary for success in a competitive America. According to them, such portrayals had endorsed the racist myths of Negro dependency and incompetency, which continued to nail contemporary black Americans to the cross of racism. So, Fogel and Engerman intended to reconstruct "black achievement." Their book was a great public success, promoted and acclaimed for its rediscovery of slavery by the use of computers and high-tech procedures.[22]

Historians were often less enthusiastic. Unquestionably, Fogel and Engerman's charges regarding "traditional" history did not sit well with those accused. For one thing, it was pointed out that what historians had written about slavery was merely about slaves, not about black Americans in the present. As well, it was objected that Fogel and Engerman's charges set up "straw men," because historians had not interpreted slavery as *Time on the Cross* contended they had.[23]

Certainly by the 1970s most American historians were already emphasizing black achievement under adversity. Fogel and Engerman's "new history" was by no means new in that regard. But *Time on the Cross* seemed significantly to downplay the obstacles to slave achievements. According to its contentions, hard-working slave men had the opportunity for upward mobility within the system, that is, to move up from field labor into less menial and more "managerial" positions such as overseers, slave-drivers, and artisans.

Herbert Gutman objected: "Sambo, it turns out, was really a black Horatio Alger." And Fogel and Engermen were charged with presenting, in David Brion Davis's words, "a sanguine view of slavery, including its economic viability and its relative lack of deprivation . . . as defined by the standards of capitalist economics." But perhaps Kenneth Stampp best summed up the objections in this new skirmish of the battle of images, by arguing that *Time on the Cross* "contributes little to the destruction of myths of false stereotypes by replacing the racist caricatures of free black workers with cooperative, diligent, success-oriented slaves, 'imbued like their masters' with the values of a Victorian bourgeois class." According to Stampp, Fogel and Engerman had thereby returned "to a very old-fashioned concept of the acquiescent slave, and to all of its potentially racist implications."[24]

However, in the controversy over *Time on the Cross*, despite and, in part, because of all the attention to images defined as racist, the question of sexist images did not arise. In fact, the parties to this debate charged each other with everything and anything but sexism. This study had said more about slave women than most other contemporary studies. But what it said was noncontroversial because it largely fleshed out the prevailing consensus, casting the slave woman's experience as one determined by her subordinate relationship to men.

According to Fogel and Engerman's own statistics, opportunities for upward mobility were largely denied to slave women. While 80 percent of female slaves were field-workers, those who worked in the plantation Big House as domestics served in such traditional female roles as laundresses, cooks, and nurses. In contrast, male slave domestics were given the more prestigious jobs, such as gardeners and coachmen.

These historians did not question whether the enslaved shared their definitions of status. Instead, they argued that the sexual division of the slave labor force reinforced a slave society in which the dominant role was played by men. Slave culture was patriarchal. In further exemplification of this, they observed that slave husbands were listed before wives in plantation record books, and that housing, clothing, and garden plots were allocated in the names of the husbands. It followed, from the perspectives of these historians, that the slave family was alive and well, that is, two-parented and patriarchal. That the master appeared to see the slave man as "the head of the family" seemed, in this book, to show that the slaves saw it that way as well.[25] This was clearly a striking change from Elkins's emphasis on the master's treatment and perception of slave men. But it said nothing about how slave women saw it, and little as well about slave perspectives in general.

In any case, the slave woman's perspectives were not of interest in the controversy over this book. What did inspire some attention was the question of whether her sexuality and reproductive potential were "manipulated" by masters. That is to say, the old question reemerged of whether or not slave "breeding" was prevalent. According to Fogel and Engerman it was not. But others disputed this contention. As well, many sought to explain the self-sustaining, "natural increase" of the American South slave population in comparison with the failure of slaves to reproduce elsewhere in the Americas. In this context, the ensuing flood of quantitative "new history" studies brought masses of new statistics to a revival of the old focus on black female sexuality. As a matter of fact, historians moved with vigor into a debate about the causes of the American slave woman's high rate of reproduction.

The tone and perspectives of this debate may be discovered, for example, in a 1978 examination by James Trussell and Richard Steckel of whether slaveholders "manipulated" slave fertility. As these historians pointed out, the slave woman's own experience and perspectives were not their interest. They sought, rather, to ascertain whether masters' manipulation had a significant demographic impact, and concluded that it did not. On the basis of dietary and height-by-age statistics, they argued that slave girls began menstruation at about age fifteen. Assuming the usual period of infertility following menarche to be three years, the mean age of slave women at first birth should have been about eighteen if masters did successfully cause them to become pregnant as soon as the women were physiologically able. However, their mean age at first birth was 20.6. Therefore, it followed that masters were either unsuccessful in manipulating the female slaves' "reproductive behavior," or else they did not attempt to do so.[26]

On the other hand, Richard Sutch's interpretation of similar quantitative data suggested that slave women were bred by masters like livestock. Examining the slave trade from the older slave states to the expanding Southwest, in the former Sutch discovered abnormally high ratios of female to male slaves. He also found that plantations and farms with this unbalanced sexual composition included very large numbers of children. In his view, such data revealed that many slave women conceived children by men to whom they were not wed, showing widespread manipulation by masters of their sexuality. He concluded that masters deliberately promoted slave polygamy and promiscuity, thus rejecting Fogel and Engerman's insistence that masters encouraged slave monogamy and stable family life as the most efficient ways of promoting slave reproduction.[27]

Sutch and Herbert Gutman led the attack on *Time on the Cross*, arguing that it was much too soft on slavery. In their view the statistics revealed an average female slave age at first birth at 19.4, which suggested that slave women often became pregnant as soon as they were physically able.[28]

However, Fogel and Engerman, and others such as Herbert Klein, held their own on the opposite side of the battlefield, trooping in further statistics about the role of lactation periods in "fertility differentials" and other factors affecting the slave woman's "fecundity" and birthrates. The one clear area of agreement between the two sides was that slave sexual behavior should no longer be seen as immoral. However, the one side interpreted slave morality in terms of black emulation of white, Victorian norms, while the other side emphasized that slave departures from Victorian sexual mores were not immoral. As Gutman and Sutch argued, the sexual behavior of the enslaved was regulated and ordered by slave community norms, while "most slaves found prenuptial intercourse and even prenuptial pregnancy and childbirth compatible with subsequent monogamous marriage." However, both sides were in agreement in rejecting the old image of depraved slave "promiscuity" as a myth.[29]

In short, the slave woman was definitely no longer a Jezebel. But in the "new history" studies, she often figured much like the brood mare of old, whether or not she was bred by her master, or on her own gave birth to broods of offspring. To summarize, throughout slavery historiography and by the close of the 1970s, Afro-American women figured essentially in two ways. First, they were cast in the image of true womanhood, which as Barbara

Welter has pointed out, prescribed the nineteenth-century female "virtues" of piety, purity, submissiveness, and domesticity.[30] It is a telling comment on American culture that during the 1970s, this version of the "black lady" characterization was presented again as the most positive of images of womanhood. While some historians pointed to different definitions of sexual "purity," it was not in dispute that slave women were characterized by domesticity and deference to male dominance. Second, slave women figured as reproductive animals and sex objects. The only question in this regard was whether or not their sexual behavior was "manipulated" by the master.

These images may look very different. But in actuality they are related, in the sense that both emphasized the black woman's maternal role and both cast her historical role as fundamentally passive. She did not act, and certainly did not act on her own behalf. As the ladylike wife and mother, she was supportive of males and their initiatives. As the brood mare she was acted upon by men and by her own biological destiny. In both images, she was cast and marginalized as a profoundly relative creature. The meaning of her existence was defined by her relationship to males and male-defined needs and interests. *Her* interpretation of and role in the shaping of her own historical experience remained very obscure.

In short, despite the commitment of the new historiography to discovering the slave's perspective and the Afro-Americans' roles as active agents of history, the perspectives and roles that emerged were largely in accordance with male-centered definitions of meaning and significance, and in accordance with the emphasis on a manly historical identity. In striking contrast to the traditional historiographic story that had long emphasized black female strength and familial dominance—and usually in a negative light—by the closing decades of the twentieth century the black woman was shrinking into near invisibility as, in images of her, a domestic and/or reproductive prop for male-centered action.

This is not to dismiss the value of this revisionist scholarship, or to ignore that the new history discovered masses of data of relevance to black women's history. It is to observe that this scholarship by no means reconstructed that history. It is to point out that in the battle against racism, sexist premises, arguments, and conclusions generally went without notice or concern. Rather, as in the past, the attack on racist mythology continued, in effect, to employ the mythology of gender as a key weapon. Circling back to the abolitionist and early black intellectual tradition, once again, myths of womanhood were put to use in the war against myths of race. And thus, as a fully human, historical personage, the black American woman became an invisible, shrinking woman.

NOTES

1. Robert Harris, "Coming of Age: The Transformation of Afro-American Historiography," 118; Van Deburg, *Slavery and Race*, 140, 160, 158.

2. Nathan Huggins, "Afro-American History: Myths, Heroes, Reality," in Nathan I. Huggins, Martin Kilson, and Daniel M. Fox, eds., *Key Issues in the Afro-American Experience* (New York: Harcourt Brace Jovanovich Inc., 1971), 13.

3. Joel Williamson, "Black Self-Assertion Before and After Emancipation," in ibid., 225, 232, 233.

4. John Blassingame, *The Slave Community* (New York: Oxford University Press, 1972), 12–13, 88, 82, 85; and ibid., revised 1979 edition, 178.

5. Ibid., 1979 edition, 260.

6. Earl Thorpe, *The Mind of the Negro: An Intellectual History of Afro-Americans* (Westport, Conn.: Negro Universities Press, 1970; orig. pub. 1961), 242.

7. Ibid.,

8. Eldridge Cleaver, *Soul on Ice* (New York: Delta/Dell Pub. Co., 1968), 162.

9. Eugene Genovese, *Roll, Jordan, Roll: The World the Slaves Made* (New York: Vintage Books, 1976; orig. pub. 1972), 355, 361. See also 353–61.

10. Ibid., 482, 450, 493, 356, 360.

11. Harris, "Coming of Age," 120.

12. James Anderson, "Aunt Jemima in Dialectics: Genovese on Slave Culture," *Journal of Negro History* 61 (1976): 99.

13. David Brion Davis, "Slavery and the Post–World War II Historians," in Sidney W. Mintz, ed., *Slavery, Colonialism, and Racism* (New York: W. W. Norton & Co., 1974), 9.

14. Gutman, *The Black Family*, note 7, p. 632.

15. Genovese, *Roll, Jordan, Roll*, 500–501.

16. Ibid., 450, 491, 493.

17. Davis, "Slavery and the Post–World War II Historians," 14, 11.

18. Genovese, *Roll, Jordan, Roll*, 461, 462, 464, 471.

19. Ibid., 415.

20. Robert Fogel and Stanley Engerman, *Time on the Cross: The Economics of American Negro Slavery*, 2 vols., (Boston: Little, Brown & Co., 1974) 1: 5, 128, 130–35, 138; Peter Kolchin, "Review of *Time on the Cross*," *Journal of Social History* 9 (1975): 108.

21. Fogel and Engerman, *Time on the Cross* 1:138; Kolchin, "Review," 108.

22. Fogel and Engerman, *Time on the Cross* 1:158; see also 258–59, 263–64.

23. See especially Kenneth Stampp, "A Humanistic Perspective," in Paul David et al., eds., *Reckoning with Slavery: A Critical Study in the Quantitative History of American Negro Slavery* (New York: Oxford University Press, 1976), 12, 13.

24. Herbert Gutman, *Slavery and the Numbers Game: A Critique of Time on the Cross*, (Chicago: University of Illinois Press, 1975), 1; Davis, "Slavery and the Post–World War II Historians," 13; Stampp, "A Humanistic Perspective," in David et al., *Reckoning with Slavery*, 27, 28, 30.

25. Fogel and Engerman, *Time on the Cross* 1:142.

26. James Trussell and Richard Steckel, "The Age of Slaves at Menarche and Their First Birth," *Journal of Interdisciplinary History* 8 (1978): 477–505.

27. Richard Sutch, "The Breeding of Slaves for Sale and the Westward Expansion of Slavery, 1850–1860," in S. L. Engerman and E. D. Genovese, eds., *Race and Slavery in the Western Hemisphere: Quantitative Studies* (Princeton, N.J.: Princeton University Press, 1975), 173–210.

28. Herbert Gutman and Richard Sutch, "Victorians All? The Sexual Mores and

Conduct of Slaves and Their Masters," in David et al., *Reckoning with Slavery*, 134–62.

29. Ibid., 142; see also, for example, Herbert S. Klein and Stanley L. Engerman, "Fertility Differentials between Slaves in the United States and the British West Indies: A Note on Lactation Practices and Their Possible Implications," *William and Mary Quarterly* 35 (1978): 357–74; Fogel and Engerman, "Recent Findings in the Study of Slave Demography," *Sociology and Social Research* 63 (1979): 566–89; Steven E. Brown, "Sexuality and the Slave Community," *Phylon* 42 (1981): 1–10.

30. Welter, "The Cult of True Womanhood," 151–74.

8

Black Studies/Women's Studies: Discovering Black Women's History?

In the closing decades of the twentieth century, Afro-American women have figured in American historiography in a happier light than ever before. But they have emerged much like the pancake-box Jemima, lighter and brighter, yet still opaque as real women. Yet during the 1960s and 1970s, the rise of the black movement and the women's movement had seemed to promise that a new attention would finally be brought to the woman who, in effect, overlapped both groups. It appeared likely that these movements would work together finally to place black women in history. This chapter intends to examine why this promise was not borne out by the results.

Long underpinning the structural barriers to racial and female equality in American scholarship has been the marginalization of both groups in the told story of American history. But with the rise of black consciousness and feminism during and after the radical 1960s, both groups demanded a radical rewriting of history that would revise this marginalization. The rise of black studies and women's studies programs in colleges and universities signified the striving by both groups fully to include themselves in American scholarly discourse. Both strove to establish a full presence in the past to support their demand for a full presence in the present.

Yet while seeming to share much the same struggle, the black movement and the women's movement did not work together, outside or inside or academe. Black studies and women's studies were not quickly accepted as legitimate fields of scholarly inquiry by the academic establishment. Instead, proponents of both were frequently viewed as radical and unwanted upstarts. Thus, each was in the position of having simultaneously to define itself and defend its right to existence. This situation also put them into a competitive position, competing with each other for funding, institutional recognition, and public attention. However, that the new black studies and women's studies programs more often seemed to be rivals than allies was also promoted by deeper divisions outside of academe.

It is well to recognize, first, that while from their birth in the 1960s women's studies have been associated with feminism, feminism has been very suspect from some Afro-American perspectives. Often seen as a white woman's movement, some have seen it as antiblack. For example, according to Nathan Hare's 1978 article in *The Black Scholar*, entitled "Revolution Without a Revolution," feminism was a self-serving, white woman's movement which "sought to exploit the spirit, the metaphor, and the rhetoric of the black movement." Moreover, in Hare's words, "the white woman sleeps with the enemy." According to this article, the feminist call for equal employment opportunities for women was at the expense of the black man's opportunity "to prevail and compete in a perpetually patriarchal society." Moreover, as Hare pointed out, the call for female economic independence made a pretense of virtue out of what had always been the black woman's necessity. And he warned that the women's movement was an antimale movement that would turn the black woman against her man. Briefly, this article emphasized that feminism deserved no support from Afro-American women.[1]

Iva Carruthers went even further in arguing that "the white feminist movement" stemmed from a "Jewish elite." An "insiduous" force, its attempt to engage black female support was said to be "leading us further down the path of Aryan control of our families."[2]

While Afro-American women were warned to remain aloof from the feminist movement, their role in the black movement remained marginalized. In the words of Nathan Hare, "the black man will be able to bring the woman along in our common struggle. . . . The black woman . . . can be the black man's helper." Her place was apparently essential to support the struggle, especially as mother, producing and nurturing the troops. And in Iva Carruthers's view, "what greater service . . . could a woman have than to be barometer and perpetuator of a son's development as a child, husband, and father?" In this context, whatever promoted black feminism was seen as a threat to the black movement.[3]

Thus, Frances Smith Foster and Charles Henry have pointed to perceptions of women's studies as promoting black feminism, as responsible for underpinning the exclusion of black women's studies from black studies programs. According to them, the exclusion stemmed from assumptions that the "developmental efforts of Black women's studies is the beginning of Black feminism."[4]

Certainly, what Paula Giddings has called the "male-conscious ethos" of this era was often expressed by Afro-American intellectuals, in conjunction with the identification of black power with the affirmation of black manhood. According to Michele Wallace, coincident with the rise of a cult of "black macho," lacking the socioeconomic power to demonstrate his manly attributes, the contemporary black male's response was often to scapegoat his woman. In Wallace's words, "his problem was that she was not a 'woman.' " Wallace and Giddings have argued that in this context, the Moynihan Report's "Black Matriarchy" thesis was not without appeal to many Afro-American men. The report seemed to point to a dominant, damaging black womanhood in a way that could support views that the black woman was the black man's problem.[5]

According to Giddings, the scholarly result of this outlook was that "sociologists, psychiatrists, and the male literati accused Black women of castrating not only their men but their sons. . . . Black women were unfeminine, they said."[6] To examine some contemporary black-authored studies tends to bear out Giddings's assertion.

Moreover, even those who presented themselves as critics of Moynihan's thesis could seem, oddly, to embrace and endorse the image of a domineering, emasculating black womanhood. For example, in their 1968 book *Black Rage*, William Grier and Price Cobbs commenced by attacking the Black Matriarchy thesis. As these Afro-American authors objected, "the black woman has been the salvation of many a family. To call such a family matriarchal, as many have done, is to obscure the essential maternal function."[7] Yet their book went on to repeat and embellish the timeworn historical portrait casting the black women's past and present in a matriarchal light.

Black Rage intended to explain the ghetto uprisings of the late 1960s. In essence, it argued that these represented a kind of psychological liberation through violence. However, in this book, the liberation often seemed more to free black men from black women than from the damaging effects of racism.

The authors reiterated the familiar Negro pathology thesis, arguing that repressed anger had historically led to black self-contempt. This was presented as the legacy of slavery. But as to how this legacy had been perpetuated for so long, the answers provided by this book seemed to point more to bad black womanhood than to white racism. Apparently generations of Afro-American mothers had continued the slave woman's socialization of her offspring in docility. The slave woman had done this to protect her child from the master; she had to "hurt him physically and emotionally and demand that he respond in an obsequious helpless manner." But after slavery's abolition, the black mother was said to have continued this damaging treatment, continuing "systematically to drive our manliness from our sons."[8]

In their portrayal of the familiar stock characters of emasculated men and castrating women as the cast of Afro-American history, these authors provided no hard evidence as substantiation. Instead, they simply referred to a taken-for-granted black women's history according to which, for example, she had always welcomed the white man's attention. Attracted to his power and sexually excited by him, "this type of passive submission, strongly colored by eroticism, has historically characterized the relationship between black women and white men." Furthermore, historically valued only as a "sexually convenient laboring animal," according to this book the black woman could not grow into a "healthy, mature, womanhood." In short, the book proclaimed that "the answers lie in the past."[9]

The primary question that *Black Rage* appeared to be trying to answer was why the Afro-American woman was continuing to damage her man as a man, thus perpetuating "the scars and wounds of yesterday." The answers provided argued that she did so because her own femininity had been so damaged by history. Given her "degraded self-perceptions," she was said to have eventually given up, neglecting her appearance and becoming obese: "Femininity is only imperfectly grasped by most black women." As a result, she focused on the only womanly function still open to her, that is, motherhood. Throwing herself into the "asexual maternal role," she smothered and crippled her child's growth into manhood.[10]

Black women's history reemerged in this book with its familiar cast, featuring the depreciated, depraved sex object who slept with the enemy, the brutalized brood mare, the failed mother, and the unfeminine emasculator of black men. Again, these demeaning, depowering images were written into the story that emphasized the black woman's immense power to damage her man and her people. All this was still being presented in the late 1960s as factual. And on its cover, *Black Rage* sported the *New York Times* laud that it was among "the most important books on the Negro to appear in the last decade."

Similarly, the black sociologist, Calvin Hernton, had no hesitation about using this prefabricated black woman's history to bear out his analysis of the present. According to his 1965 book, *Sex and Racism in America*, under slavery the "African woman was transformed into a beast. . . . The Negro woman became 'promiscuous and loose,' and could be 'had for the taking.' " Hernton's quoted material came from W. B. Cash's 1941 book, *The Mind of the South*. As well, drawing upon John Dollard's 1937 book, *Caste and Class in a Southern Town*, he pointed to the black woman's "unconscious desire" for sex with white men.[11]

Hernton's story went on to recount the familiar picture of the black woman's "strong matriarchal drive," which he described as "studdism," rendering the masculinization explicit. Naturally in this account, feeling "castrated," the black male fled into the arms of white women. In short, this sociologist drew freely from the old stock of images to flesh out his view of damaging black matriarchy. It seemed that virtually anything and everything could be said about contemporary black women so long as their supposed failures were blamed on their history. In Hernton's words, "What can one expect? After all, throughout the entire span of her experience on American soil, the Negro woman has . . . had to fend for herself as if she were a man." On its cover, this book bore a host of plaudits ranging from *Playboy* to Nat Hentoff's praise of its exposure of the "intertwining myths of sex and race."[12]

Some might point out that such literature did much more to perpetuate than to challenge myths of sex and race. Certainly Paula Giddings is not unfair in charging that Hernton, Grier and Cobbs, "and others, continued to rationalize their compulsions by projecting inadequacies on Black women."[13]

Such black male perceptions may help to explain the continuing exclusion of black women's history from the era's developing black studies programs. It may also be that this was not so much a matter of misogyny as a matter of not wishing to discuss a history assumed to be so contradictory to the reconstruction of a prideful Afro-American past. During the 1960s and early 1970s the only alternative vision of black women's history was provided by the new slavery studies which, as we have seen, left slave women largely invisible except as domestic props to the man-centered action. And as Afro-Americanist historiography moved beyond slavery into the postemancipation decades, black women's history continued to be profoundly marginalized.

Chapter titles such as "Black Men in the Urban Age" in *From Plantation to Ghetto* by August Meier and Elliott Rudwick were representative of their contents. The fleeting appearances of Afro-American women were only in traditional female roles of those who supported their men, as in Saunders Redding's *The Negro* (1967). In this text Afro-American patriotism in wartime was emphasized. Negro men worked in the war industries and "did all that was asked of them and more." As for Negro women, they "knitted sweaters, scarves and caps for the army."[14]

George Rawick stands out as the sole male critic of gender bias in contemporary Afro-American historiography. In a 1978 anthology of responses to Blassingame's *The Slave Community*, Rawick alone criticized that text as demonstrating a "totally and exclusively male perspective." As he pointed out, for Blassingame "slaves" meant "men . . . unless he specifies women, as he does very rarely." Black women were included by Blassingame only "as lovers, wives, and mothers," not "as workers or as central figures in the struggles in the black community." In contrast, as Rawick observed, the modern women's movement was using "a poster that reproduces an image of Harriet Tubman with a long rifle. I think that might be a good symbol for all black struggle." However, contemporary Afro-American historiography seemed to turn a deaf ear to such suggestions.[15]

In short, the black movement did not promote attention to placing black women *in* history. Quite the contrary. And as Foster and Henry found, even into the early 1980s black studies programs remained "reluctant to distinguish the Black woman's experience from those of Black males. . . . The few textbooks on Black Studies confine their discussion of Black women to traditional African society or combine it with an examination of the Black family."[16]

Nevertheless in its call for a discourse that reflected female perspectives, the women's movement seemed to promise that it, at least, would include black women in the feminist reconstruction of the history of American women. However, this was not the case. As women's studies established a growing, if precarious, foothold during the 1970s, they were no more inclusive of Afro-American women than were black studies. In 1974, for example, out of over four thousand women's studies courses, less than 1 percent examined black women, and only four of this tiny group had an historical focus. As Gloria Hull and Barbara Smith have pointed out, by 1976 only eleven percent of the courses offered by the fifteen established women's studies programs in colleges and universities examined minority women or issues of race. Even in the early 1980s, as Francis Smith Foster and Charles Henry have noted, women's studies remained almost exclusively white in both faculty and curriculum.[17]

In search of explanations for this exclusion that go beyond simply labeling the contemporary women's movement as antiblack, it may be noted, first, that feminist scholarship, like other fields of scholarship, was influenced by existing intellectual resources. By the 1960s, to the extent that these sources pointed at all to the presence and role of women in American history, they identified American women as white.

The identification of the history of American women as the story of white women dated back to the earliest challenges to the omission of women from traditional historiography. In 1926, for example, in *New Viewpoints in American History*, Arthur Schlesinger had called for attention to the "role of women in American history." Yet which women he had in mind was revealed in his sympathy with contemporary female "amazement that Congress should be willing to experiment with two million illiterate black men as voters while denying the ballot to women." Black women, forced to be no less illiterate, were de facto excluded from such arguments for female enfranchisement. Moreover, Schlesinger wrote approvingly of extending the vote to women because they were "better prepared for their new responsibilities than . . . the black men [who were] on an infinitely lower plane of public morality and individual fitness." That black women continued to be disfranchised after female enfranchisement was not noted by this historian. For him, it seemed to be a given that women were white and blacks were male, while black women remained in a no-man's, no-woman's land.[18]

The same conceptualization remained prevalent a half century later amongst those who pioneered in drawing attention to the history of American women—and these were initially frequently male pioneers. For example, in William O'Neill's 1969 history, *Everyone Was Brave*. Afro-American women remained excluded even from "everyone." Rather, O'Neill wrote of women's "shocked" recognition that "men would so humiliate them by supporting votes for Negroes but not for women." The female suffrage issue was characterized similarly in Page Smith's *Daughters of the Promised Lands: Women in American History* (1970): this book also provided its readers with such "facts" as that

The great Negro migration to the industrial centers of the country began at the same time as the influx of women into industry. If women had not been available, the Negroes . . . would almost certainly have been drafted into the industrial army. As it was there were other recruits. [19]

Again, women were identified as white. Yet this book also reiterated the old identification of blacks as the feminine race. According to this historian, while "the nature of women" often "affects their judgment and inclines her to . . . achieve her ends by guile," "there is a similar quality . . . among Negroes. . . . They are instant 'soul brothers.' " So, the old equation of blacks and women reemerged, which worked against the discovery of either group as full and diverse people in American history. [20]

Until at least the 1970s, when Afro-American women were mentioned at all in such "women's histories" it was largely in terms of the familiar types, and in particular, as matriarchs. According to Andrew Sinclair, for example, after slavery's abolition the freedwomen became "all the more self-sufficient and powerful," and this "matriarchal tradition has persisted until modern times." The Afro-American woman was said to have been "dominant over the husband and the children," while "the man played the role of the resentful dependent." In addition, according to Sinclair's history, "the principle of matriarchy in Negro society" was what had retarded the liberation of the Negro, since "Negro women, like all women, tend to conservatism." However, Sinclair found some cause for hope in the modern black movement, since the Negro revolt, he wrote, was as much against the dominance of black women as against white supremacy. Therefore it was "likely that Negro men will achieve increasing equality with their own women folk and with American society." In short, once again black female dominance was presented as the primary impediment to Afro-American equality. The adoption of patriarchy still seemed essential to black success. [21]

On the other hand, by the 1970s male- as well as female-authored women's historiography demonstrated increasingly feminist perspectives that challenged the equation of patriarchy with the "natural" order. And women's historiography often pointed to the past to show change in the status and roles of women over time, demonstrating gender as a social and cultural construct.

For example, in his 1972 history, *The American Woman,* William Chafe argued that swelling female labor-force participation had challenged traditional views of masculinity and femininity and provided "a foundation for seeking equality." And "once women were propelled out of their traditional role, they would not go back." Yet Chafe's thesis was beset by the dilemmas of how to fit in black women. Recognizing that they had always been in the labor force, he also observed that they still "longed for the opportunity to devote full-time to their traditional roles as wives and mothers." However, the dilemma was apparently dismissed by this book's ready recourse to the familiar image of matriarchy. That is to say, according to Chafe, Afro-American women were already singularly liberated because of their dominance in the home. With regard to this contention, Chafe's usual practice of providing plentiful substantiating documentation was supplanted by brief reference to the Moynihan Report and to E. Franklin Frazier.[22]

The ready acceptance of matriarchy as the historical order of things among black Americans was by no means limited to male-authored stories of women in American history. This conventional academic wisdom had been reiterated, for example, in Eleanor Flexner's pioneering 1959 study of the nineteenth-century women's rights movement, *Century of Struggle*. In this book the slave woman reemerged in full force as the "mistress of her cabin" and as already liberated from "the spirit of subordination to masculine authority." On the other hand, Flexner stood out in her unique recognition of the contribution to female liberation by Afro-American women ranging from teachers and professionals back to "Harriet Tubman and her great contemporary, Sojourner Truth." Flexner pointed out that as abolitionists and women's rights activists, black women deserved "better than the oblivion to which they have been assigned."[23]

Flexner's call for such recognition, however, went largely without emulation during the following decades in women's history, in large part, it would seem, because the Afro-American woman was presupposed to be too strong and free to be of interest in terms of the experience of white American women. It was not until the early 1970s that any historian turned to examine her history. Then it was Gerda Lerner, whose pioneering documentary study *Black Women in White America* was published in 1972.

Lerner began by pointing out that Afro-American women had historically borne the double burden of sexual and racial discrimination. Lerner noted as well in a later study that contemporary black women ranked lowest among all American sex-race groupings in socioeconomic status, whereas, "matriarchy, by definition, means power by women: decision-making power, power over their own lives, power over the lives of others; power in their communities. To speak of black matriarchy in contemporary society is a cruel hoax."[24]

Nonetheless, in the 1972 documentary, and also in her later article, "Black Women in the United States: A Problem in Historiography and Interpretation," Lerner presented Afro-American women as, historically, a singularly advantaged group when compared to both white women and black men. Her findings argued that more jobs and educational opportunities had been open to them than to the latter. Schooled in "self-sufficiency," and free from oppression by black males who were powerless, black women "have higher status within their own group than do white women in white society." It followed for this historian that "the greater inequality in relations between black men and black women" served to "explain the resistance most black women feel toward . . . the Women's Liberation movement." According to Lerner, it was not until the late nineteenth century, "after the development of the Negro women's club movement that feminist consciousness first appeared" among them. But even then, this consciousness remained "an exceptional attitude. . . . Black women always expressed a clearer solidarity with their men than did white women."[25]

To summarize, this major white feminist scholar's pioneering reconstruction of black women's history seemed in some ways to confirm the traditional story—but in a positive light—arguing that "independent, self-reliant, and adapted to survival," the Afro-American woman was historically "liberated in her own mind," and hence, nonfeminist.[26]

Lerner's contentions would come under fire. She would be charged, for example, with treating black women 'as if they were only black or as if they were only women," and with "inadequate conceptualization of questions confronting historians investigating black women." In Jacquelyne Jackson's view Lerner was even guilty of "shoddy scholarship." But beneath the passionate tone of such critiques lay perceptions of her work as "perpetuating an image of the mythological black woman."[27]

Certainly Lerner seemed simultaneously to reject the black matriarchy thesis and yet also to perpetuate the nonfeminist, Amazon image of Afro-American womanhood. But she strove to challenge what she perceived as the image in which black women most often had figured in American historiography: "When they do appear in history at all it is merely as victims, as helpless sufferers of conditions imposed on them by others."[28]

As we have found, however, in actuality the mythology of black womanhood was by no means cast in this image of helpless female victimization. Instead, the contemporary black woman's image as a domineering matriarch reflected decades of social-science and historical literature which had overwhelmingly portrayed her as singularly strong, self-sufficient, and even powerful enough to be responsible not only for the supposed pathologies and problems of her race, but also for the downfall of white men.

In short, Lerner was mistaken in her view of the imagery to be countered and challenged. The Afro-American woman had long been included in history in a way that had cast her as more powerful and "liberated"—as distinctly defeminized and overwhelmingly *other*—than "American" women. Her slave-woman image had in all versions of history emphasized her dominance over the black man. Thus, not only had she been historically depicted as a deviant from true womanhood in symbolizing the opposite of sexual "purity," but also she had emerged as, de facto, excluded from the cast of victims and resisters of male supremacy.

Indeed, the black woman's image as both defeminized and nonfeminist constituted a great divide preventing the new women's studies from recognizing her as an American woman, despite the rhetoric of sisterhood. Certainly, so long as women's historiography traced women's story as one of "suffering sisterhood," black women did not readily fit into the picture.

Given the casting of this group of women overwhelmingly as *other*, it becomes more explicable that in the midst of the explosion of women's studies, the concept of black women's studies continued to face a wall of apathy or hostility. As Henry and Foster have pointed out, both "black nationalists and white feminists have tended to denounce it [black women's studies] as an obstacle to unity." Neither group seemed able to bring culturally pluralist perspectives to bear upon the reconstruction of history. Instead, each treated the concept of black women's history as if it was divisive and threatening to the establishment of a collective sense of identity. The result has been, in Bell Hooks's words, that "when black people are talked about the focus tends to be on black *men*, and when women are talked about the focus tends to be on *white* women. Nowhere is this more evident than in the vast body of feminist literature."[29]

From Gerda Lerner's perspective in the early 1970s, the dearth of attention to Afro-American women in the new women's historiography stemmed largely from the dearth of available sources, which reflected the racism of the past, not of the contemporary women's movement. As she observed, because "the kinds of sources collected depend to a large extent on the predilections, interests, prejudices, and values of the collectors and historians of an earlier day," the Afro-American woman's records remained buried, or scattered and inaccessible. However, the dearth and inaccessibility of sources were also the case for American women in general, and yet the white woman's history was being reconstructed with vigor. But Lerner herself may have revealed the presupposition that black women's history was other than "women's history" in calling for historians to "unearth, compile and organize" the sources for reconstructing it, as "those writing women's history" had already done.[30]

In part, as Audre Lorde observed, the assumption remained that "racism is a Black Woman's problem . . . and only we can discuss it." And as Bell Hooks has pointed out: "When black people are talked about, sexism militates against the acknowledgement of the interests of black women; when women are talked about racism militates against a recognition of black female interests." Hooks is correct that the result has been to perpetuate both racism and sexism:

Using the term "women" even if . . . referring solely to the experience of white women . . . perpetuates racism in that it denies the existence of non-white women in America. It also perpetuates sexism in that it assumes that sexuality is the sole self-defining trait of white women.

Hooks does not seem unfair in charging that "white women liberationists did not challenge this sexist-racist practice—they continued it."[31]

However, the dynamics of sexism and racism have also worked in a different sense to promote the marginalization of black women's history by both the black movement and the women's movement. These dynamics are reflected and deeply rooted in the decades of historiography that had by the radical 1960s shaped, endorsed, and perpetuated the Afro-American woman's image as a singularly empowered other. This was for both the black movement and the women's movement a threatening image. It was equally challenging to the black movement's emphasis on manliness and to the women's movement's emphasis on sisterhood. It was also profoundly out of step with the focus of both upon forging a collective historical identity.

To examine the discourse associated with these two major movements for liberation further illuminates the continuing spell of the past over the present. The power of old images of Mammy and her kin has, ironically, promoted the marginalization of black women in American history well into contemporary times.

NOTES

1. Nathan Hare, "Revolution Without a Revolution: The Psychology of Sex and Race," *The Black Scholar* 13 (1982; reprinted from vol. 9, 1978): 16, 18.

2. Iva Carruthers, "War on African Familyhood," in Roseann P. Bell, Bettye J. Parker, and Beverly Guy-Sheftall, eds., *Sturdy Black Bridges: Visions of Black Women in Literature* (New York: Anchor Press/Doubleday, 1979), 9, 15.

3. Hare, "Revolution Without a Revolution," 16; Carruthers, "War on African Familyhood," 13.

4. Charles P. Henry and Frances Smith Foster, "Black Women's Studies: Threat or Challenge?" *The Western Journal of Black Studies* 6 (1982): 16.

5. Paula Giddings, *Where and When I Enter*, 314–15; Michele Wallace, *Black Macho*, 42.

6. Giddings, *Where and When I Enter*, 319.

7. William Grier and Price Cobbs, *Black Rage* (New York: Basic Books, Inc., 1969), 41.

8. Grier and Cobbs, *Black Rage*, 19–20, 143–44, 62.

9. Ibid. 82, 83.

10. Ibid., 19–20, 82, 40.

11. Calvin C. Hernton, *Sex and Racism in America* (New York: Grove Press, 1978; orig. pub. 1965), 124, 129.

12. Ibid., 135, 136, 163.

13. Giddings, *Where and When I Enter*, 321.

14. August Meier and Elliott Rudwick, *From Plantation to Ghetto* (London: Constable, 1970); Saunders Redding, *The Negro* (Washington, D.C.: Potomac Books, Inc., Publishers, 1967), 44.

15. George P. Rawick, "Some Notes on a Social Analysis of Slavery: A Critique and Assessment of the Slave Community," in Al-Tony Gilmore, ed., *Revisiting Blassingame's "The Slave Community": The Scholars Respond* (Westport, Conn.: Greenwood Press, 1978), 21.

16. Henry and Foster, "Back Women's Studies," 16.

17. Hull and Smith, "The Politics of Black Women's Studies," in Hull, Scott, and Smith, *But Some of Us Are Brave*, xxvii; Henry and Foster, "Black Women's Studies," 15–21.

18. Arthur Schlesinger, *New Viewpoints in American History* (New York: The Macmillan Co., 1926), 146, 158.

19. William O'Neill, *Everyone Was Brave: A History of Feminism in America* (Chicago: Quadrangle Books, Inc., 1971; orig. pub. 1969), 6; Page Smith, *Daughters of the Promised Land: Women in American History* (Boston: Little, Brown & Co., 1970), 290.

20. Smith, *Daughters*, 326.

21. Andrew Sinclair, *The Emancipation of American Women* (New York: Harper and Row, 1965), 351, 352.

22. William Chafe, *The American Woman: Her Changing Economic and Social Roles* (New York: Oxford University Press, 1972), 253, 221, 200.

23. Eleanor Flexner, *Century of Struggle: The Women's Rights Movement in the United States* (Cambridge, Mass.: Harvard University Press, 1966; orig. pub. 1959), 22, 96, 98.

24. Lerner, *Black Women in White America*, xxiii; Lerner, "Black Women in the United States: A Problem in Historiography and Interpretation," in Gerda Lerner, *The Majority Seeks Its Past: Placing Women in History* (New York: Oxford University Press, 1979), 79.

25. Lerner, *Black Women*, xxiv; Lerner, "Black Women in the United States," 80, 73.

26. Lerner, "Black Women," 80, 81, 73–74.

27. Jacquelyne J. Jackson, "A Critique of Lerner's Work on Black Women," *Journal of Social and Behavioral Science* (1975): 71, 74.

28. Lerner, "Black Women," 63.

29. Henry and Foster, "Black Women's Studies," 16; Bell Hooks, *Ain't I a Woman*, 7. Emphasis added.

30. Lerner, "Black Women," 63–64, 65.

31. Audre Lorde, "The Uses of Anger," *Women's Studies Quarterly* 9 (1981): 7; Hooks, *Ain't I a Woman* 7–8.

9

Rediscovering the Black Family: New and Old Images of Motherhood

While the history of Afro-American women remained obscure, the Afro-American family attracted renewed interest during the 1970s, in part because of the controversy over the Moynihan Report. In many ways the report had come, in the words of Elmer Martin and Joanne Mitchell Martin, at precisely the "wrong time in history." Published in 1965, during a period when black Americans moved toward a positive self-identity and when the civil rights movement pointed to national responsibility for black inequality, the report "absolved the government and the dominant society of major responsibility for the oppression of blacks, provided white racists with fresh ideological ammunition to use against blacks, and implied that blacks were inferior and not ready for freedom."[1]

At least, this is how Moynihan's *The Negro Family: The Case for National Action* was interpreted by the Martins and by many of its critics during the following years. The Moynihan Report appeared to be a damaging and dangerous policy document stamped with government approval, which, in effect, "blamed the victim." It seemed to blame black American culture, and particularly black family pathology, for continuing Afro-American inequality. Moreover, the Negro pathology thesis was out of step with the times. The black movement challenged the crippled, "crushed people" portrayal associated with that timeworn thesis by testifying to the resources and strengths of black Americans.[2]

The pathology thesis was not quickly or easily dismissed. As a 1974 study of family sociology textbooks found, the texts were still "perpetuating the myths." However, the 1970s saw a veritable revolution in interpretation of the modern Afro-American family with Robert Hill's publication of *The Strength of Black Families* (1972), reflecting the new emphasis on familial health.

In contrast to the old equation of black deviance from white middle-class norms as pathological and dysfunctional, the new black family studies increasingly emphasized Afro-American diversity—including familial and sexual departures from white norms—as a positive thing. In this context, the "otherness" of contemporary black womanhood could also be examined and reinterpreted in a positive light. This reinterpretation of the present helped to pave the way for the discovery of Afro-American women's historical diversity.[3]

During the 1970s a veritable explosion of sociological studies agreed that the old portrayal of the "matriarchal" Afro-American family was "social mythology."[4] Some combated the matriarchal mythology by arguing that most contemporary Afro-American families were two-parented and male-headed. As John Scanzoni pointed out, two-thirds of all urban black families included both husband and wife. He pointed to paternal dominance and the socialization of offspring in what were essentially traditional American values and mores. Similarly, Robert Staples and others emphasized male dominance in black families of all classes. This body of research presented the contemporary Afro-American family as essentially like other American families, nuclear and patriarchal in structure and norms.[5]

In fact, by the mid-1970s it was becoming the new social-science orthodoxy that the "black matriarchy" was a myth. However, it was increasingly argued that it did not follow that the black American family emulated white American norms. Instead, many argued that in its differences lay its strength.

The new emphasis on the diversity and distinctiveness of Afro-American families reflected the rejection of the old panacea of racial assimilation. As the color blindness hoped for by the civil rights era was like a mirage, and as it became much less credible and desirable to see blacks as whites with black skins, the black movement pointed to a proud identification of racial difference. In this context cultural pluralism was increasingly recognized, explored, and embraced.

In 1968 Andrew Billingsley pioneered in bringing this perspective to bear upon the Afro-American family.[6] During the decade that followed, the family institution's uniqueness was reinterpreted not as a problem, but as what enabled it to function so well to preserve the health of black Americans in a racist, classist, and sick society. Thus, in 1978 the *Journal of Marriage and the Family* devoted an entire issue to black family studies, in acknowledgment that,

perhaps as an aftermath to the pervasive criticism of the controversial Moynihan Report, there has been a shift in perspective on the part of social science researchers . . . based on a conceptualization . . . that black families are . . . different in many ways from white families, but possessing a value system, patterns of behavior, and institutions which can be described, understood, and appreciated for their own strengths and characteristics . . . and which serve the peculiar survival needs of a group which continues to suffer discrimination, prejudice, and subtle institutional racism.[7]

It was from this new, positive emphasis on black familial distinctiveness that the Afro-American woman began to emerge in a positive light that did not merely reshape her image into the dominant vision of good womanhood. From cultural pluralist perspectives, her strengths and central familial role could even be reinterpreted as assets rather than liabilities.

In particular, Joyce Ladner pointed the way to this revisionism. As this black sociologist emphasized, it was not black "deviation" from white norms that was the problem, but racial discrimination and poverty. In her 1971 study, *Tomorrow's Tomorrow*, she set out to provide a study of Afro-American women "which does not indict them for all kinds of alleged social problems, which, if they exist, they did not create." While Ladner rejected the concept of black matriarchy, she did not ignore the prevalence of matrifocality among the low-income subjects of her research, or argue that most black families were nuclear in structure. In fact, what was quite distinctive about many black families, in her view, was their extended structure and inclusion of a wide, supportive network of relatives and friends. Her findings argued that central to this were women supporting and identifying with other women.[8]

As Ladner observed, "the extended family, including aunts and grand-mothers, often serves as strong a function in preparing young girls for womanhood as do their mothers and fathers." Thus, Ladner found that black women identified the meaning of "womanhood" for themselves and each other. According to her findings, central to their definition was motherhood, in or out of wedlock. Unwed mothers and their children were supported rather than stigmatized as immoral. Ladner pointed to "a different set of moral codes" centered upon the "humanist value" attached to children and motherhood. And she argued that in this regard, in their extended female support system, and in their self-valuation, Afro-American women were actually in the vanguard of the "sexual revolution."[9]

Furthermore, according to Ladner, freed from the traditional constraints imposed upon women, allowed the "emotional well-being that Women's Liberation groups are calling for," and enjoying an "inner resourcefulness," black women "have always been free." Turning to history, she argued that by surmounting generations of oppression, the Afro-American woman had developed an "obstinate strength and ability to survive," while her "cultural heritage" was instrumental in shaping her modern identity in a most positive sense.[10]

Emphasizing the important roles played by women in traditional African socioeconomic and political life, Ladner pointed as well to their central role in the West African family. The African woman was most highly valued "as child bearer and perpetuator of the ancestral heritage." Ladner argued that this heritage was strengthened rather than weakened by the slave experience in America. Slavery made the slave woman "the backbone of the family," responsible for her offspring "in the absence of a sustained husband-father figure."[11]

In short, as American sociology had long been doing, Ladner also hearkened back to the past to strengthen her interpretation of the present. She reiterated the familiar image of the mother as central to the slave family. However, her story then took a very different direction, arguing that because the Afro-American family survived and emerged from slavery as an extended, maternally organized institution, *therefore* this institution had made and continued to make a great contribution to Afro-American survival of oppression. According to her story, history's legacy was not a damaged and damaging black womanhood, but women with a tradition of motherhood, work, and a "peculiar humanistic character and quiet courage."[12]

While not based upon any new historical research, Ladner's was a striking new interpretation of black women's history. It also circled back to W.E.B. Du Bois's vision of an empowered black womanhood. However, some argued that it simply constituted historical romanticization. In the view of Ann Chandler Howell, for example, it was not history that had shaped the contemporary black woman's experience, but the continuing lack of viable alternatives to work and motherhood. According to Howell, children were valued because they were the only thing the black woman could call her own; and, "further, the implication on the part of the author that there are no promiscuous black females is simply foolhardy." Nonetheless, as this critic also acknowledged, Ladner's interpretation did encourage reevaluation of the myths of black womanhood.[13]

Certainly by the mid–1970s the old myths of family pathology had been dismissed by the explosion of studies that interpreted black family distinctiveness in terms of survivalist resiliency and strength. It was this emerging new consensus that crystallized into Alex Haley's 1976 historical novel, *Roots*, celebrating black family history as an epic story of survival and heroic achievement.[14]

Therefore, as Elmer and Joanne Martin observed, the Afro-American family had been virtually transformed into a Horatio Alger success story. However, in their view a "full and realistic" understanding of the institution required "a perspective broader than either the strength-resiliency or pathology-disorganization perspective will allow."[15]

It is true that the emphasis on strength and resiliency was very new. As Eleanor Engram's study of the Afro-American family in one half-century of research has further demonstrated, a vast body of scholarly literature had by the 1970s cast the family in an overwhelmingly negative light. And as Engram has pointed out, the literature had done so on the basis of both racial and sexual presuppositions. It had been presupposed by a host of researchers that because deprived of his traditional breadwinner and instrumental roles, the black male was stripped of self-esteem and family ties. By the same token it was presupposed that the black woman's instrumental economic role led to marital discord, sexual promiscuity, and neglect of her maternal and expressive functions. In Engram's view, these social scientists had been blind to the self-valuation provided to impoverished peoples by nonmaterial rewards such as children and parenting. Moreover, assuming the natural passivity of women, researchers had ignored the role of sexuality as a source of female as well as male self-esteem. Certainly Engram's findings confirm that in black family studies, the assumptions and values of researchers had repeatedly led to post hoc and speculative conclusions which, in effect, functioned to endorse the mythology of black racial inferiority. Thus, she has pointed to half-century of black family research as confirming that race is "man's most dangerous myth."[16]

However, how black women have figured in this discourse suggests that the mythology of gender has been equally dangerous and reveals the combination of both sets of myths as near lethal. In truth, this literature reflected, endorsed, and perpetuated a negative, disempowering image of Afro-American womanhood, supported by a caricatured and dehumanizing story of black women's history. In this context, whether or not the revisionist black family studies of the 1970s presented a fully realistic picture of the health of contemporary Afro-American culture, they pointed the way to a humanizing discovery of racial and sexual diversity.

By the 1970s it was no longer credible to point to any black matriarchy. As a vast mass of data showed, Afro-American women were at the bottom of the American sex-race hierarchy in terms of all socioeconomic indices. Whether single-parent mothers or not, Afro-American women could not plausibly be labeled as matriarchs. Unable either to dominate or to count upon the support of males, it was ludicrous to associate them with this conceptualization of female power.

It also became clear that marriage by no means brought black women any matriarchal power. By the end of the 1970s, 60 percent of Afro-American women compared with 49 percent of white American women living in husband-wife households were in the labor force. Forty-two percent of the former compared with 31 percent of the latter worked at full-time jobs. Yet the median income of these black two-earner families was but 80 percent of that of all American families. The black woman's presence in the work force only masked the extent of Afro-American disempowerment and inequality more generally.

The data clarified that the black female worker remained concentrated in low-status, low-paying service jobs. As was revealed by the 1981 census statistics, the median income for full-time work was, for white men $21,178, for black men $14,984, for white women $12,665, and for black women, $11,438. The data showed, too, that Afro-American women earned less than all other race-sex groupings at the same level of education, and that their unemployment levels were substantially higher than those of either black men or white women. Their health was poor, and black infant mortality rates remained substantially higher than among nonblack Americans.

In sum, a host of statistics and studies argued that poverty and powerlessness were the primary problems for contemporary Afro-American women, not their supposed inadequacies as women and the "dysfunctionality" of the Afro-American family. Quite the contrary, in books such as Carol Stack's *All Our Kin: Strategies for Survival in a Black Community* (1974) the strength and resiliency of black motherhood emerged as pillars of tenacious black health in a classist and racist America. And as Walter Allen pointed out, in light of their "heroic" contribution to the "health of the black community researchers must ask why . . . so few women fail rather than asking why so few succeed."[17]

Whereas the black woman had once been labeled as a depreciated sex object who had internalized the society's damaging treatment and image of her, she was now seen as enjoying a high self-esteem. In her 1980 study, *Black Women: Do They Cope Better?*, Lena Wright Myers essentially answered, yes. Her findings argued that the old image of black female self-contempt was but another myth. Overall, the revisionist family sociology of the 1970s, together with attention to the facts exposing black matriarchy as a myth, promoted a new vision of Afro-American womanhood that was fully consistent with the new emphasis on the vitality, strength, and health of contemporary Afro-American culture.[18]

Historians, too, reflected and furthered this emphasis on the health of black culture, as they turned to examine the Afro-American family in history. Leading their rediscovery of the culture as healthy and vital was Herbert Gutman. He charged in 1975 that the old emphasis on the black family's ill health was "a tangle of sociological jargon and misused historical evidence."[19]

Gutman strove in particular to demolish the thesis of the black matriarchy as merely one of the "myths about the Afro-American family." The 1965 Moynihan Report was a major catalyst for his important, revisionist study, *The Black Family in Slavery and Freedom, 1750–1925*. Published in 1976, Gutman noted that his book "was stimulated by the bitter public and academic controversy surrounding Daniel P. Moynihan's *The Negro Family in America*." Accordingly, this historian set out to falsify the thesis that "the slave household developed a 'father-less,' matrifocal pattern sufficiently strong to become self-sustaining over time."[20]

Gutman's findings indicated that while the slave family was an extended institution which included a wide range of kind and adopted kin, it was fundamentally structured as a two-parent and male-led institution, and continued as such after slavery's abolition. He charged that E. Franklin Frazier's portrayal of postslavery households as typically comprised of grandmother, daughters, and grandchildren reflected "very inadequate historical evidence." Instead, he argued that the absent-father, maternally organized household remained very rare among both rural and urban blacks until at least the

Depression era. In short, according to Gutman's research, whatever the patterns of modern Afro-American family life, historically this institution had continued the slave's high valuation of "the completed, immediate family." Far from being disorganized and dysfunctional, the stability and strengths of the black family had helped black Americans to survive not only slavery and continued racist oppression, but also the traumas of migration, urbanization, and the dislocations of modernization.[21]

In presenting this striking reinterpretation of black family history, Gutman's book dismissed the old story that emphasized slave sexual promiscuity and moral depravity. In this way, it also comprised a powerful attack on the slave woman's Jezebel image. As Gutman demonstrated, while slave sexual mores did depart from those of the dominant culture, they were not, therefore, "immoral." Instead, they reflected black definitions of moral order which, for example, did not attach a stigma to prenuptial intercourse, but which did often lead to premarital pregnancy being followed by marriage. And marital fidelity was expected by slaves and freedpersons alike. Gutman's findings refuted Frazier's portrayal of "unfettered" motherhood also by showing, for example, that during the closing decades of the nineteenth century, a high percentage of the single black women in Southern cities had no children at all, suggesting that "sexual abstinence, not promiscuity was common."[22]

Gutman's book contained many findings of relevance to black women's history; for example, that slave women widely knew of and practiced abortion techniques and used contraceptive strategies. Yet frequently such important findings were relegated to footnotes by Gutman.[23]

However, Gutman's intention was not to discover the black woman's historical experience. Instead, his focus on falsifying the myth of black matriarchy by discovering evidence that black culture was historically and fundamentally patriarchal pervaded this book. For example, Gutman provided copious evidence of the black man's authoritative role in the family, including a very lengthy section arguing that slave children were commonly named after the father's side of the family.

Gutman's book complemented the new slavery studies, which were restoring the slave community to health, by reshaping slave women into the image of domesticity and deference to male authority and initiatives.[24] The androcentric thrust of these studies was perhaps epitomized by Justin Labinjoh's argument that the slave husband's dominance was demonstrated by the fact that male slave runaways sometimes returned to rescue their wives to freedom. According to Labinjoh, had his wife dominated him, the slave husband would have run away all the faster rather than returning to rescue her.[25] One can only wonder how a Harriet Tubman would fit into such a contention.

In any case, in the post-Moynihan decade American historiography moved toward consensus regarding, in Joan Aldous's words, "the new paradigm that families did exist under slavery." And despite the controversies over Fogel and Engerman's *Time on the Cross*, Aldous noted approvingly in her 1976 review of this book that its "major contribution" was to "legitimize" this paradigm by demonstrating that slave families were "customarily nuclear and not female-centered as the old paradigm held." Moreover, she argued, it "is important that sociologists be made aware of this new paradigm," since they "have often used an incorrect view of the slavery period in their search for an explanation of black families today."[26]

While Aldous was right about American sociology, her comments revealed a leap of faith in believing that now, historians had discovered the truth. In actuality, the historiography presenting this new "paradigm" had undertaken little or no research that revealed the role and perspectives of Afro-American women under slavery. Slavery historiography now seemed dogmatically intent on replacing the image of matriarchy with patriarchy, as if to deny the possibility of cultural diversity at the very time when the new sociology was emphasizing it. In fact, the boundaries of the new antimatriarchy orthodoxy emerged even in Herbert Gutman's revisionist black family history. This seemed to equate matrifocality with matriarchy, and thus to argue that any notion that slave families were often parented by the mother alone was as mistaken as the belief that two-parented families were mother-dominated.

Gutman's book was based largely upon research focused on big plantations with a balanced sex ratio; that is, ones that included about the same number of slave men and women. Theoretically, therefore, any slave could find a spouse on the same plantation. However, Gutman found that on a typical, large Louisiana plantation, almost one-fifth of slave children lived "in households headed by women who had all their children by unnamed fathers." Still, he claimed that this was an atypical phenomenon. Such evidence of matrifocality was presented as merely a "deviation from the community's norm." Moreover, the possibility that these mothers had chosen to remain single was not considered. Instead Gutman simply noted that "it is unclear whether women formed such households by design or default." His book then terminated the discussion, at the very point where his findings began to raise questions about the roles and perceptions of black women themselves.[27]

However, Gutman's interest lay elsewhere, in slaying the myth of the black matriarchy, although by the mid–1970s his focus seemed misplaced to some, who argued that the Moynihan thesis had already been so reduced in credibility that Gutman's book seemed to "overkill" an obviously mistaken interpretation. From this perspective, "what is lacking in Gutman's treatment is an explanation of the durability of the myth of slave matrifocality." In other words, according to new contentions, not only matriarchy but also matrifocality were myths.[28]

Among contemporary family historians, Peter Laslett was virtually alone in questioning the new orthodoxy, which emphasized "stable" two-parent, father-led slave families. He pointed out, for example, that on the smaller plantations and farms—where about half of Southern slaves lived—unbalanced sex ratios frequently led to marriages between persons living on separate properties, and thus led to mother-centered families. As well, his findings argued that a slave mother's children were often conceived by several different fathers, indicating a pattern of serial polyandry in which it was only the mother who provided family continuity. Furthermore, Laslett suggested examining the seemingly shocking possibility that a slave child need not have a socially recognized father at all.[29]

Otherwise, slavery historiography continued mostly to emphasize the black man's paternal authority and manly status in history. Generally, mother-led families and slave women in self-assertive roles had become historically nonexistent. Or, it may be that matrifocality and strong slave women were too akin to the myth of the black matriarchy to be acceptable to contemporary historians. In any case, while contemporary historiography shared the new emphasis on black family strength, its attention to historical diversity did not yet extend to the question of gender and female departures from patriarchally defined femininity. Black women's history therefore continued to remain marginalized in this discourse. During the closing decades of the twentieth century, it has remained largely up to Afro-American women to discover their past for themselves.

NOTES

1. Elmer P. Martin and Joanne Mitchell Martin, *The Black Extended Family* (Chicago: University of Chicago Press, 1978), 108.

2. See, for example, William Ryan, *Blaming the Victim* (New York: Pantheon Books, 1971).

3. M. F. Peters, "The Black Family: Perpetuating the Myths. An Analysis of Family Sociology Textbook Treatment of Black Families," *Family Coordinator* 23 (1974): 349–57; Robert Hill, *The Strength of Black Families* (New York: Emerson Hall Pub., 1972). Studies of black family "pathology" from the mid–1960s to the end of the decade include, for example, K. B. Clark, *Dark Ghetto* (New York: Harper & Row, 1965); Lee Rainwater, "Crucible of Identity: The Negro Lower-Class Family," in T. Parsons and K. B. Clark, eds., *The Negro American* (Boston: Beacon Press, 1965), 160–204; Jessie Bernard, *Marriage and Family Among Negroes* (Englewood Cliffs, N.J.: Prentice-Hall, 1966); H. Rodman, "Family and Social Pathology in the Ghetto," *Science* 161 (1968): 756–62; and David A. Schulz, *Coming Up Black: Patterns of Ghetto Socialization* (Englewood Cliffs, N.J.: Prentice-Hall, 1969).

4. W. Tenhouten, "The Black Family: Myth and Reality," *Psychiatry* 33 (1970): 145–73.

5. John Scanzoni, *The Black Family in Modern Society: Patterns of Stability and Security* (Chicago: University of Chicago Press, 1971); Robert Staples, "The Myth of the Black Matriarchy," *The Black Scholar* 1 (1970): 9–16; Staples, *The Black Family: Essays and Studies* (Belmont, Calif.: Wadsworth, 1971). See also Katheryn Thomas

Dietrick, "A Reexamination of the Myth of Black Matriarchy," *Journal of Marriage and the Family* 37 (1975): 367–74.

6. Andrew Billingsley, *Black Families in White America* (Englewood Cliffs, N.J.: Prentice-Hall, 1968).

7. Marie. F. Peters, "Notes from the Guest Editor," *Journal of Marriage and the Family* 40 (1978): 655. This issue provides an excellent reflection of the new consensus and a bibliography of revisionist sources.

8. Joyce Ladner, *Tomorrow's Tomorrow*, xx.

9. Ibid., 43, 201, 274, 239.

10. Ibid., 35, 239, 280, xxiii.

11. Ibid., 8, 11, 17.

12. Ibid., 280.

13. Ann Chandler Howell, "Review of Ladner's *Tomorrow's Tomorrow: The Black Woman*," *Journal of Marriage and the Family* 34 (1972): 562. See also Joyce Ladner, *The Death of White Sociology* (New York: Vintage Books, 1973), and Ladner, *Tom's Tom* (New York: Doubleday, 1972).

14. Alex Haley, *Roots: The Saga of an American Family* (New York: Doubleday & Co., 1976).

15. Martin and Martin, *The Black Extended Family*, 113, 114.

16. Engram, *Science, Myth, Reality*, xii, 141.

17. These statistics are presented in Harriette Pipes McAdoo, ed., *Black Families* (Beverly Hills, Calif.: Sage Publications, 1981), 107–23; and in Marynick Palmer, "White Women/Black Women," 151–70. Carol Stack, *All Our Kin: Strategies for Survival in a Black Community* (New York: Harper & Row, 1974); Walter R. Allen, "The Social and Economic Statuses of Black Women in the United States," *Phylon* 42 (1981): 40.

18. For example, see Florence B. Bonner, "Black Women and White Women: A Comparative Analysis of Perceptions of Sex Roles for Self, Ideal-Self and the Ideal-Male," in Willa D. Johnson and Thomas L. Green, eds., *Perspectives on Afro-American Women* (Washington, D.C.: ECCA Publications, Inc., 1975), 34–47; and Vernaline Watson, "Self-Concept Formation and the Afro-American Woman," in ibid., 81–91; Lena Wright Myers, *Black Women: Do They Cope Better?* (Englewood Cliffs, N.J.: Prentice-Hall, 1980).

19. The new attention to and wealth of sources in black family history may be found, for example, in the *Journal of Interdisciplinary History* 6 (Autumn 1975), an issue devoted to this new field of scholarly inquiry. Herbert Gutman, "Persistent Myths about the Afro-American Family," in Michael Gordon, ed., *The American Family in Social-Historical Perspective*, 3d edition (New York: St. Martin's Press, 1983; reprinted from *Journal of Marriage and the Family* 6 (1975): 462).

20. Gutman, "Persistent Myths about the Afro-American Family." For his criticism in this article of E. Franklin Frazier's analysis, see esp. 459–62. Gutman, *The Black Family*, xvii.

21. Gutman, *The Black Family*, 433, 444.

22. Ibid., 636.

23. Ibid., 81–82.

24. See, for example, Eugene Genovese, "The Slave Family, Women—A Reassessment of Matriarchy, Emasculation, Weakness," *Southern Voices* 2 (1974): 9–16.

25. Justin Labinjoh, "The Sexual Life of the Oppressed: An Examination of the Family Life of Ante-Bellum Slaves," *Phylon* 35 (1974): 375–91.

26. Joan Aldous, "Review of *Time on the Cross: The Economics of American Slavery*," in *Journal of Marriage and the Family* 38 (1976): 190.

27. Gutman, *The Black Family*, 115, 116, 117.

28. Vernon Burton and Joseph L. Love, "Review of *The Black Family in Slavery and Freedom, 1750–1925*," *Journal of Social History* 11 (1978): 432.

29. Peter Laslett, "Household and Family on the Slave Plantations of the United States," in Peter Laslett, *Family Life and Illicit Love in Earlier Generations: Essays in Historical Sociology* (Cambridge: Cambridge University Press, 1977), 233–60.

10

Toward Discovering Slave Women

To discover how Afro-American women have figured in the literature of fact is to confirm that on the printed page, black Americans have long been equated with slaves. However, the slave-women cast of this history has not consisted merely of female versions of Sambo, or Uncle Tom and his kin. The women have been linked to male figures in significant ways. Yet, the women have been distinguished from their male counterparts, in particular by being integrally associated with motherhood and with a peculiar power or strength.

These attributes have largely been shown in an overwhelmingly negative light, with the exception of Mammy, who was seen as devoting her strength to the service of whites. Otherwise, the black woman's historical power has, in image, promoted the downfall of both black and white men, and ruined her offspring and people generally. Her slave-woman image has displaced the slave man as father and confirmed the emasculation of Sambo. It has functioned to confirm and perpetuate the identification of blacks as a people characterized by female dominance and male weakness—as the "feminine" race. Her image has served to endorse the equation of black inequality with "Negro pathology," reflecting a black sexual environment that turned the rightful order of things upside down.

In turn, the pathology thesis has presented Negro moral reform—the establishment of the rightful order of the sexes—as essential to racial progress. Exonerating the present from blame and responsibility for overturning racial inequality, a vast body of scholarly literature has pointed to Afro-American "cultural inferiority" as the legacy of history. Thus, the persistent "failure" of black Americans has been presented as inherently resistant to change, and as unlikely to be changed except by restoration of patriarchy to the black home.

While irrational on the level of reason, the web of images pervading this discourse has been characterized by an odd coherence on the level of racial and sexual mythology. To trace its embeddedness in the literature of fact in the age of Jim Crow is to arrive at the image of Black Matriarchy not with surprise but with a sense of recognition and déjà vu.

This composite image and its incorporation into a story of damaging womanhood has not gone without opposition. But early black historiography largely countered it with images of damaged slave femininity. Thus, even this oppositional discourse has inadvertently fleshed out the figure of a flawed, defeminized womanhood which has supported the Black Matriarchy mythology of a woman both damaging and unwomanly.

It is not surprising that as Afro-American history came of age in the civil rights era with its emphasis on discovering a past worthy of Afro-American pride, it discovered manly slave men and womanly slave women. It is only surprising that in the new slavery studies midwifed by the radical 1960s, female slaves were reshaped so compellingly into the traditional image of true womanhood that their own perspectives and experience of history remained obscure. But given the contemporary zeal to slay Mr. Sambo and Mrs. Matriarch, Afro-American women figured as more marginalized in history than ever. With the new black family studies' emphasis on the strengths of cultural diversity, the slave family was restored to health. But it was restored in a patriarchal light that left slave women invisible as diverse and fully human historical personages. And functioning more as rivals than as allies, initially the black movement and the women's movement did not encourage attention to Afro-American women.

Nonetheless, the consciousness-raising effects of these movements eventually did in combination promote the growth of black women's studies. This was a development charged with political and cultural significance. As Barbara Smith and Gloria Hull have pointed out, for a group so long named by others and so typified by the image of mindlessness, even to name its independent, intellectual endeavor as "Black women's studies" has been to proclaim that these women "exist—and exist positively—a stance that is in direct opposition to . . . culture and thought on the North American continent." In the words of these authors, "like any politically disenfranchised group, Black women could not exist consciously until we began to name ourselves."[1]

Indeed, by the 1980s, Afro-American women were turning to name themselves in the past as well as the present. Outside of the mainstream, but steadily, by the 1980s black women's history was becoming less a subfield of black or women's studies, than a separate field and scholarly discipline in its own right.

The reconstruction of black women's history has been and continues to be a feminist endeavor. As Elizabeth Fox-Genovese has pointed out, "adding women to history is not the same as adding women's history."[2] Feminist perspectives point to the necessity of not merely adding woman's "contribution" to a history in which what is noteworthy continues to be defined by male-centered definitions of significance. The new black women's history furthers the endeavor instead, to bring full attention to female perspectives, and therefore to place women's history *in* history.

The new history also reflects and forwards black feminist perspectives in the sense in which these have been described by Beverly Guy-Sheftall, as "a sensitivity to the peculiar conditions under which black women live because of the damaging effects of racial, sexual, and class oppression."[3] However, as we shall see, black women's history constitutes no threat to black history or women's history. Quite the contrary, it richly reveals new dimensions of both.

The development of black women's history has been inspired by the impulse to rectify the exclusion of these women from the story of the past. As Ruth Bogin and Bert James Loewenberg observed in 1976, "not only do black women seldom appear in treatments of black history, but historians have been content to permit the male to represent the female in almost every significant category." And in the words of Paula Giddings, "we have been perceived as token women in Black texts and as token Blacks in feminist ones." Hence, the new black women's historiography demonstrates a strong sense of "a mission to tell a story largely untold."[4]

Yet the questions and subtext of this historiography had also been shaped by the fact that the story has been too largely told, or rather "mistold" by decades of American scholarship. Despite the lack of specific attention to how black women's history has figured in historiography, it has by no means gone without recognition that Afro-American women have been preassigned a prefabricated story. As La Frances Rodgers-Rose pointed out, the sociological story casting them as "matriarchal, domineering . . . superstrong" made it difficult to "hold on to the reality of black women's history in America." But this has also, as she and others have recognized, made it all the more crucial to do so. To reconstruct black women's history correctly has been all the more essential in order to, in the words of Frances Smith Foster, "obliterate the sense of inferiority foisted upon Black women through a 400-year American defamation campaign."[5]

The dual sense of a story simultaneously not told and "mistold" has been a major catalyst and shaping force of the new black women's historiography, providing compelling reasons both to discover the facts, and also to interpret them in ways that challenge the old myths.

Today's black women's historiography moves far beyond slavery. But the reconstruction of the story of slave women and their legacy remains central to its endeavor. Indeed, for Afro-American women, slavery history remains all too relevant. It is this that constituted the beginning of the black woman's experience in America. And it is this that has provided the foundations for the prefabricated and damaging history so long assigned to Afro-American women. Moreover, slavery is for many women as close as yesterday. La Frances Rodgers-Rose reminds us that "slavery only ended in 1863—my great grandmother was born a slave."[6]

The reinterpretation by such women of old facts, and their discovery of new ones, has already shaped a transfigured vision of the slave woman, and thereby constructed rich new foundations for the reconstruction of black women's history long after slavery. It is now time to examine what has been discovered, and perhaps also to point to some of the questions that still remain to be asked.

In the emerging reconstruction of the history of the American slave woman, Africanity has been a pervasive theme, suggesting that it is necessary to begin her story in Africa itself. This has meant rejecting Stanley Elkins's argument that the African cultural heritage could not survive the traumatic experience of the transatlantic Middle Passage, let alone American slavery. Instead, as Deborah White has argued, "both sexes did not travel the passage the same way." While vulnerable to sexual attack by sailors, the African woman was usually left unshackled on the quarter deck, while the men were chained and packed en masse into the suffocating conditions of ship holds.[7]

It is clear that African men substantially outnumbered women on the Middle Passage. According to Herbert Klein, this pattern resulted from the home society's high valuation of its women, who were of vital importance in West African societies, not least as slaves. As *Women and Slavery in Africa*, edited by Claire Robertson and Martin Klein, has shown, women had frequently been slaves in Africa. Thus, the Middle Passage predominance of male "cargo' may well reflect, as Klein has suggested, "that the role of women in the economy and society gave them a higher value, especially as slaves, than men."[8] The new black women's historiography has generally not investigated the slave-woman role of women in Africa itself. Instead, it has emphasized the authority of women in African societies.[9]

Historians like La Frances Rodgers-Rose have emphasized that women played central socioeconomic and cultural roles in the West African societies from which most American slaves were drawn. It was largely women who cultivated the crops and were instrumental in the marketplace as traders; they controlled such industries as the production and selling of pottery and cloth. Their domestic labor for the family unit was equally important. But in cultures that valued the well-being and survival of children above all else, motherhood was the most important of roles. That women and children often lived together in separate quarters also made the mother-child bond the closest of African relationships. Assuring the future of the tribe as mothers, women linked past and present, joining the tribe to the ancestors, and so played an important role in African religions and rituals.

As well, according to Rodgers-Rose, living and working so closely together, African women gained from each other a sense of mutual support, self-reliance, and self-esteem. Relationships with men were less central to the African woman's self-identity and self-valuation than in Western societies, and marital relationships were more egalitarian. In this context, the African woman was primarily devoted to the well-being of her family as an extended kinship group.[10]

This, in outline, is the portrayal of African women that has emerged in the new black women's history. While some might see this as a romanticized portrait, it does seriously challenge the old image of the African woman as a degraded and depreciated sexual slave. Black women's historians have argued that she carried this positive cultural heritage to America, since in Rodgers-Rose's words, "once individuals have been socialized, their basic personalities are established." Therefore, "to fully understand the Black woman during slavery and even certain behavioral aspects of the Black woman today, we need to know about her female African forbears."[11]

It is not suggested by recent studies that her African heritage readily and fully survived the influence of the American South's "peculiar institution." Nonetheless, several studies point to the persistence of African traditions and values. As Jacqueline Jones has argued, for example, Afro-American slaves continued the African valuation of "women's work" which contrasted with its devaluation in Western culture. And she argues that the enslaved "created—or preserved—an explicit sexual division of labor based on their own preferences."[12]

Jones has also argued that while their lessening productivity devalued older slave women for their masters, their aging only enhanced their status among the enslaved, who continued the African tradition of reverence for elders. In such authoritative roles as conjurer, healer, and midwife, these respected female elders passed on the old wisdom and skills. Serving "as a tangible link with the African past," the grandmothers "preserved the past for future generations of Afro-American women." "Combining an African heritage with American exigencies," the high valuation of family, motherhood, and kinship and community ties remained central to American slave culture.[13]

Recent studies argue that the exigencies of American slavery in some ways worked more to reinforce than to destroy the African heritage, so that motherhood remained, in Deborah White's words, "the black girl's most important rite of passage, and mothers were still the most central figures in the black family." Because of the larger numbers of African men than women carried to America, in the colonial era the unbalanced sex ratio of blacks meant that slave spouses often necessarily lived on separate farms. Thus, as White has pointed out, sex-segregated living and child-rearing arrangements actually preserved African customs and the importance of motherhood.[14]

On the other hand, some have pointed to early conditions more favorable to the development of two-parent slave families. Before the invention of the cotton gin and the rise of "King Cotton," slavery in the South underwent little expansion and the internal slave trade remained small-scale. Mary Beth Norton has noted that colonial slave families were not broken up on the scale that they would be in the nineteenth century. In her view, "at least from the standpoint of their female members, enslaved families could well have been more geographically stable than those of free white people." Moreover, upon marriage the colonial-era black woman did not, like the white woman, leave the place where she had been raised to live with her spouse. That she was tied as a slave to the home plantation meant that, unlike her white counterpart, she continued to live close to her kin, and this "gave slave marriages a kind of familial insurance against catastrophe."[15]

Norton's work has also emphasized the essentially similar experience of early American white and black women. According to her, the "common experiences of femininity made women in many ways more alike than different." However, Norton's *Liberty's Daughters: The Revolutionary Experience of American Women, 1750–1800* may also reveal the pitfalls of an emphasis on similarities.[16]

Despite Norton's intent to "include both blacks and whites," when her book turned to examine the new patterns of women's lives that appeared in the revolutionary and postrevolutionary eras, black women became all but invisible in her text. As Norton has observed, changing "American notions of womanhood" came both to elevate and restrict "femininity" to woman's domestic and maternal role. But the evolution of the nineteenth-century cult of true womanhood de facto excluded slave womanhood. Whatever revolutionary changes the American Revolution ushered in for Afro-American women did not emerge in Norton's book.[17]

The Revolution was associated with the abolition of slavery in the new American nation's northern states. Nevertheless as Debra Newman's article, "Black Women in the Era of the American Revolution in Pennsylvania," suggests, it is likely that emancipation did not lead to major change in the experience of northern black women. Certainly it brought little freedom from the menial domestic labor and unequal status assigned to them. In short, while the American Revolution may be significant in the periodization of white women's history, it may be a much less significant event in the context of black women's history.[18]

Just as the periodization of women's history must often be differently defined than in traditional history, so also the history of black women must find its own distinct periodization, in accordance with the major events and forces that shaped it. These likely include abolition of the slave trade to Africa in 1808 and the rise of King Cotton and expansion of slavery into the Southwest. These developments promoted the growth of the Old South's internal slave trade, and had an impact upon the experience of slave women in significant ways, increasing the rate of black family separation by selling family members, and also increasing the master's valuation of the slave woman's reproductive potential.

At the same time, white fears for the security of slavery, increased by the Nat Turner slave rebellion of 1831 and by the rise of Northern abolitionism, also promoted a rigidification of the South's "peculiar institution" during the antebellum decades. In this context, the Old South's self-romanticization promoted the ideology of slavery as a paternalistic, extended, white-black familial institution. But the lives of the enslaved became subject to more scrutiny and regimentation than ever. Blacks became more firmly defined as natural and perpetual slaves. Thus, according to Paula Giddings, "although the slaves may have been physically better off than before, the psychological effects of the new slavery were potentially devastating."[19]

Giddings has argued that in the Old South the Victorian family ideal prescribed the roles of women ever more rigidly, with the white woman's obedience to the family patriarch reinforced by consigning black women "to the other end of the scale, as mistresses, whores or breeders." Thus, at a time when overt rebellion against slavery was less feasible than ever, according to Giddings the slave women's resistance became "more covert or internalized . . . spurning their morally inferior roles of mistress, whore, and breeder—though under the 'new' slavery they were 'rewarded' for acquiescing in them." In her view, their resistance was "fundamentally feminist" because by rejecting these "rewards," they were basically rejecting the notion that they were the property of men.[20]

The slave woman's resistance to slavery has been a major theme of black women's history since it was first introduced by Angela Davis's 1971 essay, "Reflections on the Black Woman's Role in the Community of Slaves." Written while Davis was in prison, this pioneering article was not based upon primary sources. Nonetheless, it showed how the story of slavery could be reinterpreted to discover slave women as no less heroic than slave men, when heroism was redefined from female perspectives. While Davis adamantly rejected the myth of the black matriarchy, she also rejected the alternative vision in which the slave woman "played no significant role" in the slave community.[21]

Davis argued that, forced to work as the equal of her man in the fields, the slave woman was all the more aware of their shared oppression and all the more a resister of it. But she expressed her resistance distinctively, as a woman, pointing the way to what Davis's later essay, "The Legacy of Slavery," called "standards for a new womanhood." In particular, the "woman's work" she performed for her own family was her act of defiance and self-affirmation against the prescribed "men's work" she performed in the fields for her master. The slave home became "a house of resistance," because as mother she was uniquely capable of embedding the combative ethos into the family by her socialization of her children.[22]

In the early 1970s Davis was also early to draw attention to the politics of sexual abuse. Rape was white terrorism directed against the slave woman, and exploitation of her sexuality was a political act against the black man. Davis emphasized as well in her later writings that when white men had unlimited power to use the bodies of black women, "there could hardly be a basis for 'delight, affection and love.' " But no passive victim in Davis's story, the slave woman fought back—in particular as the "custodian" of the black home. Thus Davis urged modern black women not to be misled by fear of the matriarchy mythology into abandoning their tradition of "heroic resistance" to oppression. [23]

Similarly, the slave woman has emerged in a heroic light in numerous studies. Some have reconstructed her as an overt rebel. According to Mary Ellison, for example, slave women "fought unremittingly" and constituted "an army of resistance." [24] On the other hand, others have explored the distinct and subtle ways in which slave women resisted oppression in accordance with the particular weapons available to them as women.

As Deborah White has pointed out, bondswomen often resisted slavery in quite different ways than slave men. They were less likely to become slave runaways, because pregnancy and their responsibility for the care of children undermined their ability and will to escape. Of those who did run away, many did so when they had reason to expect to be separated from their children by sale. They were more apt to oppose the system, for example, by feigning illness, a strategy that played to the master's concern for their reproductive health. [25]

It is often pointed out, too, that the slave woman's resistance strategies reflected that she was differently oppressed than the slave man. She was doubly oppressed in that both her productive and reproductive capacities were used and abused. Because these two areas of exploitation were the twin pillars of slavery, her resistance to the one was resistance to the other as well. For example, according to Darlene Hine, in response to forced miscegenation and her assigned brood-mare role, female resistance tactics included abortion, and in some cases, infanticide. Hine has argued that the slave woman thereby "negated through individual or group action her role in the maintenance of the slave pool," and challenged the slaveocracy's worldview by rejecting her prescribed roles. In Hine's view these strategies reflected her "awareness of the sexual/economic nexus inherent in her dual role in the slave system." She therefore shaped her resistance "consciously and with full awareness of the potential political and economic ramifications involved." [26]

Not all would attribute to the slave woman such an advanced state of political consciousness. But the strength and ingenuity of her resistance to slavery testifies on its own behalf in the new historiography, falsifying her old image as collaborator with white oppression in or outside of the white man's bed and kitchen. However, not everyone would agree that her resistance was "feminist." Instead, some writers argue that the family-centered slave community was the dominant force in her life, and this, in effect, made her nonfeminist. Or so Jean Friedman's findings suggest.

Friedman has argued that the same emphasis on family ties was shared by all Southern women, white and black, undermining the recognition by both of the oppression of women. Because slavery functioned to emphasize the mother's reliance on kin, and also to force the bondswomen to work in the same roles and closely with men, slave women related to one another largely as family members. For black as for white Southern women, the values and discipline of the evangelical, family-oriented church, together with the kinship-centered community, promoted sex integration rather than sex segregation. Maintaining the regular and traditional interaction of women and men rather than promoting woman-to-woman relationships, Old South society worked against the formation of a distinct woman's consciousness and culture. In this way, Friedman's findings argue that Southern women of both races remained nonfeminist.[27]

Without doubt recent studies confirm that black and white women did not relate to each other as "suffering sisters." But Elizabeth Fox-Genovese has gone further than most in suggesting that the plantation mistress had little to suffer. This historian has combated the portraiture of the "lady" as suffering the double burden of patriarchy and slavery, forced not only to endure the master's oppressive rule but also the arduous responsibilities of managing and dealing with slaves. Instead, Fox-Genovese has pointed to the forced labor of the enslaved, which propped up the lady's leisured and advantaged life and promoted her vested interest in slavery. As this historian has argued, contrary to the paternalistic mythology, which cast the plantation mistress as the good mother and protector of the enslaved, these women were quite ready to resort to brutality, and were "more crudely racist than their men." In short, these white women were by no means "slaves of slaves. . . . They lived—and knew they lived—as privileged members of a ruling class." Fox-Genovese has emphasized the realities of power as profoundly dividing white and black women. Others have come to the same conclusions.[28]

Briefly, while Ann Scott's pioneering 1970 study, *The Southern Lady*,[29] verged upon portraying Southern white women as closet abolitionists and feminists, it has become increasingly clear that the black woman was without white female allies. Instead, some recent studies emphasize that slave women and men worked closely together to defend and protect each other. For example, Jacqueline Jones has argued that they fought the master's unisexual assignment of work roles and blurring of black gender identity by maintaining the African-rooted sexual division of labor in the slave quarters. This assigned "women's work" to women, while "at home men and women worked together to support the father's role as provider and protector." Thus, in Jones's view, it was the "father-mother, husband-wife nexus" that reflected and shaped slave perceptions about "what men and women should be and do."

It was in this context that the enslaved could best provide for one another, in opposition to white control of their lives.[30]

Jones's discussion of the aftermath of slavery helps to advance this thesis. As was presented by postbellum white Southerners as evidence of the Negro's refusal to work unless forced, the freedwomen initially left the fields and retreated en masse to the home—until necessity forced them back to field work and domestic service to whites. Jones has supported today's reinterpretation of this withdrawal as, in effect, a black strike against white control. But her findings argue further that the freedwomen were by no means forced back into the home by the freedman's attempt to assert male dominance. Instead they went home because of their shared opposition to demands that they continue to work for the white man and in the white family's kitchen. They thereby continued to express the preference of the enslaved that women be "wives and mothers first" as a manifestation of the struggle for black autonomy. In short, for the ex-slave woman, domesticity was by no means equated with a diminishment of status and self-esteem. By her own definition, freedom did not mean

individual opportunity or independence in the modern sense. Rather, freedom had meaning primarily in a family context. . . . Freedwomen derived . . . a newfound sense of pride from their roles as wives and mothers. Only at home could they exercise considerable control over their own lives.[31]

To summarize, Jones has reinterpreted slavery's legacy as promoting the postslavery black woman's prideful identity and love of family. And this historian's empowering vision of the feminine strength and continuity of the black woman's struggle is best conveyed by the title of her book's discussion of slave women, "My Mother Was Much of a Woman."[32]

New directions for rediscovering the slavery roots of Afro-American women's history may be found equally in other texts, especially Deborah White's *Ar'n't I a Woman? Female Slaves in the Ante-Bellum South*. White's research has begun from the reasonable but often overlooked premise that the slave woman's perspectives, role, and status may best be ascertained by examining what she actually did. She did perform largely the same agricultural work as slave men. White's findings argue that her productive equality, the importance in the black community of her maternal role and "woman's work" in the home, and her authoritative roles in slave religion and as midwife and slave doctor advanced a striking egalitarianism in the slave quarters, and promoted high self-esteem among slave women.[33]

As well, the continued practice of "marrying abroad," that is, of having spouses on different units, and of mothers raising offspring in matrifocal units, has been particularly emphasized by White. In contrast to Friedman, White has argued that these patterns emphasized the importance of woman-to-woman relationships, as did the frequency and closeness with which slave women worked together in domestic tasks ranging from washing to sewing.

Drawing upon anthropological theory, White argues that under such conditions women rank and identify themselves primarily vis-à-vis other women, and make their decisions and choices on the basis of female group mores. Hence, she has emphasized the development among slave women of a distinct consciousness of collective, female self-reliance, and a sure sense of identity as feminine. According to this historian, slave women "developed their own female culture, that is, a way of assigning value that flowed from the perspective they had on Southern plantation life."[34]

Challenging the perspective that rescued black femininity by rendering it subordinate to black masculinity, White has emphasized the bonds of womanhood and a strong consciousness of female strength as central to the black woman's survival of slavery as woman. Her findings have persuasively argued that to restore Afro-American culture to good health, it is not necessary to restore it historically to patriarchy. White's analysis shows that such discoveries are possible when the presuppositions under attack are not approached from points of view that equate female strength with male weakness. Instead, historians such as White and Suzanne Lebsock have explicitly challenged that paradigm.

As Lebsock has observed, because of the sensitivity of American culture to any appearance of reduced male power, Afro-American women have been mislabeled as matriarchs no matter how disadvantaged and powerless they are. The stigma of pathology has been attached to households in which black women have raised children without spousal assistance. And Lebsock has charged that American historians have largely reflected and endorsed this prejudice against matrifocal families. She has also observed that historians have followed "a dangerous line of defense" in rescuing the black family to health by casting it as a traditional, two-parent institution.[35]

In her 1984 book, *The Free Women of Petersburg*, Lebsock has pointed to extensive patterns of matrifocality among free black women of the Old South. In Petersburg, Virginia, the majority of free black households were female-headed, while the same pattern has also been discovered in other antebellum Southern towns and cities. In part, it was unbalanced black sex ratios in urban communities that forced these women to raise their families without spouses. But in part, according to Lebsock, they remained single as a matter of choice.

They had good reason not to relinquish their often recently gained freedom from slavery by handing it and their earnings over to a husband. As Lebsock has found, over half of them, in comparison with under ten percent of white women, were gainfully employed, although largely in low-paid, low-status jobs in the tobacco factories or as washerwomen for whites. However, self-supporting and self-reliant, they found acceptance and status within the black community as single mothers, and exercised power—albeit over small stakes.

Struggling against impoverishment and racial discrimination, they were by no means matriarchs. At the same time, they by no means adopted patriarchal values and norms. Instead, they found and valued their separate identity and self-sufficiency as women.

Lebsock's findings regarding free black women and those of Deborah White regarding slave women are complementary. Their research argues that it is a major mistake to ignore matrifocality as a prevalent historical family type among black Americans, or to assume that it is identifiable as pathological. As these historians point out, matrifocality has for too long been confused with matriarchy, and assumed to mean the rule of men by women. White has encouraged recognition that it merely means that in their maternal role, black women have historically been the focal point of family relationships, continuity, and survival.[36]

In sum, the new black women's historiography reflects and encourages strong revisionist perspectives. It reveals new dimensions of the past in a far richer way than this book can encompass or convey. The wealth of recent studies can merely be touched on. This summary cannot begin to point to today's explorations of black women's history long after slavery's abolition. However, my purpose is to emphasize that slave women are finally emerging in American history as women who played a full role in the struggle of the enslaved to shape their own identities and destinies.

It finally is no longer necessary to reshape Afro-American women into the old image of true womanhood in order to falsify the old images of Jezebels, matriarchs, and all their assorted kin. Instead, today's ongoing discovery of American slave women argues that it was they, in Angela Davis's words, "who passed on to their nominally free female descendants a legacy of hard work, perseverance and self-reliance, a legacy of tenacity, resistance and insistence on sexual equality—in short, a legacy spelling out standards for a new womanhood."[37]

While such women may be interpreted as nonfeminist, it can no longer be assumed that they were already too empowered and free to need liberation. Rather, theirs was a strength that struggled for expression against great odds. Perhaps the labels of feminism become irrelevant in this context.

Undoubtedly, the new historiography points increasingly to the futility of such labels, at the same time as it slays the old myths of sexism-racism. Liberating Afro-American women from their "hell of a history," it also reveals new dimensions of both women's history and Afro-American history. It confirms that, as Gerda Lerner has pointed out, "enslavement has meant something different for men and women." And, perhaps as Michael Mullin has suggested, new directions toward the discovery of black history may best be found by considering the possibility that "gender differences may count most."[38]

Reconstruction of the black woman's experience of slavery is by no means complete. Because history is a continuing dialogue between generations, it probably never will be. Nonetheless, it seems likely that in this field women will continue to name themselves in a way that denies neither their oppression nor the strength of their struggle against it, but that does deny the dehumanizing images that have cast the Afro-American woman as deserving of her oppression because she is flawed and not womanly.

It is clear that given her history in American scholarship, the Afro-American woman has come a long way, and against great odds, toward defining her own identity. The myth-making role of late nineteenth-century American scholarship was finally directly confronted a century later by this revisionist history which, by its very writing, has falsified the Afro-American woman's preassigned past. The old myths have been slain most definitively by turning them inside out, rendering them more empowering than disempowering: discovering the black woman's historical strength as rooted in the bonds of womanhood; the slave woman's performance of "man's work" and use as a sexual animal as forwarding her commitment to resisting oppression as a woman; her forced procreation as only forwarding her self-esteem as a mother; her self-assertion as an asset to her people; and her power as residing in her courage.

Unmistakably, the timeworn mythology of a slave-rooted, damaged and damaging black womanhood by no means reflects the history of Afro-American women. However, it does reveal how the Old South alleviated its anxieties about recognizing slaves as women. It does illuminate how a patriarchal and white-supremacist society has long continued to justify and control its fears of those who challenge the dominant definitions of order. In the history it has assigned to Afro-American women, American scholarship has been a telling mirror of this culture, and of both change and continuity over time in America's sexual and racial values.

NOTES

1. Hull, Scott, and Smith, *All the Women Are White*, xvii.

2. Elizabeth Fox-Genovese, "Placing Women's History in History," *New Left Review*, no. 133 (1982): 6.

3. Beverly Guy-Sheftall, "Review of *All the Women Are White, All the Blacks Are Men, But Some of Us Are Brave*," *Journal of Negro History* 57 (1982): 271.

4. Ruth Bogin and Bert James Loewenberg, eds., *Black Women in Nineteenth-Century American Life: Their Words, Their Thoughts, Their Feelings* (University Park and London: Pennsylvania State University, 1981; orig. pub. 1976), 4; Giddings, *When and Where I Enter*, 5.

5. La Frances Rodgers-Rose, ed., *The Black Woman* (Beverly Hills, Calif.: Sage Publications, 1980), 10, 11, 12; Frances Smith Foster, "Changing Concepts of the Black Woman," *Journal of Black Studies* 3 (1973): 449.

6. Rodgers-Rose, *Black Woman*, 16.

7. White, *Ar'n't I a Woman?*, 19, 63–64.

8. Claire C. Robertson and Martin A. Klein, eds., *Women and Slavery in Africa* (Madison: University of Wisconsin Press, 1983), 36.

9. See, for example, Jean Noble, "What Is Africa to Me," in Jean Noble, *Beautiful Also are the Souls of My Black Sisters* (Englewood Cliffs, N.J.: Prentice-Hall, 1978), 3–36.

10. Rodgers-Rose, *Black Woman*, 15–17.

11. Ibid., 16, 15.

12. Jacqueline Jones, *Labor of Love, Labor of Sorrow: Black Women, Work, and the Family from Slavery to the Present* (New York: Basic Books, 1985), 41.

13. Ibid., 40, 41, 43.

14. White, *Ar'n't I a Woman?*, 107, 108.

15. Mary Beth Norton, *Liberty's Daughters: The Revolutionary Experience of American Women, 1750–1800* (Boston: Little, Brown & Co., 1980), 66, 67.

16. Norton, *Liberty's Daughters*, xvi.

17. Ibid., xiii, 296.

18. Debra Newman, "Black Women in the Era of the American Revolution in Pennsylvania," *Journal of Negro History* 6 (1976): 276–89.

19. Giddings, *When and Where I Enter*, 42.

20. Ibid., 43.

21. Angela Davis, "Reflections on the Black Woman's Role in the Community of Slaves," *The Black Scholar* 3 (1971): 5.

22. Ibid., 8; see also Davis, "The Legacy of Slavery: Standards for a New Womanhood," in Angela Davis, *Women, Race and Class* (New York: Vintage Books/Random House, 1983; orig. pub. 1981).

23. Davis, "The Legacy of Slavery," 26; "Reflections on the Black Woman's Role," 15.

24. Mary Ellison, "Resistance to Oppression: Black Women's Response to Slavery in the United States," *Slavery and Abolition* 4 (1983): 56,61.

25. White, *Ar'n't I a Woman?*, esp. 70–79.

26. Darlene Hine, "Female Slave Resistance: The Economics of Sex," *The Western Journal of Black Studies* 3 (1979): 126, 127.

27. Jean Friedman, *The Enclosed Garden: Women and Community in the Evangelical South, 1830–1900* (Chapel Hill: University of North Carolina Press, 1985), esp. 68, 79, 80, 83.

28. Fox-Genovese, *Within the Plantation Household*, 47–48, 35, 145. Similar findings are presented in Suzanne Lebsock, *The Free Women of Petersburg: Status and Culture in a Southern Town, 1784–1860* (New York: W. W. Norton & Co., 1984).

29. Ann Scott, *The Southern Lady: From Pedestal to Politics, 1830–1930* (Chicago: University Press, 1970).

30. Jones, *Labor of Love*, 36, 41, 32.

31. Jones, *Labor of Love*, 58.

32. Ibid., 13.

33. Deborah White, *Ar'n't I a Woman?*; see also White, "Female Slaves: Sex Roles and Status in the Antebellum Plantation South," *Journal of Family History* 8 (1983): 248–61.

34. White, *Ar'n't I a Woman?*, 121.

35. Lebsock, *The Free Women of Petersburg*, 89. See also George Blackburn and

Sherman Recards, "The Mother-Headed Family among Free Negroes in Charleston, South Carolina, 1850–1860," *Phylon* 42 (1981): 11–19.

36. White, "Female Slaves," 256; *Ar'n't I Woman*, 106–8. See also, for earlier attention to slave matrifocality, Loren Schweninger, "A Slave Family in the Ante Bellum South," *Journal of Negro History* 60 (1975): 29–44.

37. Davis, "Standards for a New Womanhood," 29.

38. Gerda Lerner, "Women and Slavery," *Slavery and Abolition* 4 (1983): 184; Michael Mullin, "Women and the Comparative Study of American Negro Slavery," *Slavery and Abolition* 6 (1985): 38.

Conclusion

To explore how Afro-American women have figured in a century of American historiography is largely to discover a history of disfigured images. While these may be interpreted in various ways, it is clear that they remain just that—images—not facts. Because until recently the realities of the black woman's past have inspired little if any attention, her history remained a void in which anything and everything could be written. But much of what has been written has frozen this woman in time, as a perpetual slave woman.

Just as the female slave was so vulnerable to use and abuse, so also black women's history has been vulnerable to much use and abuse. In effect, it has been shaped in the image of Jezebel who deserved what she got because she was other than womanly. And the image of black womanhood as other than womanly has served to confirm black manhood as other than manly, and thus to confirm that the Negro was other and less than fully deserving of racial equality.

The spinning together of sexual and racial identity has deeply pervaded the thesis of black cultural inferiority, perpetuating the equation of racial and sexual relations as analogues. Fed by the snowball effect of American scholarship and the mingling and mixing of history and sociology, this persistent arguing by analogy long continued to circle back to the old vision of the Negro as the feminine race. In oppositional discourse this had been rendered as a positive image—as a metaphor symbolizing the redeeming qualities salvaged from a legacy of suffering. However, during the age of Jim Crow this was recast into the vision of pervasive Negro pathology and cultural ill health as the lasting, crippling legacy of slavery. Well into contemporary times, this literature of fact signified its endorsement of this vision by reiterating the black matriarchy as the controlling metaphor of this crushing legacy.

The crushed-people portrayal was finally contradicted and challenged by the post–World War II Negro revolution. During the radical 1960s, historians turned to revise the past dramatically by reconstructing a healthy, manly, black historical identity. But their radicalism did not go far enough to acknowledge the presence of women and female diversity in that revised past. The very zeal to slay the myth of the Black Matriarchy left the realities of slave women fundamentally undiscoverable, unless they conformed to the new paradigm casting Afro-American cultural health in terms of male historical agency and paternal authority.

In sum, in almost a century of American historiography the Afro-American woman largely emerged in image only, and in representations revealing much about what, from patriarchal perspectives, women ought to be and ought not to be. And her image has been serviceable not only to supporters of white supremacy, as a prop of racial inequality, but also in the battle against racism. The latter has by no means escaped the timeworn practice of using patriarchal images of womanhood to forward racial arguments and causes.

The result for Afro-American women is that they have long continued to be portrayed from the outside, with little attention to their inner lives and perceptions. The shaping of the black woman's story has revealed much more about the pictures in the minds of its shapers than about the diversity and complexity of her realities. Until recently, this story has circled perpetually back to the old slave-woman image, cast in Alice Walker's words, as "the 'mule' of the world . . . handed the burdens that everyone else . . . refused to carry."[1]

Ironically, as "mule" the Afro-American woman has been in her image an Eve-like figure, assigned responsibility for the sins of whites and blacks alike. This includes the Mammy, updated into the domineering matriarch who is assigned responsibility for the persistence of black pathology and racial inequality. As Barbara Christian has pointed out, such female stock characters actually reveal much about the society's "definition of woman." The slave woman constituted a contradiction to patriarchal definitions in her performance of man's work and exclusion from female "purity." Moreover, as Christian has argued, she was threatening to male-defined order because she represented the areas—"sexual, maternal, and emotional—in which women naturally could exhibit power." To label her, in effect, as a non-woman was to preserve the society's desired image of woman.[2]

American historiography has long perpetuated this slavewoman image of the Afro-American woman as less than a woman. This image was not definitively challenged until women, and especially Afro-American women, turned to discover their history and to define the meaning of womanhood for themselves. In this context, it has become increasingly possible to discover slave women as diverse human beings of the past. Yet it should also be noted that the new historiography has yet to free itself entirely from the myths of the past. Indeed, the very myths which are now under attack continue to shape what is discovered or discoverable, when no one would wish in any way to appear to confirm the now unacceptable images. Black women's historians have not been entirely able as yet to heed Alice Walker's advice "not to be tricked, seduced, or goaded into verifying by imitation or even rebuttal, other people's fantasies."[3]

Mammy may epitomize the result of the new historiography, as a slave woman character who has finally been so deleted from the pages of history that her very existence is now dismissed as a fiction and fallacy. As Afro-American history came of age, it relegated her to the historical dustbin, as an Uncle Tom figure who collaborated with the enemy and contradicted the emphasis upon collective black resistance to racist oppression. In imagery, the Mammy has been a woman too strong to confirm black masculinity. Yet the new black women's historiography has also stigmatized and avoided this figure, because she personified not only the ideal slave, but also, in Deborah White's words, "the ideal woman, Mammy was an ideal symbol of the patriarchal tradition." In this context, the Mammy has become doubly an anathema. To discover any real, living woman of the past existing behind the disempowering, racist-sexist legend is apparently a discovery no one would wish to make.

However, Mammy's deletion from the past has represented a transfiguration of Aunt Jemima in form and not in substance, because not substantiated by new historical research. While according to Catherine Clinton there is no "hard evidence" that this "mythic creation" had any objective historical reality, no one has sought such evidence. Recently, only Elizabeth Fox-Genovese has dared to present the Mammy as a real historical personage. As she has argued, the plantation mistress did rely on slave women to nurse and nurture her offspring and to do much of the domestic work that the white woman saw herself as performing. Thus, according to Fox-Genovese, "although 'mammies' may not have been surrounded with the romantic aura that the whites promoted . . . they indisputably existed and cut a wide swath."[4]

However, elsewhere in recent studies the Mammy's existence has remained consigned to the realm of myth. In total, any attention devoted to Mammy in today's texts adds up to but a few pages, with the exception of White's *Ar'n't I a Woman?*, which devoted more paper to arrive at the same consensus, that the old slave Mammy is only a myth,[5] that such a relatively empowered slave woman in reality had no historical existence.

Mammy's stigmatization may help to explain why, despite increasing attention to the black woman's history of work, vast numbers of Afro-American women who continued long after slavery to work in Mammy-like roles for whites—as washerwomen, maids, and nurses—have as yet won very little attention. The historical experience and role of these black female domestics have recently been of interest largely only to David Katzman. His *Seven Days a Week* provides an excellent introduction to the courage and ingenuity of their struggle to forge a life for themselves and their families, establishing themselves, for example, as day workers rather than live-in servants. But attention to such women remains very limited so long as the old slave Mammy remains so stigmatized a figure. Thus, there may be reason to write the Mammy back into the past, if she is there to be found. However, she will not be found if we do not first ask if she is there.[6]

In part the difficulty resides in the fact that Mammy seems most readily discoverable in the same sources that have endorsed this figure as an emblem of racial and sexual mythology. Nonetheless, it does not necessarily follow that because reflecting, in Bell Hooks's words, "the ultimate sexist-racist vision,"[7] slave mammies are but fictional characters. And if they are there to be found, they too may be found in the same variety of sources in which slave women have now been discovered—in a multitude of roles, including as the heads of families.

However, mammies may remain undiscoverable until the struggle to slay the old myths seems less compelling. And while these old faces of racism-sexism have been exposed and largely dismissed by the scholarship of today, they may not be definitively buried so long as they live on in American culture. Yet it seems a mistake to let Eldridge Cleaver's telling of "the secret of Aunt Jemima's bandanna" remain, in effect, the last word on the Mammy in a way that leaves the old pancake-box figure free to live on in the American popular mind.[8]

Black women's historians have inherited a great deal of disempowering and stigmatized baggage, however. Part of the struggle of black women's history to establish its presence as scholarship may well involve escaping the spell of old images that, viewed as enemies that must forever and always be vanquished, can continue to restrict what is discoverable. As Sarah Wright has observed of this legacy, " 'Gone With the Wind' is not our story. . . . Our history is not gone with the wind, it is still with us." Thus, she has advised, "writers, be wary of those who tell you to leave the past alone and confine yourselves to the present moment."[9]

So long as the popular media still reflect the continuing inequalities of American society, the timeworn myths may nevertheless survive scholarly dismissal. It may well be that, as Trudier Harris has observed, "the most relevant historical question of all is why the todays of black Americans are so much like the yesterdays."[10] American scholarship cannot single-handedly undo and remake the culture's perceptions of race and gender, despite its earlier role in shaping these into society's official beliefs. Nonetheless, this discourse can provide and endorse alternative images of reality that point away from a perpetual repetition of the past.

Such new directions emerge most of all in the historian's discovery of diversity and change. And it is especially in this sense that, as it comes of age, black women's history falsifies, in Trudier Harris's words, "those historical and sociological cubbyholes into which living black women have been shoved." But this demythicizing process will be all the more effective by heeding Alice Walker's advice that "to isolate the fantasy we must cleave to reality . . . embracing both the dark self and the light."[11]

This may mean acknowledging the damage done by a history of oppression to black women and men together. Today's historiography largely presents a story of heroic survival of slave womanhood and manhood. Yet it should be noted that one recent study has powerfully questioned this happy reemployment of Afro-American history; that study is Elizabeth Fox-Genovese's *Within the Plantation Household*. Published in 1988, this book argues that we have gone much too far in dismissing the damaging results of slavery because "the ways in which various authors want the story to end impinges on every effort to write it."[12]

In Fox-Genovese's view, recent historiography has "minimized the consequences of enslavement for the relations between slave women and men." As she has tellingly recognized, "most of the male historians . . . did their best to make those women fit into their own preconceptions . . . a cross between middle-class domesticity and the virtuous woman of Proverbs." Moreover, in her view, "recent work on Afro-American slave women has . . . paid inadequate attention to the consequences of class and racial oppression for slave women's sense of themselves as women." In her words: "We do not experience gender in the abstract, but in relation to others: To be a woman is to be a woman in relation to men." But slavery's "unmanning" of the bondsmen left the slave women "no satisfactory social definition of themselves as women." And the institution "negated womanhood as an ideological category. In the absence of an ideology . . . of gender differences, female slaves lost a vital part of the basis for gender solidarity and identification."[13]

As Fox-Genovese has emphasized, the slave woman's experience of sexual abuse and forced labor did not support her roles as wife or mother or daughter. The slave family did not provide firm institutional grounding for female gender identity. The master's power undermined the slave women's sense "of the links between their relations with men and their roles and identities as women." Neither the slave man nor the female slave's sexual identity could protect her. Instead, as she confronted her master, "the trappings of gender slipped away. The woman faced him alone. She looked on naked power."[14]

Fox-Genovese's findings do not support the crushed-people portrayal. Instead, they emphasize the struggle of the enslaved to shape their own identity, and argue that they constructed a community life that protected them from complete depersonalization. However, her findings argue that while slavery did not cripple black Americans "as a people," it "did cripple many thousands of individual men and women, and did have heartrending consequences for the relations, roles, and identities of all." In short, this book must powerfully "challenge us to recognize class and race as central, rather than incidental, to women's . . . sense of themselves as women." And as Fox-Genovese has pointed out, "either the power that some people exercise over others has consequences or it does not."[15]

The consequences of the white supremacist abuse of power and of the historical assault on the gender identity of Afro-Americans are not very evident in the new black women's historiography. Instead, the consequences of the ugly mythology of sexual racism are revealed in this literature's emphasis on "the light self." To embrace the dark self and the light may mean embracing images that few would wish to embrace. It does require that all women consider how we "have symbolized black and white women and what the power of these symbols is."[16]

It also means that the timeworn practice of arguing by analogy—equating blacks as women and women as blacks—must be abandoned. These analogues have for far too long underpinned the use and abuse of black female emblems signifying the proper place of each group of Americans, in a way that has endorsed the unequal placement of both.[17] But perhaps we may learn from the blind spots in our predecessors' vision. The Afro-American woman's "hell of a history" in American historiography may at least, in this sense, still be of use.

To conclude, Michele Wallace is both right and wrong. She is right that Afro-American women have been preassigned a "hell of a history." But she is wrong to advise that it follows that history "will continue to be written without us. The imperative is clear: Either we will make history or remain the victims of it." The writing of history is integral to the making of history, and it can either perpetuate the power of the past over the present or, in pointing to a new vision of the past, point to a new vision of the future as well. In Catherine Clinton's words, "we have still to transcend the legacy of slavery," and therefore we continue "condemned perhaps not to repeat history but certainly to rewrite it."[18]

The rewriting of the history of Afro-American women may finally inspire the historian's questions, even of Mammy: Did she exist, and if so, who was she? How did she see and shape her experience and role? Indeed, we may finally escape the power of a mythology with too much history to live down, to face up fully to today. And thus eventually, perhaps, Mammy and all of her kin may fully emerge as women who, both despite and because of their oppression and suffering, struggled to make their own history in diverse and profoundly human ways.

NOTES

1. Walker, *Our Mothers' Gardens*, 237.
2. Christian, *Black Woman Novelists*, 18.
3. Walker, *Our Mothers' Gardens*, 312.

4. Clinton, *The Plantation Mistress*, 201–2; Fox-Genovese, *Within the Plantation Household*, 137.

5. White, *Ar'n't I a Woman?*, 58.

6. David Katzman, *Seven Days a Week: Women and Domestic Service in Industrializing America* (New York: Oxford University Press, 1978). For the author's attempt to encourage attention to the Mammy see " 'My Ol' Black Mammy' in American Historiography," in Caroline Matheny Dillman, ed., *Southern Women* (New York: Hemisphere Pub. Corporation, 1988).

7. Hooks, *Ain't I a Woman*, 84.

8. Cleaver, *Soul on Ice*, 162. It should be noted that recently, the pancake-box image has been further updated by the Quaker Oats Company. Aunt Jemima is not only lighter and brighter, but is now being depicted without her bandanna. What this signifies about the future of the Mammy's image remains to be seen.

9. Sarah E. Wright, "The Negro Woman in American Literature," *Freedomways* 6 (1966): 16.

10. Trudier Harris, "Work and the Family in Black Atlanta," *Journal of Social History* 9 (1976): 325.

11. Trudier Harris, *From Mammies to Militants: Domestics in Black American Literature* (Philadelphia: Temple University Press, 1982), 4; Walker, *Our Mothers' Gardens*, 312.

12. Fox-Genovese, *Within the Plantation Household*, 49.

13. Ibid., 48, 29, 373, 301.

14. Ibid., 193, 374.

15. Ibid., 29, 39, 50.

16. Palmer, "Black Women/White Women," 155.

17. For attention to the use, and ultimately, the misuse of the analogue of women as slaves in feminist discourse, see Jean Fagan Yellin, *Women and Sisters: The Antislavery Feminists in American Culture* (New Haven, Conn.: Yale University Press, 1989).

18. Wallace, *Black Macho*, 250; Clinton, *The Plantation Mistress*, 231.

Selected Bibliography

This selected bibliography is intended to provide a guide to the critical sources found to be most useful in the writing and conceptualization of this book. Literature that has been treated largely or entirely as primary source material is not included here, but is fully listed in the chapter endnotes following discussion in the text.

SOURCES

Alaya, Flavia. "Victorian Science and the 'Genius' of Woman." *Journal of the History of Ideas* 38(1977): 261–80.

Allen, Walter R. "The Social and Economic Statuses of Black Women in the United States." *Phylon* 42(1981): 26–40.

Aptheker, Bettina. *Woman's Legacy: Essays on Race, Sex, and Class in American History.* Amherst: The University of Massachusetts Press, 1982.

Aptheker, Herbert. *Afro-American History: The Modern Era.* New York: The Citadel Press, 1971.

Auerbach, Nina. *Woman and the Demon: The Life of a Victorian Myth.* Cambridge, Mass.: Harvard University Press, 1982.

Barnes, Barry. *Interests and the Growth of Knowledge.* London: Routledge and Kegan Paul, 1977.

Beal, Frances M. "Slave of a Slave No More: Black Women in Struggle." *The Black Scholar* 6(1975): 16–24.

Beatty, Bess. "Black Perspectives of American Women: The View from Black Newspapers, 1865–1900." *The Maryland Historian* 9(1978): 39–50.

Bell, Roseann P.; Parker, Bettye J.; and Guy-Sheftall, Beverly, eds. *Sturdy Black Bridges: Visions of Black Women in Literature.* New York: Anchor Press/Doubleday, 1979.

Berzon, Judith R. *Neither White Nor Black: The Mulatto Character in American Fiction.* New York: New York University Press, 1978.

Blassingame, John. *The Slave Community: Plantation Life in the Antebellum South*. Rev. ed. New York: Oxford University Press, 1979.

Blassingame, John, ed. *New Perspectives on Black Studies*. Urbana: University of Illinois Press, 1971.

Bogin, Ruth, and Loewenberg, Bert James, eds. *Black Women in Nineteenth-Century American Life: Their Words, Their Thoughts, Their Feelings*. University Park: Pennsylvania State University Press, 1981.

Bond, Jean Carey, and Gregory, Carole E. "Two Views of Black Macho and the Myth of the Superwoman." *Freedomways* 19(1979): 13–26.

Cade, Toni, ed. *The Black Woman*. New York: Mentor/New American Library, 1970.

Canary, Robert, and Kozicki, Henry. *The Writing of History: Literary Form and Understanding*. Madison, Wis.: University of Wisconsin Press, 1978.

Christian, Barbara. *Black Women Novelists: The Development of a Tradition, 1892–1976*. Westport, Conn.: Greenwood Press, 1980.

Clinton, Catherine. *The Plantation Mistress: Woman's World in the Old South*. New York: Pantheon Books/Random House, 1982.

Davis, Angela. *Women, Race and Class*. New York: Vintage Books/Random House, 1983.

Davis, David Brion. "Slavery and the Post–World War II Historians." In *Slavery, Colonialism, and Racism*, edited by Sidney W. Mintz. New York: W. W. Norton & Co., 1974.

Delamont, Sara, and Duffin, Lorna. *The Nineteenth-Century Woman: Her Cultural and Physical World*. London: Croom Helm, 1978.

Dietrick, Katheryn Thomas. "A Re-examination of the Myth of Black Matriarchy." *Journal of Marriage and the Family* 37(1975): 367–74.

Diggs, Irene. "Du Bois and Women: A Short Story of Black Women, 1910–1934." *A Current Bibliography on African Affairs* 7, no.3(1974): 260–303.

Dill, Bonnie Thornton. "Race, Class, and Gender: Prospects for an All-Inclusive Sisterhood." *Feminist Studies* 9(1983):130–50.

Dillman, Caroline Matheny, ed. *Southern Women*. New York: Hemisphere Publishing Corporation, 1988.

Douglas, Mary. *Purity and Danger*. London: Routledge, 1966.

Ellison, Mary. "Resistance to Oppression: Black Women's Response to Slavery in the United States." *Slavery and Abolition* 4(1983): 56–63.

Engram, Eleanor. *Science, Myth, Reality: The Black Family in One-Half Century of Research*. Westport, Conn.: Greenwood Press, 1982.

Evans, Sara. *Personal Politics: The Roots of Women's Liberation in the Civil Rights Movement and the New Left*. New York: Vintage Books/Random House, 1980.

Fitzgerald, Frances. *America Revised: History Textbooks in the Twentieth Century*. Boston: Little, Brown & Co., 1979.

Foucault, Michel. *The Archeology of Knowledge*. New York: Pantheon Books, 1972.

———. *The History of Sexuality*. Vol. 1, *An Introduction*, trans. R. Hurley. New York: Pantheon Books, 1978.

Fox-Genovese, Elizabeth. "Placing Women's History in History." *New Left Review* no. 133 (May-June 1982): 5–29.

———. *Within the Plantation Household: Black and White Women of the Old South*. Chapel Hill: The University of North Carolina Press, 1988.

Fredrickson, George. *The Black Image in the White Mind: The Debate on the Afro-American Character and Destiny, 1817–1914.* New York: Harper & Row, 1971.

Friedman, Jean E. *The Enclosed Garden: Women and Community in the Evangelical South, 1830–1900.* Chapel Hill: University of North Carolina Press, 1985.

Friedman, Lawrence. *The White Savage: Racial Fantasies in the Postbellum South.* Englewood Cliffs, N.J.: Prentice-Hall, 1970.

Fullinwider, S. P. *The Mind and Mood of Black America: Twentieth Century Thought.* Homewood, Ill.: The Dorsey Press, 1969.

Genovese, Eugene D. "The Influence of the Black Power Movement on Historical Scholarship: Reflections of a White Historian." *Daedalus* 99(1970): 473–94.

————. *Roll, Jordan, Roll: The World the Slaves Made.* New York: Vintage/Random House, 1976.

Gerster, Patrick, and Cords, Nicholas, eds. *Myth and Southern History.* Chicago: Rand McNally College Pub., 1974.

Giddings, Paula. *When and Where I Enter: The Impact of Black Women on Race and Sex in America.* New York: William Morrow & Co., Inc., 1984.

Gilmore, Al-Tony, ed. *Revisiting Blassingame's "The Slave Community": The Scholars Respond.* Westport, Conn.: Greenwood Press, 1978.

Gutman, Herbert G. *The Black Family in Slavery and Freedom, 1750–1925.* New York: Vintage Books/Random House, 1977.

Guy-Sheftall, Beverly. "Review of *Ain't I a Woman*, by Bell Hooks." *Phylon* 44(1983): 84–85.

Gwin, Minrose C. *Black and White Women of the Old South: The Peculiar Sisterhood in American Literature.* Knoxville: University of Tennessee Press, 1985.

Harley, Sharon, and Terborg-Penn, Rosalyn, eds. *The Afro-American Woman: Struggles and Images.* Port Washington, New York: Kennikat Press, 1979.

Harris, Robert. "Coming of Age: The Transformation of Afro-American Historiography." *Journal of Negro History* 67(1982): 107–21.

Harris, Trudier. *From Mammies to Militants: Domestics in Black American Literature.* Philadelphia: Temple University Press, 1982.

Hawks, Joanne V., and Skemp, Sheila L., eds. *Sex, Race and the Role of Women in the South.* Jackson: University Press of Mississippi, 1983.

Helmreich, W. B. *The Things They Say Behind Your Back.* New York: Doubleday and Co., 1982.

Henry, Charles P., and Foster, Frances Smith. "Black Women's Studies: Threat or Challenge?" *The Western Journal of Black Studies* 6(1982): 15–21.

Hine, Darlene C. "Female Slave Resistance: The Economics of Sex." *The Western Journal of Black Studies* 3(1979): 123–27.

Hooks, Bell. *Ain't I a Woman: Black Women and Feminism.* Boston: South End Press, 1981.

————. *Feminist Theory: From Margin to Center.* Boston: South End Press, 1984.

Hull, Gloria T.; Scott, Patricia Bell; and Smith, Barbara, eds. *All the Women Are White, All the Blacks Are Men, But Some of Us Are Brave: Black Women's Studies.* New York: The Feminist Press, 1982.

Jackson, Jacquelyne Johnson. "A Critique of Lerner's Work on Black Women." *Journal of Social and Behavioral Science* (Winter 1975): 63–89.

Janeway, Elizabeth. *Man's World, Woman's Place.* New York: William Morrow and Co., 1971.

Johnson, Willa D., and Green, Thomas L., eds. *Perspectives on Afro-American Women.* Washington, D.C.: ECCA Publications, Inc., 1975.

Jones, Jacqueline. *Labor of Love, Labor of Sorrow: Black Women, Work, and the Family from Slavery to the Present.* New York: Basic Books, 1985.

Jordan, Winthrop. *White Over Black: American Attitudes Toward the Negro, 1550–1812.* New York: W. W. Norton & Co., 1977.

Katzman, David. *Seven Days a Week: Women and Domestic Service in Industrializing America.* New York: Oxford University Press, 1978.

Keller, Evelyn Fox. *Reflections on Gender and Science.* New Haven, Conn.: Yale University Press, 1985.

King, Mae. "The Politics of Sexual Stereotypes." *The Black Scholar* 4(1973): 12–23.

Ladner, Joyce. *Tomorrow's Tomorrow: The Black Woman.* Garden City, New York: Doubleday, 1971.

Lane, Anne J., ed. *The Debate Over Slavery: Stanley Elkins and His Critics.* Urbana: University of Illinois Press, 1971.

Laslett, Peter. "Household and Family on the Slave Plantations of the United States." In Peter Laslett, *Family Life and Illicit Love in Earlier Generations: Essays in Historical Sociology.* Cambridge: Cambridge University Press, 1977.

Lebsock, Suzanne. *The Free Women of Petersburg: Status and Culture in a Southern Town, 1784–1860.* New York: W. W. Norton & Co., 1984.

Lerner, Gerda. *The Majority Finds Its Past: Placing Women in History.* New York: Oxford University Press, 1979.

———. "Women and Slavery." *Slavery and Abolition* 4(1983): 173–98.

———, ed. *Black Women in White America.* New York: Vintage Books, 1973.

Levy, David W. "Racial Stereotypes in Antislavery Fiction." *Phylon* 30(1970): 265–79.

McAdoo, Harriette Pipes, ed. *Black Families.* Beverly Hills, Calif.: Sage Publications, 1981.

Mapp, Edward. "Black Women in Films." *The Black Scholar* 4(1973): 42–46.

Martin, Elmer P., and Martin, Joanne Mitchell. *The Black Extended Family.* Chicago: University of Chicago Press, 1987.

Mencke, John G. *Mulattoes and Race Mixture.* New York: UMI Research Press, 1976.

Moses, Wilson Jeremiah. *Black Messiahs and Uncle Toms: Social and Literary Manipulations of a Religious Myth.* University Park, Pa.: Pennsylvania State University Press, 1982.

———. "Civilizing Missionary: A Study of Alexander Crummell." *Journal of Negro History* 60(1975): 229–51.

Moss, Alfred A., Jr. *The American Negro Academy: Voice of the Talented Tenth.* Baton Rouge: Louisiana State University Press, 1981.

Mullin, Michael. "Women and the Comparative Study of American Negro Slavery." *Slavery and Abolition* 6(1985): 25–40.

Myrdal, Gunnar. *An American Dilemma.* 2 vols. New York: McGraw-Hill Co., 1944.

Newby, I. A. *Jim Crow's Defense: Anti-Negro Thought in America, 1900–1930.* Baton Rouge: Louisiana State University Press, 1973.

Noble, Jean. *Beautiful Also Are the Souls of My Black Sisters.* Englewood Cliffs, N.J.: Prentice-Hall, 1978.

Norton, Mary Beth. *Liberty's Daughters: The Revolutionary Experience of American Women, 1750–1800.* Boston: Little, Brown & Co., 1980.

Palmer, Phyllis Marynick. "White Women/Black Women: The Dualism of Female Identity and Experience in the United States." *Feminist Studies* 9(1983): 151–70.

Peters, M. F. "The Black Family: Perpetuating the Myths: An Analysis of Family Sociology Textbook Treatment of Black Families." *Family Coordinator* 23(1974): 349–57.

Pinkney, Alphonso. *The Myth of Black Progress*. New York: Cambridge University Press, 1984.

Rainwater, Lee, and Yancey, William, eds. *The Moynihan Report and the Politics of Controversy*. Cambridge, Mass.: MIT Press, 1967.

Robertson, Claire C., and Klein, Martin A., eds. *Women and Slavery in Africa*. Madison: University of Wisconsin Press, 1983.

Rodgers-Rose, La Frances, ed. *The Black Woman*. Beverly Hills, Calif.: Sage Publications, 1980.

Saveth, E. N. *American History and the Social Sciences*. New York: Collier-Macmillan Ltd., 1964.

Smith, John David. "A Different View of Slavery: Black Historians Attack the Proslavery Argument, 1890–1920." *Journal of Negro History* 65(1980): 298–311.

———. *An Old Creed for the New South: Proslavery Ideology and Historiography, 1865–1918*. Westport, Conn.: Greenwood Press, 1985.

Smith-Rosenberg, Carroll. *Disorderly Conduct: Visions of Gender in Victorian America*. New York: Oxford University Press, 1985.

Smith-Rosenberg, Carroll, and Rosenberg, Charles. "The Female Animal: Medical and Biological Views of Woman and Her Role in Nineteenth-Century America." *Journal of American History* 60(1973–74): 322–56.

Stampp, Kenneth M. "Rebels and Sambos: The Search for the Negro's Personality in Slavery." *Journal of Southern History* 37(1971): 367–92.

Stanfield, John H. *Philanthropy and Jim Crow in American Social Science*. New York: Greenwood Press, 1985.

Staples, Robert. *The Black Family*. Belmont, Calif.: Wadsworth, 1971.

———. *The Black Male's Role in American Society*. San Francisco: The Black Scholar Press, 1982.

———. *The Black Woman in America: Sex, Marriage and the Family*. Chicago: Nelson-Hall Publishers, 1973.

———. "The Myth of the Black Matriarchy." *The Black Scholar* 1(1970): 9–16.

Steady, Filomina Chioma, ed. *The Black Woman Cross-Culturally*. Cambridge, Mass.: Schenkman Pub. Co., Inc., 1981.

Sterling, Dorothy, ed. *We Are Your Sisters: Black Women in the Nineteenth Century*. New York: W. W. Norton, 1984.

Terborg-Penn, Rosalyn. "To Find a Place in History." Review of *We Are Your Sisters: Black Women in the Nineteenth Century*, ed. by Dorothy Sterling, and of *Labor of Love, Labor of Sorrow: Black Women, Work and the Family from Slavery to the Present*, by Jacqueline Jones. *The Women's Review of Books* 2, no. 10 (1985): 10–11.

Thomas, Alexander, and Sillen, Samuel. *Racism and Psychiatry*. New York: Brunner/Mazel Publishers, 1972.

Van Deburg, William L. *Slavery and Race in American Popular Culture*. Madison: University of Wisconsin Press, 1984.

Vicinus, Martha, ed. *Suffer and Be Still: Women in the Victorian Age.* Bloomington: Indiana University Press, 1972.

Walker, Alice. *In Search of Our Mothers' Gardens.* New York: Harcourt Brace Jovanovich, 1983.

Wallace, Michele. *Black Macho and the Myth of the Superwoman.* New York: Warner Books, 1980.

Weber, Shirley N. "Black Power in the 1960s: A Study of Its Impact on Women's Liberation." *Journal of Black Studies* 11(1981): 483–97.

Weinstein, Allen; Gatell, Frank Otto; and Sarasohn, David, eds. *American Negro Slavery: A Modern Reader.* 3d ed. New York: Oxford University Press, 1979.

Welter, Barbara. "The Cult of True Womanhood, 1820–60." *American Quarterly* 18 (1966): 151–74.

White, Deborah. *Ar'n't I a Woman?: Female Slaves in the Ante-Bellum South.* New York: Norton, 1985.

———. "Female Slaves: Sex Roles and Status in the Antebellum Plantation South." *Journal of Family History* 8(1983): 248–61.

White, Hayden. *Tropics of Discourse: Essays in Cultural Criticism.* Baltimore: The Johns Hopkins University Press, 1978.

Wiebe, R. H. *The Search for Order.* New York: Hill and Wang, 1967.

Williams, Vernon J., Jr. *From a Caste to a Minority: Changing Attitudes of American Sociologists Toward Afro-Americans, 1896–1945.* Westport, Conn.: Greenwood Press, 1989.

Williamson, Joel. *The Crucible of Race: Black-White Relations in the American South Since Emancipation.* New York: Oxford University Press, 1984.

———. *Miscegenation and Mulattoes in the United States.* New York: The Free Press, 1980.

———. *A Rage for Order: Black-White Relations in the American South Since Emancipation.* New York: Oxford University Press, 1986.

Wood, Peter. " 'I Did the Best I Could for My Day': The Study of Early Black History during the Second Reconstruction, 1960 to 1976." *William and Mary Quarterly* 35(1978): 185–225.

Yellin, Jean Fagan. "Du Bois' 'Crisis' and Woman's Suffrage." *Massachusetts Review* 14(1973):365–75.

———. *Women and Sisters: The Antislavery Feminists in American Culture.* New Haven, Conn.: Yale University Press, 1989.

Index

About the Author

PATRICIA MORTON is Associate Professor in the History Department at Trent University, Ontario, Canada. Her previously published journal articles include, among others: "From Invisible Man to 'New People': The Recent Discovery of the American Mulatto," "The New Police Historiography," " 'My Ol' Black Mammy' in American Historiography," and "Southern Women."